Nehemiah

STATESMAN AND SAGE

מגיד
MAGGID

Dov S. Zakheim

Nehemiah

Statesman and Sage

Maggid Books

Nehemiah
Statesman and Sage

First Edition, 2016

Maggid Books
An imprint of Koren Publishers Jerusalem Ltd.

POB 8531, New Milford, CT 06776-8531, USA
& POB 4044, Jerusalem 9104001, Israel
www.korenpub.com

The publication of this book was made possible
through the generous support of *Torah Education in Israel.*

ISBN 978-1-59264-369-1, *hardcover*

A CIP catalogue record for this title is
available from the British Library

Printed and bound in the United States

In loving memory of Irving and Beatrice Stone,
who dedicated their lives to the
advancement of Jewish education.
We are proud and honored to continue in their legacy.

Their Children, Grandchildren, and Great-Grandchildren
Cleveland, Ohio USA

To my grandchildren

עטרת זקנים בני בנים

Grandchildren are the crown of their elders

(Proverbs 17:6)

– The Author

Contents

Preface

This volume is the product of my long-standing fascination with Nehemiah. During my years as a graduate student, while simultaneously preparing for rabbinic ordination, I contemplated the possibility of one day serving in government. I admired Nehemiah as a man who made a lasting mark both as a statesman and as a religious leader, one whose activities offered an enduring example for later generations to emulate. As I moved up the ranks of officialdom, Nehemiah continued to offer a compelling model of what leadership and religious commitment were all about. I found his example inspiring – and I still do.

I first lectured on Nehemiah while a graduate student in Britain in the early 1970s. However, the immediate impetus for this volume was a series of *shiurim* on the Book of Nehemiah that I gave at my synagogue on Shabbat between Minḥa and Maariv over the course of several years. These began while I was serving as deputy undersecretary of defense in the Reagan administration. I taught Nehemiah with additional materials a second time when I was in the Pentagon again, this time serving as undersecretary of defense in the George W. Bush administration. In both cases, my experience in government brought home to me, and I suspect to my listeners, the relevance of Nehemiah's memoir – for that is what it would be called today – to the strategic, economic, and social challenges of our own times, particularly those confronting the State of Israel. Highlighting the lessons that the past can offer for contemporary governance can be an especially useful exercise; for example, about the time that I completed this book, the Oxford historian (and warden of my former college) Margaret Macmillan likewise identified lessons for addressing contemporary political developments in her highly acclaimed, recently published history of the years leading up to the First World War.[1]

While lecturing on Nehemiah as a senior Jewish official in the government of the world's only superpower, I found that my experience enabled me to offer my audience a special perspective on the challenges that Nehemiah confronted, the way he dealt with them, and the politics of governance. Indeed, since Nehemiah's day there have not been all that many Jews who both completed their rabbinic studies and served as government officials in the Diaspora. There is a difference between government officials and government advisers. Advisers have no legally binding power; officials do. Moreover, until recently, Jewish advisers often served governments that were hostile to Jews.

There have, of course, been Jews who achieved the highest ranks in democracies, among them prime ministers of Italy and France. There have been Orthodox Jews who reached pinnacles almost as high: today they include Secretary of the Treasury Jack Lew. And, of course, rabbis, all of them Orthodox, have long served as ministers in the government of Israel, and have done so since its establishment in 1948. But what fascinated my listeners at synagogue, and led many of them to suggest that I restructure my *shiurim* into a book, was that I was an ordained (*musmakh*) rabbi who held junior ministerial rank. Not only did I hold such a rank, but I did so in a non-Jewish government, that of the United States, which the great Rabbi Moshe Feinstein and the Lubavitcher Rebbe both always called *malkhus shel ḥesed*, the government of lovingkindness.[2] Even Nehemiah's Persia never reached that level – though

1. Margaret Macmillan, *The War That Ended Peace* (New York: Random House, 2014).
2. Rabbi Feinstein was known to refer to the United States in this way. He employed the term in a widely distributed letter written in 1977. See William B. Helmreich, *The World of the Yeshiva: An Intimate Portrait of Orthodox Jewry*, augmented ed. (New York:

under Artaxerxes, even more than under his ancestor Cyrus the Great, it came close.

This book includes many quotations from Nehemiah, but it is not a commentary. Nor is it a biography in the usual sense of "life and times." There is simply too little material to work with: the Book of Nehemiah is certainly a memoir, but it is restricted to the author's activities as governor of the Persian province of Judah. And unlike contemporary memoirs that are limited to a particular period in the author's life, Nehemiah offers no background regarding himself, and only a skeleton sketch of his family relationships.

Accordingly, this book offers a political biography of the man, based, of course, on his own memoir, but also on the context provided by both traditional commentary and academic research. Its focus is on leadership – why and how he went about realizing what he sought to achieve. He was a man of great accomplishment. It therefore comes as no surprise that when Sir Herbert Samuel served as high commissioner of Palestine – the first Jew to have authority over the Jewish homeland since the Bar Kokhba rebellion – he was addressed by his fellow Jews as "the Nehemiah of our times."

ACKNOWLEDGMENTS

It was Harold and Hannah Levy, respectively warden and matron of the residence at Jews' College where I both lived and studied part-time during my "junior year abroad" program at the London School of Economics, who first gave me the opportunity to lecture on Nehemiah at the study groups that they organized annually for young British students. May their memory be for a blessing.

I am deeply indebted to those who painstakingly reviewed earlier drafts of this book: Adam Garfinkle, editor of *The American Interest*, a dear friend with an encyclopedic knowledge of things Jewish who has served at the highest levels of the Department of State; Erica Brown, prolific author and Judaic scholar extraordinaire, whose

Ktav, 2000), 89. For the Lubavitcher Rebbe, see Joseph Telushkin, *The Rebbe: The Life and Teaching of Menachem M. Schneerson, the Most Influential Rabbi in Modern History* (New York: Harper Wave, 2014), 159.

influence extends beyond the Jewish community to America at large; David Makovsky, analyst, peace negotiator, and one of America's leading commentators on Mideast politics in general and Israeli politics in particular. And my sons Keith (Chaim) and Roger (Reuven), both of whom are steeped in Torah as well as in politics: Keith as a former city councilman in New Jersey; Roger as a former deputy assistant secretary of defense as well as deputy staff director of the House Committee on Armed Services.

I have benefited tremendously from all the comments, critiques, and suggestions that I received; whatever errors this volume might contain are mine alone, however.

Asher Schapiro urged me to submit this volume to Maggid for publication; Matthew Miller, Maggid's leading light, seconded Asher's motion and was supportive throughout, as was my son Scott (Saadya). I am grateful to all three.

I was blessed with the top editorial and publishing team that Maggid afforded me: Deena Glickman has been a fount of substantive as well as editorial wisdom; Rabbi Reuven Ziegler and Tomi Mager were exceedingly helpful and supportive; and Robert Milch and Ita Olesker carefully proofread the text.

Aḥarona aḥarona ḥaviva, my wife, Deborah, encouraged me throughout the course of this project, as she has before, on so many other occasions, and in countless other ways.

Introduction

Nehemiah: A Leader Both Modern and Traditional

Etched high on the outer wall of Jerusalem's Old City, a few feet from the Jaffa Gate and facing the restored Mamilla district, is a brief Hebrew inscription. Unusually for a city oriented to Western tourists, it is coupled with a translation into Arabic, not English. An English rendering of the inscription would read, "On the twentieth day of the month of Tevet, 5730, the restoration of the Old City walls was completed: 'The repairing of the walls of Jerusalem went forward.'"[1] The final passage is a quotation from the Book of Nehemiah (4:1). Jewish history recognizes Nehemiah as one of the founding fathers of the Second Commonwealth, the period between 516 BCE, when the Jews sanctified the new Second Temple, and 70 CE, when the Temple was destroyed.[2] It was Nehemiah

1. Biblical translations used in the book are based on the Jewish Publication Society's *The New English Translation of the Bible* (Philadelphia: Jewish Publication Society, 1917) and *Tanakh: A New Translation of the Holy Scriptures according to the Traditional Hebrew Text* (Philadelphia: Jewish Publication Society, 1985). Translations of Talmud and Mishna are based on *The Soncino Talmud* (Chicago: Computers in Jewish Life/ Davka/Judaica Press, 1991–1993).
2. There are varying opinions regarding the dating of the Second Commonwealth. Some historians begin the era at 538 BCE, when Zerubbabel led the initial group

who successfully reconstructed Jerusalem's walls and provided for its security just over a half-century after the Temple was rebuilt. And it was Nehemiah who restored national pride and imposed a social and religious order based on tradition, justice, and decency. As Rabbi Adin Steinsaltz notes, "the arrival of Nehemiah [from the Persian capital of Susa, familiar to readers of Megillat Esther as Shushan] was crucial. Not only was he a man of great spiritual and intellectual powers, but he was also a brilliant man of action."[3]

Yet the Talmud is ambivalent about Nehemiah. It chides him for seeking too much credit for his accomplishments, seeing him as too self-serving and insufficiently modest (Sanhedrin 93b). It adds that it is for this reason that he was not credited with a book of his own. In fact, for many centuries Nehemiah's memoir was subsumed within the Book of Ezra; it was only in the Middle Ages, well after the medieval Masoretes had completed the definitive version of the Holy Scriptures, that Nehemiah was credited with his own book of Scripture. Rashi's commentary (Rabbi Shlomo Yitzhaki, 1040–1105) still addresses a single book; he notes in his comment on what is now the first verse of Nehemiah, "from here forward Nehemiah wrote this book."[4] The Church father Origen appears to have been the first to differentiate the books of Ezra and Nehemiah.[5]

---

of exiles back to Judah. See, for example, Solomon Zeitlin, *The Rise and Fall of the Judaean State: A Political, Social and Religious History of the Second Commonwealth* (Philadelphia: Jewish Publication Society, 1962), 29. Others begin about a century later, when Nehemiah flourished. In addition, some consider the Second Commonwealth to have lasted until the Bar Kokhba rebellion was crushed in 135 CE.

3. Adin Steinsaltz, *Biblical Images: Men and Women of the Book* (New York: Basic Books, 1984), 208.
4. Rashi, Neh. 1:1, s.v. *divrei Neḥemia.*
5. H. G. M. Williamson, citing Eusebius. In citing Origen's division of the Hebrew Bible, Eusebius wrote, "the first and second of Esdras, in one [book], called Ezra." Eusebius, *Ecclesiastical History*, book 6, 25, c2, trans. C. F. Cruse (Peabody, MA: Hendrickson, 2000), 214. Williamson adds that Jerome's Vulgate also credited Nehemiah with his own book, while "in the earliest Hebrew manuscripts the books are not divided"; H. G. M. Williamson, *Word Biblical Commentary: Ezra, Nehemiah* (Nashville: Thomas Nelson, 1986), xxi. Williamson further notes that both Rashi and Rabbi Abraham ibn Ezra (1089–1164) treat the two books as one. He is correct with respect to Rashi (see the entry cited in note 4), but not in the case of Ibn Ezra.

It was not until the fourteenth or perhaps even the fifteenth century that Jews treated Nehemiah as a separate book.[6]

Nehemiah certainly does not fit easily into the rabbinic mold of Jewish leaders. Although tradition asserts that he was a member of the Great Assembly,[7] his recollections deal more with practical politics and administration than with scholarship. He certainly respected religious authority – indeed, he enforced it – but he did so as an educated layman rather than as a rabbinic sage. To quote Rabbi Steinsaltz again, "his spiritual ideas did not show any real originality, but he knew how to get things done."[8] Perhaps the rabbis sensed that he embodied a threat to their authority. While they strove to make their imprint on every facet of Jewish life, Nehemiah seemed to create a boundary between the authority of the synagogue he venerated and the state he governed.

In that sense, Nehemiah was the first "modern" leader of a Jewish state. He had to cope with an array of challenges that would not be unfamiliar to any senior Israeli official today. These included national security relations with both regional neighbors and an international superpower; domestic social and economic issues; and, most peculiar (though not

6. Rabbi Chaim Joseph David Azulai (better known by his acronym, *Ḥida*), who lived in the eighteenth century, wrote that it had already been "several hundred years since the Book of Ezra was on its own and the Book of Nehemiah was on its own, and this is not happenstance, for all is from Heaven with complete precision, particularly with holy matters such as these." Cited in *Encyclopedia Talmudit*, ed. Zalman Nehemiah Goldberg (Jerusalem: Yad Harav Herzog, 5774/2014), XXXIII:181n10.
7. *Targum*, Song. 3:7; Maimonides (Rabbi Moshe ben Maimon), *Mishneh Torah, Hakdama*, and R. Menachem ben Shlomo (Meiri), *Beit HaBeḥira: Meiri im Mekorot, Tziyunim VeHe'arot*, ed. Avraham Sofer, vol. 20: Avot (Jerusalem: Haim Gitler, 1968), 19. See also the statement by R. Samuel b. Naḥman, Exodus Rabba, 51:1. Maimonides lists Nehemiah and Zerubbabel as being colleagues in the Great Assembly. Drawing upon different sources, and for the purpose of claiming that the Second Temple was built in Artaxerxes's reign, Diana Edelman also makes the case that the two men were near-contemporaries or even the same person. See Diana V. Edelman, *Origins of the "Second" Temple: Persian Imperial Policy and the Rebuilding of Jerusalem* (London: Equinox, 2005), 75, 351. For a convincing refutation of her theory, see Ralph W. Klein, "Were Joshua, Zerubbabel and Nehemiah Contemporaries? A Response to Diana Edelman's Proposed Late Date for the Second Temple," *Journal of Biblical Literature* 127 (Winter 2008): 697–701.
8. Steinsaltz, *Biblical Images*, 208.

unique, as it occurs in Israel and numerous other Middle Eastern societies), the place of religion in the governance of the state.

Nehemiah was also "modern" in the sense that characterizes Modern Orthodox Judaism today. He embodied the principle whose Hebrew formulation, *Torah im derekh eretz*, roughly translates into "observance and worldliness." It is a principle that has never gone unchallenged, either in Judaism or, for that matter, in other religions. Extreme secularists and assimilationists have always been in league with religious zealots to undermine the relevance of Jewish life and law to the changing times and generations.

Nehemiah clearly was no cloistered scholar. Neither, however, was he ready to tolerate deviation from tradition. In cleaving to what Maimonides described fifteen hundred years later as the "balanced path," Nehemiah aroused the enmity of many of his more assimilationist contemporaries and the opprobrium of his less tolerant talmudic heirs.

He continues to fuel passions to this very day. A 1971 study bemoaned the fact that Nehemiah had imparted to his coreligionists "the national, territorial side of Judaism, by which it differed from other Hellenistic forms of oriental religions." For it was this bequest, "that double character – local as well as universal – which … in its terrible consequences, yet endures."[9]

Similarly, the author of a 1998 study who devoted a lengthy introduction to the importance of historical objectivity argued that Nehemiah's legacy was not the liberal Judaism that freely partook of the surrounding culture.

> It was traditional Judaism – the Judaism of the *stetl* [*sic*] and the ghetto – which kept the religion alive. Even today the real crisis is perceived by many in such liberal societies as America where Jews are assimilating at an alarming rate…. Nehemiah remains the champion of those who argue for an exclusivist religion.[10]

9. Morton Smith, *Palestinian Parties and Politics That Shaped the Old Testament* (New York: Columbia University Press, 1971), 147.
10. Lester L. Grabbe, *Ezra-Nehemiah* (London and New York: Routledge, 1998), 179.

This is an argument with an old pedigree. Beginning with the Protestant scholar Julius Wellhausen (1844–1918), many scholars have denigrated the Judaism to which Ezra and Nehemiah were so firmly committed. Together with the books of Chronicles and Esther, they have offered Ezra and Nehemiah "as evidence in the indictment of early Judaism as an illiberal religion dominated by legalism and ritualism, a religion looking inward rather than out into the world beyond its carefully guarded confines."[11]

No doubt Nehemiah was a nationalist who was emotionally attached to the Land of Israel. And he certainly opposed intermarriage. Yet it is pure historical speculation to argue that Jewish love for the land was an artifact of the Babylonian exile, or of Nehemiah's single-mindedness. Thousands of Jews had returned to Judah before Nehemiah was born; others had never left their ancestral home.

Moreover, intermarriage was the scourge of Jewish society well before Nehemiah's day. The children of many of the leading families that had returned from Babylonia decades before his arrival in Jerusalem had married non-Jewish wives. Indeed, centuries earlier, even King Solomon had been rebuked for his many foreign wives. Certainly, for contemporary believing Jews, intermarriage remains the challenge that it was in Nehemiah's time. Were it not for the Jews' special sense of identity, they would have long since been absorbed into the Hellenistic or Christian or Muslim worlds in which they variously found themselves over the span of the centuries.[12]

Nehemiah rose to the highest levels of the Persian court precisely because he was not an insular "ghetto" Jew. Ghetto Jews remained in the ghetto, or what passed for it functionally before the first ghetto

11. Joseph Blenkinsopp, *Ezra-Nehemiah: A Commentary* (Philadelphia: Westminster Press, 1988), 35.

12. It might be argued that because both Smith and Grabbe place Nehemiah two centuries later than does Jewish tradition (and a half-century later than the estimates of Modern Orthodox Jewish scholars), their view of Nehemiah was expressed in juxtaposition to the Hellenistic culture that was beginning to emerge in the Middle East. In fact, Hellenism did not become widespread until nearly seventy years *after* Smith and Grabbe's chronological estimates, and, in any event, their later dating in no way erodes the force of the argument made above, and in some ways reinforces it.

appeared centuries later. Moreover, at no time, whether at the court or in Jerusalem, did he demonstrate any inclination to oppose in principle his coreligionists' interaction with their neighbors. He simply set some bounds to that interaction, be it about commerce on the Sabbath (which was also banned among Jews) or marriage. That was all. To call such a man some kind of *shtetl* Jew is to reflect deep-rooted cultural biases that seem to run counter to the ideals of free expression and choice.

The assertions of critics who would question the nature and motives both of those who returned from exile and those, like Nehemiah, who led them, are themselves self-contradictory and highly speculative. Their writings are riddled with the words "may," "likely," "it is probable," "it is possible." With no claim to divine revelation, their hypotheses require a degree of belief that barely falls short of that which religion demands.

AN UNSUNG HERO

It is a pity that even traditional Jews who are well versed in biblical lore have only a passing knowledge of this great man's life, times, and accomplishments. To be sure, there is a growing number of translations of his book, particularly into English, the lingua franca of the twentieth and twenty-first centuries. Yet these translations tend to fall into two categories. Either they are intended to accompany a compilation of commentaries that reflect a particular interpretation of the Talmud's view of Nehemiah and his memoirs, or they offer a synthesis of the latest trends in biblical criticism coupled with recent archaeological findings.

This volume addresses Nehemiah from a vantage point that differs somewhat from the perspectives adopted by scholars of late, or, for that matter, in the past – namely, his professional career as politician, statesman, bureaucrat, and lay religious administrator. That is, after all, clearly the way he regarded himself. Moreover, by viewing him as he was, one can also recognize the degree to which the fundamental issues with which he grappled persist. Issues of national defense and foreign relations, the allocation of domestic economic resources, and social reform have remained relatively unchanged to this day – because human nature is unchanging – and continue to confound Nehemiah's latter-day successors in office. There is a talmudic maxim that has often resurfaced in rabbinic literature: "The deeds of the patriarchs are a signal for their descendants" (*maasei avot siman lebanim*). In no book of the Scripture is this dictum consistently truer than in that of Nehemiah, the nation builder.

AN APPROACH TO READING NEHEMIAH: A WORD ON SOURCES

There has been a growing tendency in recent years among some traditional Jews to divorce all reference to secular or non-Jewish sources from commentaries that approach the Scripture from a traditional vantage point. This obscurantist approach has reached such extremes that even traditionally respected commentaries, notably that of Rabbi Don Isaac Abrabanel, have been denigrated in certain Orthodox Jewish circles for their explicit references to Christian scholars. Nevertheless, it is difficult to ignore historical reality when addressing a period for which there is a mountain of evidence consisting of contemporaneous non-Jewish original source material.

Considering that material, or even the musings of non-traditional scholars, be they Jewish or not, in no way demeans the validity and truth of the Orthodox Jewish belief that the books that comprise the Prophets and Writings (collectively known as *Nakh*) were divinely inspired and that the texts as we have them have survived intact since they were first transcribed. Nor does it exonerate the lamentable refusal of most biblical scholars even to consider the insights of the Jewish medievalists in particular, presumably on the grounds that they had a theological ax to grind and are therefore unworthy of notice. It is, at a minimum, ironic that such an attitude rarely has been adopted toward the products of Church scholarship. Perhaps even more ironic is the fact that many speculative hypotheses put forward by biblical scholars are adumbrated in the writings of Jewish rabbis and scholars whose basic premise was the divinity of the Scripture.

The motives and attitudes of secular and non-Jewish scholars notwithstanding, many have much to offer those who wish to have a better understanding of the historical context that the Scripture addresses. To believe in the truth of Scripture is to believe that it is congruent with history. History is not a validation of Scripture, which needs no validation. But surely the human experience must be consistent with its delineation in Scripture.

Rabbinic sources have no monopoly on an understanding of that experience. The Jews' miserable existence for two millennia made statecraft a vicarious exercise for all but a very few, among them, ironically, Rabbi Don Isaac Abrabanel. Moreover, the rabbis of the Talmud had little if any access to the archives of the non-Jewish powers that influenced the Judean polity. Similarly, medieval rabbis, and their successors through the pre-war years of the twentieth century, contented themselves to rely solely on their own interpretations of talmudic dicta. With so much more material available today, and a Jewish state that functions in a very real, secular world, the value of reaching beyond a neo-medieval approach to the Nehemiah story should be self-evident.

At the same time, modern scholars all too easily dismiss the Talmud and Midrash, as well as medieval and recent commentaries produced in conformity with strict Orthodox Judaism, as nothing more than unreconstructed atavism. The Talmud, its ancillary books, and the commentaries it has spawned may be ahistorical, but they are no less enlightening. They offer perspectives that might otherwise be ignored and highlight traditions that might otherwise be overlooked. To trivialize them is to undermine the very nature of the critical and analytic inquiry that modern scholars assert to be the essential feature of their endeavors.

NEHEMIAH AS MEMOIRIST

The same discussion in the Talmud that chides Nehemiah for his hubris credits him with authorship of both the book that bears his name and the Book of Ezra. Another talmudic source (Bava Batra 15a) asserts, however, that Ezra composed both books. Modern secular scholars likewise have no uniform view regarding the Book of Nehemiah's authorship. The dominant theory is that it was written by the so-called "Chronicler," the author of the Book of Chronicles and also of the Book of Ezra.[13] There are shades of difference, however, regarding the specific sources of

13. The discussion in Bava Batra 15a likewise ascribes most of Chronicles and Ezra to a common author, namely, Ezra himself, adding that Nehemiah completed the remainder of Chronicles after its listing of Ezra's own genealogy.

portions of Nehemiah, notably the section written in the first-person, termed "the Nehemiah memoir."[14] It is widely agreed, however, that at a minimum, "substantial parts of the Book of Nehemiah go back to a first-person account by Nehemiah himself (or an amanuensis writing under his immediate direction)."[15]

Most scholars argue that someone else – a "Chronicler" who also wrote Chronicles or one or more independent editors – compiled both Ezra and Nehemiah. But a recent major study of the literary style of all three books argues convincingly that Ezra and Nehemiah shared a common author *who was different* from the redactor of Chronicles. Another study argues that there were actually three variants of the Chronicler's work, at least one of which was available to Nehemiah, and one that incorporated Nehemiah's memoirs.[16]

It is possible that there were two quite separate traditions, which derived from independently written memoirs that were later fused into one. The existence of two traditions would also explain Ben Sira's placing Nehemiah among the pantheon of Jewish leaders but ignoring Ezra.[17] Ben Sira was simply reflecting Nehemiah's popularity with the masses, which stemmed from the nature of his aggressive lay leadership – the same leadership that so discomfited some of the Talmud's rabbis. Yet even on this point it appears that "the issue cannot be decided beyond reasonable doubt"[18] – an observation that, in light of the endless disputes among Bible scholars, applies to virtually all of their hypotheses.

In any event, even according to the Talmud, Nehemiah functioned as an editor as well as an author. Moreover, there is no denying that Nehemiah cited both royal decrees (or possibly extracts of those

14. R. J. Coggins, for example, speculates that the memoir was "written by someone else to do honour to Nehemiah." See R. J. Coggins, *The Books of Ezra and Nehemiah* (Cambridge: Cambridge University Press, 1976), 2–5.
15. Williamson, *Ezra, Nehemiah,* xxiv.
16. Frank Moore Cross, *From Epic to Canon: History and Literature in Ancient Israel* (Baltimore and London: Johns Hopkins University Press, 1998), 164–69, 172. See Williamson, *Ezra, Nehemiah,* xxiv–xxvii, for a discussion of the various views taken regarding the nature and authorship of the Nehemiah memoir.
17. *Ben Sira* 49:13.
18. Blenkinsopp, *Ezra-Nehemiah,* 47.

decrees) that he had not formulated and lists that he had certainly come upon somewhere – notably those naming the original returnees to Zion under Zerubbabel. As editor, there would have been no reason for Nehemiah not to splice the texts available to him, whether those relating to Ezra or decrees and lists drawn from various archives, in a manner that best suited his purposes.[19]

When did Nehemiah edit the books? It is possible that he worked on Ezra and much of his own book after the Persian king recalled him from Judah, having served as governor for a dozen years. While in Susa he might have then completed his book before returning to Judah after an unspecified passage of time. He possibly reedited the whole book after his second tour in Judah was complete, perhaps some years after 425 BCE, when Darius, whom he mentions in his memoir, succeeded Artaxerxes on the Persian throne.[20]

---

19. This is, in fact, the approach that the nineteenth-century commentator Rabbi Meir Leibush ben Yeḥiel Michel Weiser (1809–1879), known by the acronym Malbim, takes in explaining discrepancies between the corresponding lists appearing in both Nehemiah 11 and I Chronicles 9. See his commentary on Nehemiah, *Leḥem Hapeḥa* (hereinafter cited as Malbim) on Neh. 11:4, s.v. *uveYerushalayim yashvu*. As one modern scholar asserts, even Neh. 8, which virtually all biblical scholars – following the version that appears in 1 Esdras – believe is best included with the Ezra story, could simply have been moved to the Book of Nehemiah for reasons of literary structure. To be sure, academic scholars would argue that this was the work of an independent editor. Nevertheless, apart from referring to an anonymous "Chronicler," Bible scholars have no clue as to who that editor actually might have been, much less when he wrote. The placement of chapter 8 could equally have been the work of Nehemiah.
20. Nehemiah mentions Darius in conjunction with his recording a list of several High Priests beginning with Eliashiv, his contemporary (Neh. 12:22). See Peter A. Steveson, *Ezra, Nehemiah, and Esther* (Greenville, SC: Bob Jones University Press, 2011), 95, who conjectures that Nehemiah completed his book around 420 BCE. Others are less certain that the reference is to Darius II Nothus. They feel it may possibly refer to Darius I Hystaspes, who reigned prior to Artaxerxes. Still others claim that Nehemiah is referring to Darius III Codomannus, who ruled Persia from 336 to 330 BCE. The latter view is based on the belief that parts of the Book of Nehemiah were grafted onto his memoir. For a discussion, see Williamson, *Ezra, Nehemiah*, 357, 364–65. Ironically, this third view coincides exactly with the view of the Tosafists (medieval French talmudic scholars). *Tosafot*, Rosh HaShana 3b, s.vv. *shnat*, *b'oto*. See Appendix A, "Chronological Table."

We know little about Nehemiah's final days, other than a stray midrash or two. It is quite plausible that with this book he sought to leave his imprint on history in the twilight of his career, much as Josephus did several centuries later.[21]

REGARDING EZRA

Ezra son of Seraiah, the scribe and scholar,[22] is a towering figure in Jewish history who – according to Jewish tradition – was Nehemiah's contemporary. Like Nehemiah, he too requested and received royal permission from Artaxerxes to travel to Judah; unlike Nehemiah, he was not prompted to do so by residents of the province. The king authorized him to lead a group of Babylonian Jews to Judah, to bring gold and silver to be spent on offerings for the Temple, to conduct an inquiry into the situation in the province and in Jerusalem, and "to appoint magistrates and judges to judge all the people in the province of Abar Nahara [Beyond the River, i.e., Judah] who know the laws of your God, and to teach those who do not know them" (Ezra 7:25).[23] Ezra arrived in Judah, accompanied by some fifteen hundred males (8:2–20) and an unknown number of women and children, bringing funds for gifts to the Temple and a writ from the king to investigate the situation in Judah and Jerusalem. At that point he "dedicated himself... to teach laws and rules to Israel" (7:10), to revive the people's floundering commitment to religious practice, and to eradicate what he viewed as the plague of intermarriage that had affected large sections of Jewish society. The sages of the Talmud also credited him with many important innovations in Jewish law and practice.

Nevertheless, Ezra figures only fleetingly in the Book of Nehemiah, leading many critical scholars to conclude that the two men

21. The dating of Nehemiah's work, perhaps ten or more years after his return to Judah, would then be consistent with the reference to Darius II (423–404 CE) in Neh. 12:22. Nehemiah himself could thus be the third Chronicler (Chr3) to whom Cross refers (Cross, *From Epic to Canon*, 172).

22. The Hebrew term (Ezra 7:6) is *sofer*, which is usually translated as "scribe"; A. J. Rosenberg, *Daniel, Ezra, Nehemiah: A New Translation* (New York: Judaica Press, 1991), 148, translates the word as "scholar."

23. See also Williamson, *Ezra, Nehemiah*, xlvi–vii.

were not contemporaries, and that the references to their joint activities were later additions to Nehemiah's memoir. Moreover, a wealth of academic literature endlessly debates whether Ezra preceded Nehemiah in coming to Judah, in 458 BCE, or followed him, in 398 BCE or at some other date.[24]

Scholars are increasingly predisposed to the view that Ezra preceded Nehemiah to Judah.[25] The two men obviously could have functioned contemporaneously if Ezra's mission began thirteen years before that of Nehemiah. Moreover, as a recent study indicates, the ceremony over which they jointly presided (described in Nehemiah 12) makes no sense at all unless both were participants, since otherwise it "would leave one of the [two] processions [described therein] without a leader."[26]

Finally, the fact that Nehemiah was certainly self-centered – he barely credits anyone with a major role in supporting his activities as governor – in no way indicates that he would have completely disregarded Ezra's activities. Nehemiah's is a political memoir and apologia that justifies his actions as governor. It is perfectly consistent for the author of such a work to relegate Ezra's role to that of religious functionary.[27]

One thing is certain, however. Nehemiah takes less than subtle swipes at Ezra. He ends Ezra's book abruptly, with the scribe seemingly having succeeded in preventing intermarriage only to have the reader discover that Nehemiah had to cope with the same issue a mere decade later. In so doing, Nehemiah is able to contrast his own modus operandi favorably to that of the more spiritually oriented Ezra. Ezra's initiatives were short-lived; it took Nehemiah, who, unlike Ezra, arrived

24. As noted above, the Tosafists assigned a later date to Nehemiah's activities. They also argued that Ezra followed Nehemiah, because the political tranquility that Nehemiah established in Judah was a prerequisite for the success of Ezra's activities. See *Tosafot* in Rosh HaShana 3b and Rabbi Yosef Rabinowitz, *Nechemiah: The Book of Nehemiah* (Brooklyn, NY: Mesorah/Artscroll, 1990), 32.

25. For an extended discussion, see Cross, *From Epic to Canon*, 152–64.

26. Edwin M. Yamauchi, *Persia and the Bible* (Grand Rapids, MI: Baker Book House, 1990), 253.

27. It is also possible, as Bright argues, that "the two men, both decided personalities, came to have little love for each other"; John Bright, *A History of Israel*, 3rd ed. (Philadelphia: Westminster Press, 1981), 389.

in Jerusalem with an armed Persian escort, to set those initiatives on a more permanent footing. It is no wonder that the rabbis of the Talmud had such an ambivalent view of him, even as they lauded Ezra.

NEHEMIAH'S WORLD: THE JEWS IN THE PERSIAN EMPIRE

Jewry has only fond memories of the early years of the Persian Empire. The empire came into being under the leadership of Cyrus the Great, scion of Persia's Achaemenid dynasty and maternal grandson of Astyages, king of Media.[28] Cyrus initially ascended to the throne of Anshan, a Median vassal state and the seat of the Persian kingdom, in 559 BCE. While still a young monarch, Cyrus organized the neighboring tribes into a rebel force and led them against his grandfather, Astyages. At the same time, he also entered into a treaty relationship with Nabonidas, king of Babylonia, the most powerful empire of the day.[29]

Cyrus defeated Astyages, and together with Harpagus, his leading general, proceeded to conquer much of western Asia. As a result of winning the Median throne, Cyrus came into control of some formerly Assyrian territory that was also claimed by Babylonia. A clash between the treaty partners was inevitable, and a series of battles ensued, with Cyrus the victor. Cyrus then attacked Babylon itself in conjunction with a subordinate Median emir (Cyrus had reversed the relationship between the kingdoms of Media and Persia) whom Daniel calls Darius the Mede (Dan. 6:1).

Darius the Mede is nearly as popular in Jewish lore as Cyrus, though his historical identity is the subject of much conjecture and dispute.[30] He may well have been Cyrus's general Harpagus, who was a Mede,

28. The Achaemenids referred to themselves by this name because they claimed descent from a royal ancestor named Achaemenes. See Thomas M. Bolin, *Ezra, Nehemiah* (Collegeville, MN: Liturgical Press, 2012), 6.

29. Herodotus, *The Persian Wars,* trans. George Rawlinson, with an introduction by F. R. B. Godolphin (New York: Random House, 1942), chaps. 107–30.

30. Jewish tradition, as well as Christian and Islamic tradition, is unequivocal about the role the man Daniel calls "Darius the son of Ahasuerus" had in the fall of Babylon. Some talmudic sources argue that Darius was Cyrus's father-in-law. The Talmud also calculates that he was relatively old, aged sixty-two, when he took Babylon, and that

and who may have commanded one of the two Persian army groups that successfully overran Babylon in 539 BCE. There is also a midrashic tradition that he was Cyrus's father-in-law. That tradition might simply have confused "Darius the Mede" with Astyages, likewise a Mede, who was Cyrus's grandfather. Whatever his identity, one particularly colorful midrash portrays Darius and Cyrus as two biblically well-versed, excessively polite gatekeepers for Belshazzar, king of Babylonia.

> Said Cyrus to Darius, "You rule first." Said Darius to Cyrus, "That was not Daniel's intention when he stated, 'Divide your kingdom between Media and Persia. First Media and then Persia. So you rule before me.'" When [Belshazzar] heard Daniel's vision [of his imminent demise] he ordered, "Anyone who will appear here at night, even if he tells you that he is the king, behead him." That night Belshazzar developed intestinal trouble and went outside the palace to the privy, unbeknownst to the guards. When he returned they detected him and asked, "Who is that?" He answered them, "I am the king." They ruminated, "Have we not been given an order?" and they killed him. (Song of Songs Rabba 3:4)

Whatever the circumstances, and whoever he may have been, Darius quickly disappeared from the narrative. It was Cyrus's accession to the throne of the Babylonian Empire that signaled the beginning of the Jewish redemption foretold by the prophet Isaiah. In fact, in 538 BCE, within a year of his becoming emperor, Cyrus proclaimed that the Jews could return to their ancestral homeland to rebuild their Temple.

The Jews of Babylonia had arrived there in three distinct stages. King Jehoiachin (also known as Jeconiah), members of his royal court, other members of the upper classes, and many craftsmen had been

---

he died within a year of his victory. While some secular historians question his very existence, others have sought to identify him with various Median or Persian kings or generals, most of whom are mentioned in Herodotus's *Persian Wars*. Josephus claims that he was the son of Astyages, making him Cyrus's uncle. Josephus Flavius, *Jewish Antiquities*, vol. 6, trans. Ralph Marcus (Cambridge, MA: Harvard University Press, 1937), X:248, see also fn d.

taken to Babylon in 597 BCE. When Nebuchadnezzar's forces burned the Temple in 586 BCE, far more people were exiled, though there were fewer important personages among them. When Gedaliah son of Ahikam, Nebuchadnezzar's representative, was murdered, a third, much smaller wave left for Babylonia.

The Jews settled in the vicinity of the city of Nippur, near the river Kebar (which in actuality was a canal), where Ezekiel prophesied (Ezek. 1:1). Left to their own devices, free to live as a community and to cultivate land that the Babylonians had given them,[31] encouraged by the prophet Jeremiah to establish themselves in the land of their captivity,[32] the Jews displayed both the resilience and the remarkable degree of adaptability that was to mark the two millennia of the Roman exile. They quickly began to assimilate to their new surroundings and they prospered.

Moreover, Ezekiel's encouragement – along with the fact that Nebuchadnezzar's son, Evil-Merodach (Amel-Marduk), not only had spared King Jehoiachin for thirty-seven years after his capture and exile but had elevated him to a dignified position at the Babylonian court and given him a royal allowance (II Kings 25:27–30) – helped give the community a sense of dignity and purpose. It appears that the community viewed Jehoiachin as leader of a government-in-exile even before Nebuchadnezzar dethroned Zedekiah and destroyed the Temple.[33] Evil-Merodach essentially formalized Jehoiachin's position. Furthermore, Daniel's ascent under Nebuchadnezzar, and his ability to maintain his position, no doubt also sustained the community's morale. This was especially true in view of the various tribulations it confronted during the turbulence in the years that followed Nebuchadnezzar's death, when the crown changed hands several times and the empire then fell to Persia.

Morale was one thing; migration was something quite different altogether. Indeed, the Jews responded only too well to Jeremiah's injunction – the basis for the standard Jewish prayer for the welfare of

31. Elias Bickerman, *From Ezra to the Last of the Maccabees* (New York: Schocken, 1962), 5.
32. "Build yourselves houses and dwell in them, and plant gardens and eat the fruit of them, take yourselves wives and beget sons and daughters" (Jer. 29:5–6).
33. Binyamin Lau, *Jeremiah: The Fate of a Prophet*, trans. Sara Daniel (Jerusalem: Maggid Books, 2013), 133.

the government – to "seek the peace of the city whither I have caused you to be carried away captive, and pray unto the Lord for it; for in the peace thereof shall you have peace" (Jer. 29:7). They stayed put.

Cyrus appears to have rightly judged that not all Jews would choose to leave their newfound home in Babylonia, despite the fact that the final phase of their exile, and the destruction of their Temple, had taken place less than fifty years earlier. Accordingly, Cyrus's proclamation, a more complete version of which is recorded in the Book of Ezra, not only encouraged those who wished to rebuild the Temple, but added that those who chose not to return to Judah should aid those returning "with silver, and with gold, and with goods, and with beasts beside the freewill-offering for the house of God which is in Jerusalem" (Ezra 1:4). Cyrus, too, provided material support, returning all the Temple vessels that the Babylonian king Nebuchadnezzar had carried off when he destroyed the Temple (1:7–11).

As Cyrus had anticipated, the majority of the Jews in Babylonia chose not to leave their new home. Foreshadowing Jewish behavior during the entire Second Temple period – not to mention in the years preceding the creation of the State of Israel and until today – those who chose not to leave Babylonia appear to have been very supportive of the returning exiles. As Scripture records, they provided the returning exiles with "vessels of silver, with gold, with goods, and with precious things, beside all that was willingly offered" (Ezra 1:6). But while the number of returnees is not given, it appears to have been rather small – again, this is reflected in the initial migrations to Israel in the nineteenth and early twentieth centuries.

Although Cyrus had referred to the God of Israel, his proclamation was not necessarily motivated by warm feelings toward the Jews, though he clearly was not averse to them either. Many scholars speculate that the proclamation reflected the Achaemenid state's interest in having loyal nationalities defending the empire's strategic outposts. This happened to converge with the interests of those Jews in the Babylonian exile who sought to return to Judea, an area that could command access both to Egypt and the Mediterranean Sea. Whatever his intent, however, Cyrus's declaration did not result in the immediate re-creation of a Jewish Commonwealth.

The leader of the small band of Babylonian Jews who made the journey home was, as the Book of Ezra described him, a "prince of Judah" named Sheshbazzar. Evidently, he was a scion of the royal house of David who must have had both access and influence at the highest levels of the Persian court. Cyrus appointed him governor of Judah. It was to him that Cyrus returned the Temple vessels, and it was he who laid the Temple's foundation stone (Ezra 5:14–16). Unusually for the books of Ezra and Nehemiah, and generally for Scripture, he carries no patronymic; his name is Chaldean.[34] Some modern scholars argue, on the basis of a similar name that appears in Chronicles, that he was the fourth son of the exiled King Jehoiachin; others are less certain. All agree, however, that he should not be identified with Zerubbabel son of Shealtiel, also a scion of the Davidic line, who led the next group of exiles from Babylonia to Judah several decades later, and whom the emperor Darius appointed its governor.[35] In fact, apart from the few passages already cited, we know nothing more about Sheshbazzar. Even the Midrash, whose homilies and tales frequently fill scriptural lacunae, has nothing to say about him.

Sheshbazzar's mission provoked opposition from the local inhabitants of Judah. Surprisingly, given the financial support they had provided to the returnees, it appears that there was no reaction to this opposition on the part of the Jewish community in Babylonia. In any event, it is not clear what happened to the people who returned to Judah with Sheshbazzar; they seem to have accomplished little. The fate of Sheshbazzar's mission remains a mystery.

As noted, some years after Sheshbazzar's mission, another scion of the Davidic line, Zerubbabel son of Shealtiel, grandson of King

34. Modern scholars agree that it is indeed a Chaldean name, meaning "sun-god protect the sun"; *The Soncino Bible: Daniel, Ezra, Nehemiah*, with commentary by Judah J. Slotki (London: Soncino, 1951), 114.

35. Mordekhai Zer-Kavod, *Ezra UNeḥemia* (Jerusalem: Mossad Harav Kook, 1988), 9; *The Anchor Bible: Ezra/Nehemiah*, trans. and intro. Jacob M. Myers (New York: Doubleday, 1965), 9; *Olam HaTanakh: Daniel, Ezra UNeḥemia*, chief ed. Gershon Galil (Tel Aviv: Dodson-Eti, 1997), 131–32. In contrast, however, medieval commentators, such as Rashi, Ibn Ezra, and Ralbag, all argue that Sheshbazzar was simply Zerubbabel's Chaldean name.

Jehoiachin, led a larger migration of Jews to Judah intending to rebuild the Temple. The mission quickly ran into difficulties because of the opposition of the indigenous population, many of whom were descended from the Samaritans. Biblical tradition records that the Samaritans were originally heathens whom the Assyrian king Esarhaddon settled on the territory of the ten tribes that had constituted the Kingdom of Israel, some years after Sargon II had carried them off into exile.[36] Faced with savage attacks by wild lions that both they and the Assyrians attributed to God's anger at their animist practices, the Samaritans accepted the God of Israel – without, however, renouncing their own deities. Now settled in lands that had previously been populated by the Jews, the Samaritans bitterly resented the return of the exiles, viewing them as a threat to their own territorial control. For their part, the Jews rejected any overtures by the Samaritans because of the latter's syncretic beliefs.[37]

The Book of Ezra recounts that, as a result of lobbying by both the local inhabitants of Judah and their hired representatives in the Persian capital, Cyrus reversed himself and brought the Temple project to a halt (Ezra 4:2–6, 17–24).[38] According to some traditional Jewish commentators, a large portion of the community that had emigrated with Sheshbazzar in the immediate aftermath of Cyrus's proclamation was so disheartened as to return to Babylonia.[39]

In many respects, the course of these events bears considerable resemblance to the fate of the Zionist movement during the first half of the twentieth century. In both cases, the governing power – Persia

---

36. See II Kings 17:24ff. II Chronicles makes no mention of Esarhaddon's resettlement, though the book generally focuses on developments in Judah rather than the Northern Kingdom. The present-day Samaritans themselves claim to be the descendants of the Ten Tribes.

37. See Malbim, *Aliyat Ezra*, Ezra 4:2, s.v. *nivne*, and 4:3, s.v. *anaḥnu*; Zer-Kavod, *Ezra UNeḥemia*, 26–27.

38. See also Slotki, *Daniel, Ezra, Nehemiah*, 109, and Rabinowitz, *Nechemiah*, 30n3.

39. The Ran (Rabbi Nissim Girondi, 1320–1376), commenting on Megilla 1b, argues that there *may* have been a large migration back to Babylonia; see also Rabinowitz, *Nechemiah*, 34, who in citing Metzudat David (the commentary of Rabbi David ben Solomon ibn Zimra, ca. 1479–1573), is more definite about the return of the Jews to Babylonia, but also cites the Ran, failing to mention that the latter's view was only tentative.

in the ancient past, Britain more recently as the mandatory power governing Palestine – initially offered new hope to the Jewish community. As with Cyrus's proclamation, mixed political motives certainly stimulated the Balfour Declaration.[40] In both cases, leading lobbyists for the Jewish cause were Jews who were well placed at the highest levels of the non-Jewish government – Sheshbazzar and later Zerubbabel in ancient times; Chaim Weizmann and Sir Herbert Samuel in the twentieth century. In both cases, initial government support for the settlement effort succumbed to other sources of political pressure that threatened to undermine, if not abrogate, the movement to settle the Land of Israel with Jews. And in both cases opposition to Jewish settlement came not only from the indigenous population but also from its lobbyists in the capital of the governing power. In ancient times, according to various midrashic works, it was none other than Haman, the villain of the Book of Esther;[41] in the twentieth century it was the equally villainous mufti of Jerusalem, Amin al-Husseini.[42] Both men openly shared the same objective: to rid the Land of Israel of the Jewish people and ultimately to exterminate them.

It was only in 522 BCE, nearly two decades after Cyrus's proclamation, that Darius Hystaspes, who had succeeded Cyrus's son Cambyses six years earlier, reauthorized the construction of the Temple. Darius's decision, which came in the second year of his reign, was made in the face of the same strong local and national opposition that had led to the suspension of the Temple project under Cyrus. In fact, it occurred

40. There is a wealth of literature on the Declaration and the motives behind it. A great British historian summed them up neatly in a single sentence and footnote; see A. J. P. Taylor, *English History, 1914–1945* (New York and Oxford: Oxford University Press, 1965), 98 and fn 1.

41. There are several variants of this midrash. Esther Rabba (7:2) simply states that Haman advised Ahasuerus to halt construction of the Temple. *Seder Olam Rabba* (29) states that it was the sons of Haman who wrote the king opposing its construction. *Yalkut Shimoni* (II:545, on Amos 5:19), citing various midrashim, states that Haman and his son Shimshai were the ones who convinced the king to suspend the Temple project.

42. Simon Sebag Montefiore, *Jerusalem: The Biography* (London: Phoenix, 2012), 545–47; see also David G. Dallin and John F. Rothmann, *Icon of Evil: Hitler's Mufti and the Rise of Radical Islam* (New York: Random House, 2008), 39–65.

only after Zerubbabel and the High Priest Jeshua – who, despite Cyrus's change of heart, apparently never ceased to press for the reconstruction of the Temple – prompted a search of the Empire's records to validate their claim that Cyrus had granted the Jews the right to rebuild it. It was as a result of that search, which unearthed Cyrus's proclamation, that Darius issued his own edict regarding the Temple. Zerubbabel and the High Priest Jeshua, both already in Judah, thereupon completed and rededicated the Temple and restored its ritual and services.

Even when the Temple was finally completed, with Darius's support, in 516 CE, the nascent polity was virtually stillborn. Immigration dried up; intermarriage was rife. The local Jewish elites made common cause with their non-Jewish neighbors, and generally oppressed those non-elite Jews and others who had remained behind in Judah during the exile and who, as a consequence, had little economic power and even less political clout. None of these developments appears to have evoked much concern on the part of Babylonian Jewry until Ezra appeared on the scene about half a century later.

Persia itself was home to a significant number of Jews, as the Book of Esther clearly attests. However, like all the subject peoples of the Persian Empire, the Jews suffered from the vagaries of whoever occupied the Persian throne. Cambyses seems to have looked favorably upon the Jewish community, even recruiting the Jews of Elephantine, in Egypt, to serve under Persian military command,[43] while Darius allowed the Jews to complete the construction of their Temple. On the other hand, Xerxes (519–465 BCE), who is probably the Ahasuerus of the Book of Esther, was no friend of the Jewish community, nor, for that matter, of the other subject peoples of his empire. Jewish tradition dating back to talmudic times links the events in Esther to the ethnic tension in the province of Judah. Since the Book of Ezra recounts the Jews' difficulties from Cyrus's reign through that of Artaxerxes, it does appear likely that the story of Esther was somehow intertwined with the fate of the Jews in Judah. Certainly, the downfall of Haman must have proved as much of a relief to the Jews who had returned from Babylonia as to those who stayed behind.

---

43. Yamauchi, *Persia and the Bible*, 98.

The report in Esther that "many from among the peoples of the land became Jews" (Est. 8:17) underscores their continued rapid rise to social prominence once Haman was no longer on the scene. The Jews of Judah certainly appear to have done what they could to demonstrate their loyalty to their Persian masters. According to Herodotus, the "Syrians of Palestine" joined with the Phoenicians to furnish and man three hundred triremes for Xerxes's major military operation against the Greeks.[44] That these Syrians of Palestine were none other than Jews can be inferred from the fact that Herodotus describes them both as practicing circumcision[45] and as, "according to their own account, [having] dwelt anciently upon the Red Sea, but crossing thence, they fixed themselves on the sea-coast of Syria, which they still inhabit. This part of Syria, and all of the region extending from hence to Egypt, is known by the name of Palestine."[46]

It is noteworthy that the Jews in question were prepared to combine forces with the Phoenicians. Presumably these Jews were remnants of the sea-faring tribes, notably Dan, Asher, Menashe, Issachar, and Zebulun, who had survived both the Assyrian and Babylonian exiles.[47] From the Song of Deborah, some scholars have inferred that the tribe of Dan, in particular, had a long history of joint maritime missions with the

44. Herodotus, *Persian Wars,* VII:89, 530. A trireme was a galley with three tiers of oars on each side, one above the other, that was employed primarily as a warship.

45. Herodotus claims that they learned the practice from the Egyptians. F. R. B. Godolphin notes, however, "He may be excused for supposing that the Jews borrowed circumcision from the Egyptians, since they did not practice it as a regular and universal custom until after they left Egypt." See ibid., II:104, 165n53.

46. Ibid. VII:89, 530. The Phoenicians also practiced circumcision, but did not claim to have crossed the Red Sea into Palestine.

47. A number of aggadic sources indicate that some portion of the Ten Tribes remained in the Land of Israel after the Assyrian conquest. The Talmud (Megilla 14b) states that Jeremiah brought back the Ten Tribes during Josiah's reign. *Yalkut Shimoni* cites a source that claims that one-eighth of the Northern Kingdom's population was not exiled but instead migrated to Judea (*Yalkut Shimoni,* II:236). Rivka Gonen also points to the likelihood that refugees from the north streamed into Judea; Rivka Gonen, *To the Ends of the Earth: The Quest for the Ten Lost Tribes of Israel* (Northvale, NJ: Jason Aaronson, 2002), 17. It is arguable that after the Persian conquest, some members of the remnant of the ten tribes migrated back to their original territories.

Phoenicians.[48] Moreover, the two nations had a history of friendly relations dating back to Hiram's provision of materials for the construction of the First Temple. In any event, the joint force is believed to have been superior in "quality and numbers" to the rest of Xerxes's fleet; the sailors were armed with Greek-style helmets, rimless shields, and javelins. However capable the combined Phoenician-Jewish force might have been, it was insufficient to prevent Xerxes's crushing maritime defeat in the battle of Salamis (480 BCE), which brought to an end the Persian invasion of Greece.

The fact that Jews probably fought on behalf of the Persians is yet another indication that by the time Ezra led the next wave of settlement from Babylonia two decades after Salamis, they had become quite well acculturated to the Persian environment.[49] Jews had become landholders and financiers as well as tenant farmers. The records of the Murashu family of Nippur, which some scholars in the past thought may have been Jewish, include Jewish-sounding names of people who served as witnesses and of government officials, like Nehemiah, in whose time the Murashu flourished.[50] Babylonian Jews also reflected another, more troubling aspect of acculturation and assimilation: they, like their contemporaries in Judah, had begun to marry out of the faith, an ironic development given the above-noted reports of mass conversions to Judaism.

The local civilization permeated even Jewish ritual. Perhaps the most prominent case of non-Jewish influence on Jewish religious practice was the new nomenclature for the months of the Jewish year: Marheshvan, Shevat, Tammuz, and Elul, for example. Even the Talmud acknowledges that Ezra imported the names of the months from

48. Judges 5:17; see *Encyclopaedia Judaica* (Jerusalem: Keter, 1972), s.v. "Phoenicia, Phoenicians."

49. Unlike Jews drafted into the Russian tsarist army, there is no evidence that the Jews who fought for Persia were compelled to do so.

50. A brief discussion of the Murashu appears in Georges Roux, *Ancient Iraq*, 3rd ed. (London: Penguin, 1992), 411. The primary analysis of the archaeological findings that revealed the activities of the Murashu is found in G. Cardascia, *Les Archives des Murasu* (Paris: Imprimerie Nationale Paris, 1951).

Babylonia (Y. Rosh HaShana 5b). To this day, the months of the Jewish calendar bear non-Hebrew names.[51]

Ezra's lasting contribution to Judaism was his reimposition of the Scripture as the central sacred text and guidepost of Jewish life. Some scholars argue that, through various means, he also restored the Pentateuch to its original intent, if not form, by compensating in a variety of ways for the many errors that might have crept into its text over the generations.[52] What Ezra could not do, however, was reorganize the community in a way that conformed to Jewish norms. His initial attempts to terminate the practice of intermarriage with other faiths failed miserably; it was only when Nehemiah supported him that Ezra was able to combat that scourge of Jewish identity.

"Nehemiah to the rescue" might well be the subtitle of his eponymous book. He rescued the polity from external threat and internal stagnation. He salvaged Ezra's efforts to restore Judaism to the core of the Jewish experience. He rescued the nation from the loss of its identity, thereby not only improving the lot of those Jews who lived in Judah, but of Jews everywhere, from Persia to Elephantine. He so deeply implanted a sense of nationhood in the Jewish people that they were able to retain their identity through two millennia of exile. And when they returned to the city whose walls he had rebuilt, they inscribed his name, and the verses of his book, on the walls that symbolize the Jewish people's eternal commitment to his legacy.

---

51. In contrast, R. Elazar HaKappar asserted that "in the merit of four things did the Israelites leave Egypt: they did not change their names; they did not change their language; they were not steeped in debauchery; and they did not reveal their mysteries"; *Midrash Shoḥer Tov al Tehillim* (Jerusalem: Amudim, 5752/1993), 215.

52. See, in particular, David Weiss Halivni, *Revelation Restored: Divine Writ and Critical Responses* (Boulder, CO: Westview, 1997).

Nehemiah 1:1–3
Origins

WHO WAS NEHEMIAH?

Talmudic and mystical literature have assigned various identities to Nehemiah. According to one opinion in the Talmud, frequently echoed by classical and neo-classical commentators, he was actually Zerubbabel, the royal scion of David who led the returnees after Cyrus's decree in 538 BCE (Sanhedrin 38a). Since Zerubbabel lived nearly a century before Nehemiah, however, it is unlikely that the two were one and the same.

A relatively obscure midrash known as "Midrash of the Ten Kings" asserts that Nehemiah was a scion of the Judean royal family.[1] A second talmudic opinion is far more specific, claiming that he was Asir Shealtiel, who is described as the son of King Jeconiah in I Chronicles 3:17. Asir Shealtiel, the Talmud states, was another name for Zerubbabel, whose real name was Nehemiah son of Hakhaliah (Sanhedrin 37b–38a). According to the talmudic account, the king impregnated Nehemiah's mother while they were both still imprisoned by Nebuchadnezzar. However, the timelines do not support this interpretation either; Zerubbabel has himself been identified as the grandson of Jeconiah.

1. Williamson cites a similar opinion that Nehemiah was descended from a "branch" of the royal family. See Williamson, *Ezra, Nehemiah*, 179. The Hippolytus Chronicle also claimed that he was of Davidic descent; see Myers, *Ezra/Nehemiah*, lxxvi.

According to a tradition ascribed to the mystic Rabbi Isaac Luria (popularly known as the Ari, 1534–1572), Nehemiah was the reincarnation of the child born out of wedlock to David and Bathsheba.[2] Rabbi Luria built upon the tradition in the Midrash of the Ten Kings by offering a linkage to the Davidic royal family that Scripture had not identified. Equally striking is the claim by the kabbalists Rabbi Yisrael Seruk and his student Rabbi Menachem Azarya of Fano that the tannaitic leader of the Sanhedrin, R. Gamaliel, was the reincarnation of Nehemiah.[3] R. Gamaliel was the leader (prince or *nasi*) of the Jewish community after the destruction of the Second Temple, much as Nehemiah had led the community not long after its construction. Like Nehemiah, R. Gamaliel was reputed to be descended from King David according to the Midrash and Talmud.

Both mystical notions built upon the kabbalistic tradition of reincarnation (*gilgul*) in order to place Nehemiah within the flow of Jewish history. The former assertion employed the kabbalistic notion that the souls of departed children reemerge in the bodies of others. The latter drew upon the kabbalistic idea that the souls of great men reappear centuries later in the bodies of other greats.

If Nehemiah's identity is not clear, other aspects of his origin are equally shrouded in mystery. His father's name, Hakhaliah, reflects an Egyptian-Jewish background; it appears several times in Alexandrian Jewish papyri and was the name of one of Cleopatra III's generals. At the time, there was a thriving Jewish community in Egypt. The Jews who made up the garrison at Elephantine on the Upper Nile were supporters of Cambyses when he conquered Egypt; they may also have brought Temple artifacts with them to Egypt after the Babylonian expulsion in 586 BCE.[4]

2. *Margaliot Hayam* cites Rabbi Chaim Vital, in *Sefer HaḤizyonot*, who claimed that Rabbi Luria told him this in a dream. Reuven Margaliot, *Margaliot Hayam: Sanhedrin*, vol. 2 (Jerusalem: Mossad Harav Kook, 5718/1958), 144.
3. See Yisrael Yaakov ben Simḥa Bunim, introduction to the Book of Nehemiah, in *Nevi'im and Ketubim with All the Commentaries*, Orim Gedolim ed., 65.
4. Bezalel Porten, "Did the Ark Stop at Elephantine?" *Biblical Archaeology Review* 21 (May/June 1995): 54–57.

Some Modern Orthodox scholars speculate that Nehemiah's parents may have been buried in Jerusalem.[5] The family may have moved to Jerusalem, possibly from Egypt; Nehemiah, following the path of many talented men before and since, moved to the center of imperial power – Susa, the Persian winter capital. The Book of Nehemiah begins with a visit to Susa by Hanani, whom Nehemiah describes as his brother. Hanani arrives from Judah to plead for Nehemiah's support for the reconstruction of Jerusalem's deteriorated infrastructure and beleaguered Jewish community. It would not have been uncommon for Nehemiah to move to Susa while Hanani stayed behind in Judah.[6]

Ultimately there can be little doubt that Nehemiah was the scion of an important Judean family, whose reputation was well established in Susa, the Persian capital. It is doubtful – though not impossible – that had Nehemiah been merely a lowly provincial outsider, he would ever have managed to achieve so exalted a position at the court. His rank: the king's cupbearer, the position he holds at the outset of the memoir that has come down to us as his eponymous book.

To be sure, the difficulty with specific claims about Nehemiah's origins is that his memoir does not provide the extended genealogy accorded to Ezra in his own biblical volume. Such a genealogy might have been expected had Nehemiah been a true scion of the royal family.[7] Whether royal or not, however, the family's connections must have facilitated Nehemiah's rise to the post of cupbearer to the emperor, which made him the highest-ranking Jew in the Persian court.

THE ROYAL CUPBEARER: NEHEMIAH'S ROLE AT COURT

The cupbearer to the Persian emperor was an extremely powerful courtier. Like the biblical Joseph, and, for that matter, the Persian cupbearer Ahikar – whom the author of the apocryphal Book of Tobit describes as "keeper of the royal seal, calculator of the accounts" – Nehemiah was

5. Zer-Kavod, *Ezra UNeḥemia*, 69. Nehemiah makes this claim in 2:3, though he may be speaking figuratively.
6. Zer-Kavod, *Ezra UNeḥemia*, 69.
7. Cf. Coggins, *Ezra and Nehemiah*, 70.

virtually a second-in-command to the emperor.[8] Like Joseph, he too "discharged his duties without compromising his identity."[9] If Nehemiah played his cards right, he had the potential to alter Judah's political, economic, and spiritual state beyond recognition.

Nehemiah may have been one of several cupbearers; the job seems to have rotated every two years or so.[10] Cupbearers usually were drawn from the Persian elite, though Nehemiah may have been appointed precisely because he was not identified with any party involved in palace intrigues.[11] In this regard Nehemiah's experience would not have been unique in Jewish history either in those days or in later years. Mordekhai may have been elevated for similar reasons. In medieval times, Hasdai ibn Shaprut, the powerful minister and diplomat of Muslim Cordova, and Samuel ibn Naghrilla, known as Rabbi Samuel the Prince (*nagid*), vizier of Granada, likewise were outsiders who rose to the highest rank under their respective rulers.[12] There are more recent examples as well. Of particular note is Andrei Azoulay's role as the long-time senior adviser to King Hassan II of Morocco. Azoulay, a French Jewish financier of Moroccan origin, and therefore likewise an outsider, was nicknamed by his local compatriots none other than *Mordekhai HaYehudi*.[13]

Artaxerxes may have been especially sensitive about having someone tasting his wine who was not identified with any of the court's

8. Cf. Tobit 1:22. Tobit claimed that Ahikar was his nephew, and that "Essarhadon had established him as second in command." Fifth-century CE Assyrian papyri confirm the existence and role of this powerful figure.
9. Blenkinsopp, *Ezra-Nehemiah*, 211–12.
10. Galil, *Daniel, Ezra UNeḥemia*, 205.
11. Ibid.
12. Hasdai initially joined the Cordovan court as the caliph's personal physician; Samuel was selling spices in a small shop when the Granadan vizier took him on as his secretary. See Simon Dubnov, *History of the Jews from the Roman Empire to the Early Medieval Period*, trans. Moshe Spiegel, vol. 2 (South Brunswick, NJ: Thomas Yoseloff, 1968), 609–11, 623–27. See *Encyclopaedia Judaica* (Jerusalem: Keter, 1971), s.vv. "Hasdai" and "Samuel."
13. While Jack Lew's position as chief of staff to President Obama and, more recently, secretary of the treasury is not entirely identical to the roles played by his illustrious rabbinic predecessors, it certainly shares with them the unique access and influence that only the closest proximity to the leader of a state affords.

cliques. His father had been murdered by Artabanus, the commander of the royal bodyguard, after surviving an assassination attempt by two other bodyguards – Bigtan and Teresh, according to the Book of Esther. The Talmud asserts that the plot involved poisoning Xerxes's food; the Aramaic *Targum* has them poisoning Esther's wine and then stabbing Xerxes with a sword.[14]

We are not told how Nehemiah came to be cupbearer – much in the same way as we are simply informed that Joseph and Mordekhai rose to their respective and analogous roles. Nor do we know what he did before he was cupbearer or how he won the king's trust, which was a sine qua non for holding any senior office in the royal court. The Midrash of the Ten Kings asserts that Artaxerxes was attracted to him because of his royal ancestry as well as his good looks.[15] In any event, Nehemiah gives credit to no one other than himself throughout his memoir; there is no mention of a mentor or a patron.

Nor does Nehemiah tell us very much about himself, other than his father's name and his kinship with Hanani. The Scripture at times provides descriptions of its heroes: Joseph was good-looking; Saul was tall; Esau was ruddy, as was David; Elisha the prophet was bald; Eglon, the king of Moab, was fat, while his killer, Ehud son of Gera, was left-handed.

But we know nothing about Nehemiah's physiognomy. Was he tall or short, fat or thin?[16] We know of no wife, nor of any children. Nehemiah likewise relates nothing at all about his education. We are not told of teachers or mentors, yet it is clear that he must have received both a thorough religious education and some sort of general one as well. His memoir tells us that when he acted upon his brother's plea and prepared to meet with the emperor Artaxerxes to seek royal assistance for the Jews of Judah, he first prayed to God. He laced his entreaties with passages that are reminiscent, in both language and intent, of the

14. Megilla 13b; *Targum*, Est. 2:21.

15. Midrash of the Ten Kings, cited in Yisrael Yitzchak Hasida, *Otzar Ishei HaTanakh: Demutam UFe'alam befi Ḥaza"l* (*Encyclopedia of Biblical Personalities: As Seen by the Sages of the Talmud and the Midrash*) (Jerusalem: Reuven Mas, 1991), 307. This was also the case with Daniel.

16. Josephus, *Antiquities*, XVI:230, asserts that he was handsome but offers no proof for this.

pleas of Moses as well as Solomon's prayer upon the construction of the Temple. He could not have done so without a thoroughgoing knowledge of his people's sacred texts.

Nehemiah's education, as stated, could not have been limited to sacred subjects. In addition to the world of religion, Nehemiah must have also have been well schooled in the language and mores of the Persian court. Even if his position as cupbearer was his first and only royal appointment, he nevertheless must have possessed the ability to communicate with the king. He must have been able to converse in Aramaic, the region's lingua franca and the official language of the Persian court and empire, and probably Persian (actually Median) as well. Moreover, to have survived at court, he must have understood the nature of its ways, enabling him to cope with the chicanery and intrigue that have marked royal court life from ancient times until the modern era.

Several scholars, beginning with the Church father Origen, have concluded that Nehemiah was a eunuch. Their premise is that Persian royal cupbearers must have been eunuchs, because they served in the queen's presence.[17] In so doing they follow what appears to have been a mistranslation of the Hebrew word *mashke* in two manuscripts of the Septuagint.[18] Other scholars have refuted this view, not only because Haman, who fathered ten sons and was therefore no eunuch, was often in Esther's presence, but also because Persian courtiers who served as pages and bodyguards could enter the royal harem even if they were not eunuchs.[19]

Jewish tradition points to other difficulties with the eunuch thesis. Eunuchs were excluded from the Jewish community (Deut. 23:2);

17. Cf. Neh. 2:6; Myers, *Ezra/Nehemiah*, lxxvi, 96; and Bright, *History*, 380.

18. For a discussion, see Steveson, *Ezra, Nehemiah, and Esther*, 108–9. Steveson rejects the notion that Nehemiah was a eunuch.

19. See especially Yamauchi, *Persia and the Bible*, 263–64. Yamauchi argues that "no firm evidence exists that Nehemiah was a eunuch. Dogmatic statements that he was are based on a web of arguments that in many cases are untenable and in other cases are less than convincing." Williamson points out that proponents of the eunuch thesis erroneously cite as evidence the fact that Nehemiah is so described in the Septuagint. He notes, however, that the Greek word for "eunuch" is actually a scribal error. The correct word is "cupbearer" (Williamson, *Ezra, Nehemiah*, 174).

had he been one, Nehemiah's authority in spiritual matters would most likely not have been accepted by the Judahites, and especially Ezra. For the same reason, it is questionable whether the rabbis of the Talmud would have accepted the memoirs of a eunuch into the scriptural canon. Finally, it is not at all far-fetched to suppose that due to his obvious piety, Nehemiah would not have been suspected of immoral behavior with the distaff side of the royal household.

A PLEA FROM JERUSALEM

However Nehemiah may have reached his exalted status, he was firmly in place as cupbearer when the events that open his memoir took place. This does not mean that he had been on the job for a long time. In fact, the opening verses of Nehemiah would lead one to conclude otherwise.

As noted, Nehemiah's memoir begins with an encounter between Nehemiah and Hanani and his "brothers" at the citadel of Susa. It took place during the month of Kislev[20] in the twentieth year of the reign of Artaxerxes, 446 BCE. Nehemiah inquires about the state of affairs in Jerusalem: "I asked them about the Jews who had escaped," he writes, "who remained of the captivity, and about Jerusalem" (Neh. 1:2). Hanani answers his question in some detail, reporting that the city, and Judah generally, was in the throes of an extended existential crisis that had begun when the first Jews returned to Judah: "The remnant who remained of the captivity in the province are in great trouble and reproach; and the wall of Jerusalem is breached, and its gates were burned with fire" (1:3). Had Nehemiah been in power for many years under Artaxerxes, one would expect the Jewish community in Judah to have approached him much earlier. On the other hand, it would not be at all surprising if Nehemiah had been approached shortly after he assumed his position. Those desperately in need of assistance would not have wasted much time seeking a new champion.

It was a sad reality that despite the relatively comfortable position of the Jews in Persia and Babylonia, their coreligionists in

20. Kislev was the post-exilic name for this month; the name also appears in Assyrian artifacts and remains in Jewish usage until today. Prior to the destruction of the Temple, the months had different names.

Judah continued to suffer political and strategic setbacks.[21] Some years before Ezra led his returnees to Judah, Artaxerxes received a petition from the locals living in Samaria, led by Bishlam, Mithredath, Tabeel, Rehum the secretary, and Shimshai the scribe, the latter identified by the medieval commentators as none other than a son of Haman(!).[22] The petitioners accused the Jews of fomenting rebellion by seeking to rebuild Jerusalem's walls. They urged the king not only to put a stop to any further construction but also to destroy the Temple. They warned the king, "If this city is rebuilt and its walls are completed, you will no longer have any portion in the province of Abar Nahara" (Ezra 4:16).[23]

Artaxerxes, having checked the royal records at the petitioners' behest, found that "this city has from the earliest times risen against kings, and that rebellion and sedition have been rife in it" (Ezra 4:19). He ordered a halt to any work on the walls, adding "that this city is not to be rebuilt until I so order" (4:21). The complainants "hurried to Jerusalem and stopped them by main force" (4:23).[24]

It is noteworthy that Artaxerxes did not order the destruction of the Temple, as Bishlam and his colleagues had proposed. The Persian monarchs used temples as "administrative clearinghouses for

21. The parallels between the Judahites, and similarly the Jewish Yishuv under Ottoman rule, with the Jews in pre–World War I western Europe and America, living in relative comfort, are striking.

22. Cf. Rashi, Ezra 4:8, s.v. *Shimshai*. As discussed above, Shimshai is associated with his father Haman's effort to reverse Cyrus's edict granting the Jews permission to rebuild the Temple.

23. Traditional commentators, following the Talmud, identify Artaxerxes with Cyrus (as well as Darius). The talmudic view would also have Haman's son living in Samaria, and already an adult, well before the Esther story took place (since the rabbis consider Ahasuerus to be a different individual from Cyrus/Darius/Artaxerxes). Whatever Shimshai's identity, it is exceedingly difficult to make the case that one king was called Cyrus, Darius, and Artaxerxes. For a discussion, see below, chapter 3, footnote 15.

24. The following verse appears to indicate that Darius followed Artaxerxes, since it states that no further Temple construction took place until the reign of Darius. This would seem to support the talmudic view that Artaxerxes was identical with Cyrus, but would fly in the face of historical reality. It is arguable, however, that this final sentence of Ezra 4 simply refers back to a parallel occasion in the reign of Cyrus.

the collection of tribute."[25] To destroy the Temple, therefore, would have been counterproductive. More surprising, perhaps, was the fact that the king did not even order the destruction of the walls that had already been built. It is possible that Bishlam reinterpreted the king's authorization as permitting the walls to be torn down; hence he had to employ "main force" to do so.

Alternatively, it appears that as part of the king's writ, Judah lost its independent provincial status and was incorporated into the province of Samaria, whose governor, Sanballat, delegated Tobiah to look after affairs in Jerusalem.[26] And it was some time after Tobiah reached the city that the walls were destroyed. In any event, by the time Hanani and his colleagues contacted Nehemiah, the walls, and the city, were in a wretched state, and the Samaritan overlords and their henchmen were determined that matters should stay that way. The Jewish community's only hope was to induce Artaxerxes to rescind his decree. To do that, they needed someone at court; Nehemiah was that someone.

The encounter with Nehemiah took place against a backdrop of instability in the Persian Empire. Artaxerxes had been forced to agree to a humiliating peace with the Greeks in 449 BCE ("the peace of Callias"). He had finally quelled a long-standing rebellion in Egypt the very year that Nehemiah received his report from Jerusalem. The Persian emperor must have had things on his mind other than affairs in the putative capital of a tiny subprovince (Judah's total area may not have been greater than 750 square miles, less than three-fourths that of Rhode Island, America's smallest state).[27]

---

25. Bolin, *Ezra, Nehemiah*, 9.
26. Judah may not have been formally annexed, however. See Zeitlin, *The Rise and Fall of the Judaean State* (Philadelphia: Jewish Publication Society, 1962), 20.
27. Neither Ezra nor Nehemiah provides an indication of Judah's boundaries. One estimate posits that Judah extended no more than thirty miles from east to west and twenty-five miles from north to south. See Paul L. Reditt, "Nehemiah's First Mission and the Date of Zechariah 9–14," *Catholic Bible Quarterly* 56 (October 1994): 670. See also "Cities of Ancient Israel," http://www.bible-history.com/geography/ancient-israel/judea.html.

   It is possible that the province had roughly the same boundaries as the shrunken version of the Judean kingdom immediately prior to the exile; see Galil, *Daniel, Ezra UNeḥemia*, 130. Zer-Kavod, *Ezra UNeḥemia*, 28–32, notes that Jewish settlements

On the other hand, it was hardly a surprise that Nehemiah, despite his senior position in the Persian court, should have been concerned about the fate of the tiny Jewish polity. He had inherited a strong sense of Jewish identity and kept himself abreast of affairs in Judea, where, as he reported to the emperor, his ancestors were buried and part of his family resided.

We have no record of Nehemiah's formal role within the Jewish community, however. It is doubtful that he was its spiritual leader; Ezra is a more likely candidate. Nor does he appear to have been the community's secular representative to the court, the forerunner of the exilarch (*resh galuta*) of post-exilic Babylonia, or the *nagid* (prince) of the medieval Jewish community in Muslim Egypt, or the *shtadlanim* (intercessors) who represented the Jews in the royal courts of early modern Europe. Had he held such a position in Persia, Nehemiah most likely would have noted it early in his memoir. Even the talmudic assertion that he was a member of the Great Assembly does not indicate when exactly he joined that eminent body – it might have been subsequent to his journey to Judah. Rather, Nehemiah was an educated layman, well versed in Judaic studies, highly conscious of his status and that of his family within the community, and willing to put himself at the service of his people.

The fact that it was Hanani who reported to Nehemiah indicates that Nehemiah's sense of communal service reflected a family tradition. It is possible that Hanani had moved to Susa, perhaps some time after Nehemiah, and that Nehemiah had dispatched him to Jerusalem to investigate the situation there.[28] Alternatively, Hanani might have moved on to Jerusalem to join the small community of returning exiles that had been established a half-century earlier by Zerubbabel. Either way, Hanani's approach reflected the importance that the family ascribed to furthering the welfare of the fledgling, struggling Jewish polity.

Whatever the circumstances that brought him to Jerusalem, once Hanani was established there he recognized that it was a city in crisis.

---

were spread over much of the territory of the pre-exilic kingdoms of Judah and Samaria, thus extending well beyond the boundaries of the province that Nehemiah governed.

28. Myers, *Ezra/Nehemiah*, xxxii.

Hanani, joined by his colleagues and supporters, therefore turned to his powerful kinsman in the capital. They rightly viewed Nehemiah as their secular conduit to the Persian decision-making apparatus, and, more important, to the king himself; they evidently preferred him to an official Jewish communal representative. Esther had served in that role during the preceding reign of Ahasuerus (Xerxes), in contrast to her uncle Mordekhai, who was the communal leader. The notion that a high-ranking Jew would also represent his people's interests was of ancient vintage among the Jews, harking back to the days of Joseph in Egypt; the paradigm remains a powerful one to this day and is still in practice in many states throughout the world.

Nehemiah was more than a committed Jewish layman with relations in Judah who doubled as a high-ranking Persian official, however. He was also extremely knowledgeable about Jewish law and practice, as his legislative innovations relating to the Sabbath and his other ritual rulings were to prove once he was ensconced in the governor's mansion in Jerusalem. It is in this spirit that the talmudic claim regarding his membership in the Great Assembly should be understood. And it is in the same sense that he became a role model for the rabbinic scholars of future generations who served with equal distinction both the Jewish people wherever they might be found and the non-Jewish governments of the lands they called home.

Nehemiah 1

A City in Ruins

SUSA: A HISTORIC CITY

The Book of Nehemiah's first chapter opens in Susa. The setting for the narrative is significant: Hanani and his colleagues appear to have approached Nehemiah directly outside Susa's fortified citadel. The citadel contained the royal palace and other homes as well – not only of the elites but also of the lower classes. It was, in fact, a city within a city, somewhat akin to what is seen at the Tower of London today.

The city of Susa itself was not as strongly fortified. It was quite spread out, with a circumference of perhaps seven miles. The citadel was enclosed by a wall that was two and one-half miles long.[1] Like most such places around the world, it was situated in an elevated area, to make it more defensible against an attack (although, as demonstrated by the conquests of many a fortress over the centuries – for example, Quebec in the eighteenth century – elevation was never sufficient to ensure a successful defense).

Susa was the ancient capital of Elam. Located in what is now Khuzestan in southwestern Iran, just south of Dezful and north of Ahvaz, it is today called Shush. Susa came under Persian rule when it was conquered by Cyrus in 540–539 BCE. It had previously been

1. S. Goldman, "Esther," *The Five Megilloth: Hebrew Text & English Translation with Introductions and Commentary*, ed. A. Cohen (London: Soncino, 1968), 196.

under Babylonian control, and before that, Assyrian. Cambyses made Susa one of the empire's four capitals; it was a royal winter residence, though Artaxerxes spent considerable time there year-round. The citadel enclosed a magnificent royal palace that had been built by Darius Hystaspes (it was unearthed by French archaeologists in the late nineteenth century).[2]

The Book of Esther relates that Susa was a walled city, home to a large Jewish community. This is hardly surprising; the Jews had been exiled to Babylonia after the destruction of the Temple. As Esther recounts, when Mordekhai was exiled from Judah together with King Jehoiachin, he took up residence in Susa.[3] The community remained in Susa for centuries after the city fell to foreign conquerors. According to Benjamin of Tudela, who visited Khuzestan in the course of his travels in the late 1160s and early 1170s, the region was partly desolate and in ruins, but the city was still home to "about 7,000 Jews and fourteen synagogues."[4]

Nehemiah does not recount exactly how he was accosted by Hanani and the rest of the delegation from Judah; the text merely states that the delegation *arrived* (Neh. 1:2). It is possible that the Judahites contacted him through an intermediary, much as Mordekhai contacted Esther when he instructed her to approach the king on the Jews' behalf. The Roman Jewish historian Josephus Flavius, whose *Jewish Antiquities* often expanded upon the detail provided in the biblical accounts, postulated that it was Nehemiah himself who initially met the delegation. According to Josephus, Nehemiah "was walking about before the walls of Susa ... when he overheard some strangers, who were entering the city after a long journey, speaking Hebrew to one another, so he went

2. For a firsthand description of some of the excavations, see J. de Morgan, G. Jequier, and G. Lampre, *Recherches archéologiques, Ire série: fouilles à Suse en 1897–1898 et 1898–1899* (Paris: Ernest Leroux, 1900), 50–54, 58–68, 81–137.
3. There is, of course, a problem with dates, if it is assumed that Mordekhai himself was exiled with Jehoiachin. Over a hundred years passed between that king's exile and Xerxes's reign. It is possible that Est. 2:5–6, which outlines Mordekhai's lineage, refers to his great-grandfather Kish as being exiled with Jehoiachin.
4. *The Itinerary of Benjamin of Tudela*, trans. with commentary by Marcus Nathan Adler (London: Henry Frowde/Oxford University Press, 1907), 51.

up to them and inquired where they had come from."[5] Josephus does not explain what exactly motivated Nehemiah to take a walk outside the fortress walls. Nor does he provide a good reason for the Judahites to have been speaking Hebrew rather than Aramaic, the region's lingua franca; Hebrew was not in widespread use among the Jews of Babylonia or Judah. On the other hand, Nehemiah was an advocate of spoken Hebrew as a major indicator of Jewish identity.[6] One might speculate that members of Nehemiah's family and their closest colleagues conversed in Hebrew.

That Nehemiah himself sheds no light on the circumstances of the meeting should, perhaps, come as no surprise. The fact that he mentions no intermediary – in fact throughout his memoir he never mentions having consulted any powerful ally or even assistant before deciding upon a policy or course of action – indicates that from the very start he was determined to receive all the credit for any actions he might take on behalf of his people. In this regard, he acted no differently than any other politician of any era. Yet the very fact that he did so in his memoir testifies to its authenticity; memoirs invariably serve to glorify their authors. Of course, it is for this very reason that the sages rebuked him.

Nehemiah and Hanani were clearly close. Scripture describes Nehemiah as referring to Hanani as *eḥad me'aḥai*, which literally means "one of my brothers" (Neh. 1:2), though a number of traditional commentators read the Hebrew word *aḥai* as a colleague rather than a blood relative, much as the term was used by Jacob in his confrontation with Laban.[7] Nehemiah later appointed Hanani to be guardian of the gates, placing him in charge of Jerusalem's security,[8] and Hanani subsequently served as Nehemiah's temporary replacement as governor.

---

5. Josephus, *Antiquities*, XI:159.
6. This fact and its implications are discussed in chapter 14 below.
7. Cf. Rashi, Neh. 1:2, s.v. *eḥad*. See Gen. 31:37. Others call him a kinsman or countryman; see Slotki, *Daniel, Ezra, Nehemiah*, 182. Zer-Kavod, *Ezra UNeḥemia*, 69, reads the word in its literal sense. See also Ex. 2:11, in which the term clearly connotes "countrymen."
8. Kenneth G. Hoglund, *Achaemenid Imperial Administration in Syria-Palestine and the Missions of Ezra and Nehemiah* (Atlanta: Scholars Press, 1992), 215.

Some modern scholars speculate that Hanani was already guardian of the gates when he led the delegation to Susa. They argue that *aḥai* in this context indicates equality in rank. It is unlikely, however, that this would be the case, for the simple reason that the guardian of the gates of a backward provincial town hardly had the same protocol status as one of the emperor's most powerful advisers. Hanani might well have held the position of guardian, but that would not have given him access to the king's cupbearer. As in most other political contexts, what mattered (and still matters) was bonds of kinship, or at least close friendship; Hanani might not have been Nehemiah's brother, but he was certainly a kinsman.[9]

As was noted in the preceding chapter, Nehemiah had kept himself informed about developments in Judah and Jerusalem, and Hanani answered him in some detail. It is worth asking why Nehemiah himself had not made *aliya* as did so many other Babylonian Jews – whether with Zerubbabel, or with Ezra, or as individuals. We will never know, because Nehemiah does not tell us; it is possible that he had visited Jerusalem in the past, though he gives no indication of that either. There was little to prevent him from making *aliya*: he had relatives in Judah, and given his prominent social status and, as will be seen, his wealth, emigration should have been relatively painless.

Yet like many wealthy Jews of future generations, Nehemiah may have felt that he could contribute more to his people by remaining where he was. With Persia both the regional superpower and the suzerain over the land of his people, Nehemiah had a strong case for remaining in Susa, in order to better the condition of the Jews in Judah. When he queried Hanani about the "remnant who had survived the captivity," Nehemiah was specifically referring to the lower economic and social classes of pre-exilic Judean society whom the Babylonians had not bothered to expel.[10] Just in terms of his inquiry it can be seen

9. See also Williamson, *Ezra, Nehemiah,* 171.

10. It has been asserted that the "remnant" in question refers to those who had not been exiled during another population displacement that took place during the reign of either Xerxes or Artaxerxes (see, for example, Zer-Kavod, *Ezra UNeḥemia,* 69); for a refutation of this theory, see Hoglund, *Achaemenid Imperial Administration,* 51–61.

that Nehemiah, despite his own exalted status, possessed a special feeling for those less privileged than he, a sense of noblesse oblige. It was precisely in his capacity as a Diaspora Jew that he was in a position to make a difference to the politically and economically less fortunate.

THE REPORT: A TROUBLED CITY

It is hardly surprising that Nehemiah asked about Jerusalem as well. The city had not been fully resettled and was vulnerable to depredation from the surrounding countryside. It held a special magic for the Jews of the exile, representing the essence of their nationhood and the core of their religious identity; hence the passage in Psalms that Jews recite: "By the rivers of Babylon.... If I forget you, O Jerusalem" (Ps. 137:1, 5).

Hanani and his fellow delegates pointed out to Nehemiah that the downtrodden survivors were suffering at the hands of neighboring ethnic groups. As Josephus explains: "The surrounding nations were inflicting many injuries on the Jews, overrunning the country, and plundering it by day and doing mischief by night, so that many had been carried off as captives... and every day the roads were found full of corpses."[11] One modern commentator, perhaps influenced by events in the twentieth century, speculates that the situation was the result of an Arab raid.[12]

---

11. Josephus, *Antiquities*, XI:161. Louis Feldman argues that Josephus, himself a priest, was less enamored of Nehemiah than of Ezra the priest. Nevertheless, with a view to presenting both the Jews and Nehemiah in their best light to his Roman audience, Josephus presented Nehemiah's activities in a manner that would portray Jews as model citizens. At the same time, Josephus downplayed those aspects of the story that might serve as ammunition for the anti-Semites of his day. Accordingly, Feldman asserts that Josephus emphasized the lack of law and order in Judah, and particularly its roads, "inasmuch as roads were the great pride of both the Persians and the Romans." In emphasizing the instability that characterized Judah prior to Nehemiah's arrival there, Josephus' objective was to demonstrate Nehemiah's role "as the Persian king's loyal servant who gave stability to the land of Palestine." Louis H. Feldman, "Josephus' Portrait of Nehemiah," *Journal of Jewish Studies* 43 (Autumn 1992): 190–91, 201–202.
12. Smith, *Palestinian Parties*, 127–28. Blenkinsopp, *Ezra-Nehemiah*, 204, rightly notes that Smith's scenario is "a possibility, but no more than that.... All we can say... is that some serious disturbance had taken place shortly before 445 BCE the cause of which remains obscure."

Moreover, and no less troubling to Nehemiah, the "survivors" had not been warmly embraced by the returnees from Babylonia, who were materially better off. The returnees appear to have brought with them their social class consciousness, no doubt because they had constituted the pre-exilic elite. The class-based divisions only added to the community's overall vulnerability, however. The community was also vulnerable because Jerusalem was under the control of the non-Jewish authorities in Samaria, who bitterly opposed the return of the Jewish exiles from Babylonia.[13]

Some traditional commentators have argued that the Jews who returned from Babylonia were under the rule of a Jewish governor, while those who had never left were governed – and mistreated – by the satrap (imperial administrator) of Abar Nahara.[14] This theory, which cites a statement in Ezra that Cyrus appointed Sheshbazzar as governor of Judah, is actually an attempt to maintain consistency between that statement, the text of Nehemiah, the talmudic conflation of the reigns of Cyrus, Darius, and Artaxerxes, and the rabbinic tradition, articulated in the midrashic work *Seder Olam Rabba*, that the Persian Empire lasted a mere thirty-four years.[15] The talmudic and midrashic assertions are ahistorical, however.

---

13. See Myers, *Ezra/Nehemiah*, xxxiii, who notes that Sanballat, whom he terms the "commissar" of Samaria, probably considered himself Jewish, even if more religious Jews did not.
14. See Malbim, Neh. 1:2, s.v. *hapleita*. Satrapies were the main administrative units of the Persian Empire. The term was a derivation of the Persian word meaning "protecting the kingdom." The satrap was the official who acted as the king's representative. He was not exactly a ruler; he was more like a viceroy. Satrapies were subdivided into provinces. Judah was a subprovince that was incorporated into the province of Samaria. For a brief discussion, see Bolin, *Ezra, Nehemiah*, 8–9.
15. Cf. Rosh HaShana 3b, and the accompanying comments of Adin Steinsaltz in *The Talmud* (New York: Random House, 1989). See also Avoda Zara 9a and Rashi's commentary ad loc. There can be no disputing the fact that there were three kings named, respectively, Cyrus, Darius, and Artaxerxes, and that the Persian Empire lasted more than thirty-four years. The calculation in the Talmud, and in the chronology known as *Seder Olam Rabba*, appears to postulate Persian rule over Judah from 370 BCE, when Cyrus purportedly assumed the Persian throne, to 318 BCE, when Judah ceased to be a Persian province. There is an additional two-year discrepancy even in this calculation, since Cambyses is said to have ruled for that period; the commentaries

The view that the Jews were ruled by an independent governor erroneously draws upon the fact that the Jews may well have been governed by one of their own prior to Artaxerxes's decree suspending the construction of the city walls. By the time Nehemiah became an official in the Persian court, however, Judah was no longer an independent province but rather a unit of the satrapy of Abar Nahara, itself the fifth of the twenty satrapies of the Persian Empire administered from Damascus. Its administrative structure, inherited from the Assyrians, was reflected in its name: Abar Nahara literally meant "beyond the river," meaning the Euphrates.[16] Abar Nahara contained other, smaller provinces within its boundaries, notably Samaria, which itself incorporated Judah. Had there still been a Jewish governor ruling over a Jewish province, he would certainly have served as a magnet for the emigration of many, if not most, of those Jews who were oppressed in other parts of the satrapy. Furthermore, it strains credulity that a Jewish governor in charge of a province populated by Jews would not have controlled Jerusalem, the spiritual and cultural heart of the province within whose limits the Temple functioned. Finally, however reluctant Nehemiah might have been to credit others for the reconstruction of the city, it is unlikely that he would have entirely omitted mentioning a Jewish governor. Such an official would have been a natural, and powerful, ally both in the satrapy and at the royal court. Yet no such official is mentioned.

Clearly, the enmity of the locals and their leader, Sanballat, the major villain in Nehemiah, is more easily explained if they were dealing with a breakaway province, rather than with a province that had never been under their control. In our time, for example, China's hostility to Taiwan far exceeds its concerns about other territories (such as in the South China Sea) to which it also lays claim.

---

simply argue that because of its brevity, his reign was not included in the calculation. For a discussion, see various volumes of the ArtScroll series, including *Daniel*, by Hersh Goldwurm and Nosson Scherman (Brooklyn: Mesorah, 1980), *Ezra*, by Yosef Rabinowitz (Brooklyn: Mesorah, 1984), and *Nechemiah*, by Yosef Rabinowitz (Brooklyn: Mesorah, 1990); and *Seder Olam Rabba*, 462–66.

16. Thomas B. Dozeman, "Geography and History in Herodotus and Ezra-Nehemiah," *Journal of Biblical Literature* 122 (Autumn 2003): 457.

It was precisely because of the community's vulnerability to indigenous pressures that Hanani's mission appears to have been undertaken outside official channels. The local population, after initially offering to join in the construction of the Second Temple, became its fiercest opponents once the offer had been rebuffed. The locals appear to have been complicit in Haman's attempt to eradicate the Jews of the Persian Empire. Had they been aware of Hanani's attempt to contact the Persian authorities, they certainly would have blocked it.

Having reported on the state of the community, Hanani then informed Nehemiah of the city's physical condition. Apart from the Temple, nothing had been rebuilt since the exile. It was not necessarily that the city had faced any additional misfortunes, though some argue that this was the case; it had simply decayed over the previous 140 years. On the other hand, the Jews appear to have concluded that they had little option but to leave matters as they were – not just because of Artaxerxes's edict and pressure from the Samaritans, but also because they had failed to assert their national identity. Attempting to improve the city's infrastructure would not only have threatened the territorial claims of those who had seized land vacated by the Jews exiled to Babylonia, but also would have underscored Samaritan allegations that the Jews were planning to reestablish a commonwealth independent of Persia. Given the reality that, over the previous century, the Persians had faced revolts in one or another part of the empire, the Samaritan claim would have seemed credible enough, and the Jews might well have been exiled yet again. All told, the plight of the small Jewish community in Judah was not all that dissimilar to that of the nascent Jewish settlement (Yishuv) under Ottoman rule during the late nineteenth and early twentieth centuries, which found itself under constant threat from the local Arab population.[17]

17. The relationship with the Arabs grew worse under British rule. Under the Ottomans, the small Jewish population of eighty thousand lived in poverty, and the few farming communities outside the cities where most Jews lived were, for the most part, in Chaim Weizmann's words "disheartened and disheartening." For Weizmann's impressions during his first visit to Palestine in 1907, see Chaim Weizmann, *Trial and Error: The Autobiography of Chaim Weizmann* (New York: Harper & Brothers, 1949), 125–28. Arab hostility, which was already present during the Ottoman years,

FASTING AND PRAYER

Nehemiah recounts that upon hearing Hanani's tale of woe he was overcome with emotion: "I sat and wept and was in mourning for days, fasting and praying to the God of heaven" (Neh. 1:4). Though he was generally aware of developments in Judah, he may not have realized just how dire the situation had become. In particular, he may have been reacting to the damage that had been done in the aftermath of Artaxerxes's edict some years before. In that regard, his initial reaction, to sit on the ground – consistent with halakhic practice to weep, pray, and fast during a period of mourning[18] – was similar to that of Ezra upon hearing of the degree to which the Jewish community had intermarried with the indigenous peoples (Ezra 9:3–15) and to that of Mordekhai upon hearing of Ahasuerus's decree (Est. 4:1). No doubt, too, Nehemiah immediately perceived that Hanani and his associates viewed his powerful connection to the king as a vehicle for terminating the frustrating political impotence that gripped the Judean community and, as an initial step, for reversing the king's decree.

Nehemiah was not asked to make representations to the emperor, as Esther had been. That Hanani did not request this is somewhat puzzling, given the need to reverse Artaxerxes's edict. It is possible, however, that there was no need to press Nehemiah on this score; the report of Jerusalem's condition made it clear that something had to be done at court. This may well be why Nehemiah threw himself into fasting and prayer. He surely recognized that Esther's entreaties to Xerxes (Ahasuerus) had only succeeded thanks to the divine intervention that came in response to the community's fasting and prayer. As a private individual, he may have been loath to involve the entire community, as Esther had done (Est. 4:10–16), but he did follow her example in seeking divine inspiration and assistance.

exploded during the Mandatory period. For a detailed – though revisionist – review of Arab-Jewish relations under the Mandate, see Tom Segev, *One Palestine, Complete: Jews and Arabs Under the British Mandate*, trans. Haim Watzman (New York: Metropolitan, 2000). See also Montefiore, *Jerusalem*, 522–47, and Dallin and Rothmann, *Icon of Evil*, 7–38.

18. Rabbi Yosef Karo, *Shulḥan Arukh: Yoreh De'ah* 387:1. See also the *Siftei Cohen* commentary (or *Shakh*) there, s.v. *akhshav*.

Nehemiah's prayer employed a formula that has since become standardized in Jewish prayers, especially on holidays and fast days. It opened with ardent praise, followed by a confession of Israel's sins, and concluded with a reminder to God of His promise to redeem His people. In addition, several of the passages in Nehemiah's prayer, like those of contemporary prayers, echoed earlier scriptural passages, notably the prayers of Moses and Solomon.

Nehemiah began by calling upon the "Great and awesome God who stays faithful to His covenant with those who love Him and keep His commandments" (Neh. 1:5) to receive his prayer on behalf of his people. He then uttered his confession for "sins that I and my father's house have committed. We have offended You by not keeping the commandments, the laws, and the rules that You gave to Your servant Moses" (1:6–7). These verses reflect the confession of the High Priest on Yom Kippur[19] and are similar to the passage that immediately precedes the beating of the breast in the *Seliḥot* prayer of *Ashamnu*, which is recited on fast days, the Ten Days of Atonement, and Yom Kippur. In aligning himself with his people in this way, Nehemiah borrowed Moses's formula of humbly joining with his brethren in accepting responsibility for the people's transgressions.[20]

Moreover, by focusing on Israel's sins as the source of their troubles, Nehemiah demonstrated the degree to which his worldview was colored by his adoption of mainstream Jewish principles and theology, as articulated throughout Scripture and highlighted in the holiday prayer *Mipnei ḥata'einu galinu me'Artzeinu* ("Because of our sins we were exiled from our land"). The exile was due to Israel's sins; consequently, so must be their current lowly condition in Judah. Perhaps Hanani had reported on the poor religious and moral state of the people as well as on their politico-economic and security situation, and Nehemiah was identifying a specific linkage between the two, much as in later generations many rabbis would explain the dire straits in which Jews found themselves as being a result of their many sins (*avonoteinu harabim*).

19. Ibn Yahia (Gedalia ibn Yahia ben Joseph, 1526–1587), Neh. 1:6, s.v. *ḥatanu*; cf. Lev. 16, 17.
20. Cf. Slotki, *Daniel, Ezra, Nehemiah*, 184; Ex. 34:9. Daniel employed a similar approach, though at much greater length than Nehemiah; see Dan. 9:5–15.

Having referred to Israel's sins, Nehemiah then went on to cite God's dual promise: exile as punishment for their sins, but the ingathering of the dispersed once Israel repented. "Be mindful of the promise You gave Your servant Moses," he entreated God: "If you are unfaithful I will scatter you among the peoples; but if you turn back to Me, faithfully keep My commandments, even if your dispersed are at the ends of the earth, I will gather them from there and bring them to the place where I have chosen to establish My name" (Neh. 1:8–9). With respect to exile he evoked God's rebuke, or *tokhaḥa,* echoing God's warning in Leviticus that "if you will not for all this hearken unto Me, but walk contrary to Me," then I will scatter you among the nations.[21] Then, referring to the return, he adapted a passage from Deuteronomy reminding God of His commitment: "Even if your exiles are at the end of the heavens, the Lord, your God, will gather you from there" (Deut. 30:4).[22]

Nehemiah then uttered a variant of Moses's plea for forgiveness in the aftermath of the Golden Calf incident: "For they are Your servants and Your people whom You redeemed by Your great power and Your mighty hand" (Neh. 1:10).[23] Nehemiah added a personal, concluding request: "Let Your ear be attentive to the prayer of Your servant, and to the prayer of Your servants who desire to hold Your name in awe. Grant Your servant success today, and dispose that man to be compassionate

---

21. Echoing Lev. 26:27. Moses employed similar language when he warned the people in Deuteronomy (28:64) that "the Lord will scatter you among all peoples, from one end of the earth to the other."
22. The fifteenth-century Yemenite scholar, rabbi, and doctor Zechariah ben Shlomo cited this passage when arguing that geographic distance is irrelevant to those who seek God. See Rabbi Zechariah ben Shlomo HaRofeh, *Midrash HaḤefetz al Ḥamisha Humshei Torah, Ḥibro Rabbi Zekharia ben Shlomo HaRofeh: Vayikra, Bemidbar, Devarim*, ed. and trans. Meir Havazelet (Jerusalem: Mossad Harav Kook, 1992), 98. The Talmud and all traditional commentators consider the phrase "the place where I have chosen to establish My name" to be an allusion to the Temple, and Nehemiah likewise employs it in this vein. Numbers Rabba 11:8 cites this passage as evidence that the Tetragrammaton was uttered only within the Temple precincts. Interestingly, the midrash adds that when "unprincipled men multiplied" among the priests – presumably it refers to the Sadducees – utterance of "the name" was confined to the "pious of the priesthood."
23. Moses had said: "Yet they are Your people and Your inheritance, that You brought out by Your great power and Your outstretched arm" (Deut. 9:29).

toward him!" (Neh. 1:11). The first part of his conclusion is nearly identical in language to that of Psalm 130, which has since become the staple of Jewish prayer in troubled times, notably when a serious illness is involved. The request that he find favor in the eyes of "that man," namely, Artaxerxes, is a throwback to Jacob's blessing to his sons when he dispatched them to Joseph, whom he then only knew as Pharaoh's viceroy: "And God Almighty give you mercy before the man" (Gen. 43:14).

Nehemiah need not have recorded in his memoir the details of this prayer. In doing so, however, he sought to demonstrate for posterity both his knowledge of scriptural sources and his religious devotion. They were as much a part of his persona as his nationalist outlook, and would color his behavior once he departed for Judah, as we will shortly see.

Nehemiah 2:1–8

Nehemiah Petitions the King

ARTAXERXES AND THE PERSIAN COURT

The Persian court, like the courts of all absolute monarchs through the ages, was complex. At one and the same time, it served as the subject of the monarch's whims, the venue for endless intrigues by courtiers – both those who sought to endear themselves to the king and those who wished to undercut their rivals – and the administrative heart of the empire. We know little about the Achaemenid court from Persian sources; it is their Greek archenemies, with all their obvious biases, on whom we must depend for information about Persia's rulers. In addition, we have the reports in Esther, Ezra, and Nehemiah, although they are ancillary to the Jewish concerns that serve as the focus of these biblical books.

A number of biblical critics concede that the Book of Esther, which offers the most detailed Jewish description of Persian court life, must have been composed by an Achaemenid insider. Like the Greek historians, Esther describes a court bureaucracy composed of layers of officials fawning over a king – one who demands absolute obedience from them and from his wives and harem, one whose decrees can only be reversed with the greatest of difficulty, if at all.

Artaxerxes I, son of Xerxes, acceded to the throne in 465 BCE under bloody circumstances. As noted, his father had been assassinated by Artabanus, the powerful commander of the royal bodyguard, assisted by a eunuch named Aspamitres. Artaxerxes himself then murdered Artabanus and his sons. Xerxes, who is frequently identified as the biblical Ahasuerus, was a moody, mean-spirited sort who was feared – but not revered – by his courtiers and subjects. Moreover, he suffered major defeats at the hands of the Greeks, as Herodotus documents in his epic history of the Persian Wars.

On the other hand, Xerxes pursued a policy of religious tolerance throughout his empire – which is consistent with the biblical portrait of Ahasuerus, particularly after the fall of Haman early in his reign. It appears that Artaxerxes adopted his father's policy. There were a number of reasons for this. To begin with, the Achaemenids could not formulate a single law code that would serve for the whole of their empire.[1] As portrayed in Esther as well as in Ezra and Nehemiah, "the Persian monarchs in general and Artaxerxes in particular, are idealized as kings who uphold the law in Abar Nahara [in which Judah was situated] and are restricted by it."[2] In addition, the Persian tolerance for other faiths and law codes was a means of winning local support, or at least not alienating local populations. The policy of the British Empire with respect to religion was not much different – and existed for the same reasons. As matters stood, Persia was constantly faced with the need to put down local uprisings – so, too, was Britain – in addition to conducting near-constant wars with the Greeks. Any action that could mitigate the likelihood of more widespread revolt – with its concomitant drain on military resources – was more than welcome.

Artaxerxes appears to have been a more amiable fellow than his father. Nicknamed "Longimanus" because his right hand was longer than his left, he was, according to Plutarch (writing hundreds of years later), "among all the kings of Persia the most remarkable for a gentle

1. Williamson, *Ezra, Nehemiah,* xliii, citing U. Kellerman.
2. Dozeman, "Geography and History," 459.

and noble spirit."[3] Perhaps the best-known example of his generous nature was his willingness to welcome to his court Themistocles, hero of the crushing Athenian defeat of Xerxes's naval forces at the battle of Salamis, after the Greek had been expelled from his native land.[4] And, reflecting his policy of religious tolerance, Artaxerxes authorized Ezra in 458 BCE to take charge of the religious and civil affairs of Judah.

NEHEMIAH'S APPROACH

The fact that Artaxerxes had a more stable personality than his father does not mean that he was any less powerful an emperor of Persia. Herodotus translates his name as "great warrior," though in fact it means "whose rule is through truth,"[5] and he had the power to order a courtier's death merely on the basis of a passing whim.

Timing is everything; fully aware of the flightiness that characterized Oriental despots such as the Persian emperor, Nehemiah may have simply concluded that an ill-timed request was inadvisable. Such a request, especially on behalf of a people who might still be suspect in the eyes of the Persian hierarchy, might lead not only to a denial, but also to Nehemiah's own political downfall, imprisonment, or even death. In this regard Artaxerxes was no different from his predecessors, including his father, of whom, as Esther had made clear to Mordekhai in a somewhat analogous circumstance, "All the king's courtiers and the people of the king's provinces know that if any person, man or woman, enters the king's court without having been summoned, there is but one

3. Plutarch, *The Lives of the Noble Grecians and Romans*, trans. John Dryden, ed. and rev. Arthur Hugh Clough (New York: Modern Library, n.d.), 1251.
4. Thucydides, *History of the Peloponnesian War*, trans. and intro. by Rex Warner (Baltimore: Penguin, 1954), 90.
5. Tradition has it that the name was actually a royal title (cf. Rashi, Ezra 4:7, s.v. *uviyemei*). Nehemiah may have assumed that Persian practice followed that of Egypt, which designated every king as Pharaoh. This view is consistent with the talmudic tradition that Artaxerxes, Cyrus, and Darius were one and the same person. As we noted earlier, there is no historical basis for this assertion; Herodotus notes that Darius means "worker" in Persian, while Artaxerxes means "great warrior." Herodotus, *Persian Wars*, VI:98; Herodotus also notes that Xerxes means "warrior."

law for him – that he be put to death" (Est. 4:11).[6] Though Nehemiah saw Artaxerxes on a daily basis, he may well have feared that raising an unpleasant subject like the state of Jerusalem might provoke a similar response. Thus, despite his prayers for heavenly assistance, he kept his own counsel for five long months (Rosh HaShana 3a).[7] He was, in effect, behaving as officials everywhere have done over the millennia. They recognize that a superior preoccupied with other affairs of state is much less likely to grant a request. Moreover, they are reluctant to be the purveyors of bad news. Modern-day subordinates fear for their jobs; Nehemiah and his counterparts feared for their lives. That a monarch would "shoot the messenger" was no mere turn of phrase.

It is also possible that, despite his role at the royal court, Nehemiah was nevertheless insecure about his position and hesitated to broach a subject that would highlight his ethnic and religious identity. If a major reason for Nehemiah's having been granted the office of the king's wine-taster was precisely his status as an outsider who would be less likely to make a play for the throne, this very status would have

6. A case has been made that the Persian rulers "uphold the law and are restricted by it" (Dozeman, "Geography and History," 459). Such an observation can only be carried so far; there was no "rule of law" as it is understood today. The Persian kings made laws and unmade them as they wished. That Ahasuerus told Esther that "no document written in the king's name and sealed with his ring can be revoked" (Est. 8:8) did not prevent him from doing just that when Haman's plot was revealed to him.
7. Rashi (Neh. 1:1, s.v. *shnat*) confesses his uncertainty as to the date that the royal year began. The text implies that it must have begun before Kislev, since both Kislev and Nisan are identified as falling in the twentieth year of Artaxerxes's reign. Accordingly, traditional and modern scholars all assume that the year began on the first of Tishrei. Some scholars have speculated that Nehemiah heard from Hanani in the *nineteenth* year of the king's reign, so that the new royal year began sometime after Kislev, and before the events that took place during Nisan; see Wilhelm Rudolph, *Esra und Nehemia mit 3. Esra: Handbuch zum Alten Testament* (Tübingen: Mohr, 1949), 102; Blenkinsopp, *Ezra-Nehemiah,* 205; and Judson R. Shaver, *Torah and the Chronicler's History Work: An Inquiry into the Chronicler's References to Laws, Festivals and the Cultic Institutions in Relationship to Pentateuchal Legislation* (Providence, RI: Brown, 1989), 27. This view appears to be somewhat forced, and calls for emending a text that makes perfect sense if one adopts the Babylonian Talmud's identification of the royal new year, which clearly was based on familiarity with the practices of the Parthian Empire, successor to the Persians, in whose domains the talmudic yeshivas were found.

rendered it more difficult to request a royal favor on behalf of the Jews. Since the king had already granted Ezra's request to lead a group of Jews returning to Zion only thirteen years earlier, Nehemiah may have felt that another such request might represent a bridge too far for the king.

Finally, Nehemiah himself testifies to the fact that he only raised the matter after the king saw that he was troubled and asked what was wrong. His depression may have been a contributing factor to his inability to raise his concerns with the king. Depression often leads to inactivity.

Nehemiah himself offers no explanation for his hesitation. Certainly he must have understood that Hanani and his cohort were nervously awaiting a reply, and that a delayed response would only further undermine the Jews' morale. Did Hanani's delegation remain in Susa until they heard something, anything, from Nehemiah? Perhaps the entire delegation headed home. They may have been frustrated by Nehemiah's caution and lack of news. Or perhaps they considered their mission to have failed. Nehemiah is silent on this matter.

It is possible that Hanani stayed behind in Susa while the delegation returned home. Hanani may have asked for updates, which Nehemiah could not provide, since he had not raised the matter before the king. In that case, having nothing to report to Hanani, and perhaps being embarrassed by his own inaction, Nehemiah would have preferred not to dwell on the matter in his memoir.

In fact, Nehemiah refrains from mentioning anyone with whom he might have had contact, other than the king, during the months between his meeting with the delegation from Judah and the day when he finally revealed his feelings to Artaxerxes. It is perhaps understandable that he did not convey his doubts and concerns to Hanani. But was there no one in whom he could confide? Nowhere in his memoir does Nehemiah mention a spouse (perhaps the major justification for those who speculate that he was a eunuch). Yet Scripture is full of examples of both its heroes and villains consulting their spouses on major issues: witness Adam and Eve; Abraham and Sarah; Jacob and Rachel and Leah; Elkanah and Hannah; Manoah, Samson's father, and his wife; and, for that matter, Haman and Zeresh. Yet there is nary a word from Nehemiah.

Nor does Nehemiah mention any friend or relative to whom he might have looked for advice, as Moses looked to Jethro, or David to

Jonathan. Was Nehemiah a loner? Did the exalted nature of his position make it difficult for him to get others to understand the issues confronting him? Nehemiah may have thought so; his memoir certainly gives the impression that he did.

And perhaps he was right. It is impossible to convey fully the conflicting emotions that pulse through a senior government official when faced with difficult choices that have potential life-and-death implications. Such was Nehemiah's dilemma.

Nehemiah hints, and only hints, at one possible relationship apart from the one he had with the king, stating "And the king said to me, the queen also sitting by him…" (Neh. 2:6). The queen, Damasias (or Damaspia), was Artaxerxes's "first" wife, that is to say, she was the chief member of his harem, with a higher standing in court protocol than the king's other wives – much less his concubines – functioning in some respects as do the first wives of modern-day emirs in the Arabian Gulf. Moreover, the Persian queen wielded considerable influence at court, as the story of Esther makes clear. Feminine influence appears to have been particularly strong in Artaxerxes's court.[8]

Nehemiah does not give Damasias a speaking part in his memoir, but he notes her presence when he performed his duties before the king. And, as will be shown, she may have been a supporter when he entreated the king for permission to leave the court and travel to Judah. The tantalizing, if unanswered, question is: How did Nehemiah come to relate to Damasias? Was it simply because she was often present when he was serving the king? Or had they developed a separate channel of communication? Was he one of her favorites? We just do not know, because Nehemiah is silent on this matter as well.

The fact that Nehemiah had some sort of relationship with the queen is noteworthy in another respect. The rabbis of the Talmud inveighed against excessive intimacy with women, even with one's own wife (Avot 1:5). Was Nehemiah exempt from these rabbinical injunctions, as he was from others, because of his official position? The rabbis nowhere make such an argument, and they speak disparagingly of the queen, whom Nehemiah describes as *hasheigal* (Neh. 2:6). The term

8. Williamson, *Ezra, Nehemiah*, 180.

simply connotes "first wife" in Assyrian and Sumerian.[9] But the rabbis play upon a cognate Hebrew word that has a base sexual connotation.[10] Perhaps out of antipathy to the oppressive Persian rulers of their time, the rabbis seized upon the term to make a variety of disparaging observations about the monarchy, including one asserting that a *sheigal* was actually a dog (Rosh HaShana 4a). Some medieval commentators also follow this general approach, translating the word to mean someone specifically appointed to satisfy the king's coarser appetites. Needless to say, the rabbis would never countenance Nehemiah's having any sort of interaction with a woman of this sort, yet her presence when he made his request seems to indicate that he was no stranger to her.

In any event, it was when Nehemiah was setting wine before the king that he provided an explanation for his unsettled mood. Nehemiah would first take the wine from a subordinate official and taste it for security purposes before handing it to Artaxerxes.[11] One may wonder how Nehemiah, an observant Jew identified in rabbinic lore as a member of the Great Assembly, permitted himself to violate the law of *stam yeinam* by drinking wine that had been touched by a non-Jew. Later rabbinic rulings justified his behavior on the grounds that he was a senior government official,[12] paving the way

9. Slotki, *Daniel, Ezra, Nehemiah*, 188; Zer-Kavod, *Ezra UNeḥemia*, 71; Galil, *Daniel, Ezra UNeḥemia*, 207.

10. Cf. Deut. 28:30, wherein the term for illicit sexual relations in the great rebuke, or *tokhaḥa*, is written as *yishgalena*, but to preserve decency, the rabbis ordered that it be read aloud as the less offensive *yishkavena*.

11. Among those holding this view are Ibn Yahia, Slotki, and Rabbi Saadia. It is probable that this "Rabbi Saadia" is not the great tenth-century *gaon*. More likely he was a namesake who was possibly a contemporary of Rashi but in any event wrote his commentary no later than the twelfth century. For a detailed discussion see H. A. Mathews, ed., *Commentary on Ezra and Nehemiah by Rabbi Saadiah* (Oxford: Clarendon Press, 1882), i–xxiv.

12. The Jerusalem Talmud (Y. Kiddushin 35b) states that Nehemiah was exempted from the rabbinic ban on tasting non-Jewish wine. The commentary *Beit Moshe* emphasizes that the exemption did not apply to ritual wine, which is biblically banned. Although he went so far as to forbid Jews from pouring non-Jewish wine for non-Jews, Rabbi David ibn Zimra (*She'eylot UTeshuvot Radvaz* IV:1096/22) observes that Nehemiah was exempt from this ban on the basis of the general principle of his being a "royal official" (*hurmanuta demalka*).

for contemporary Jews in similar circumstances, notably diplomats representing the State of Israel.[13]

It was while serving the wine that Nehemiah dropped his guard – he "had never been out of sorts in his presence" (Neh. 2:1) and always had presented a cheerful countenance before the king.[14] For the first time since his meeting with Hanani five months earlier, the issue came to light. As the wine was being served, the king asked Nehemiah, "How is it that you look bad if you are not ill? It must be bad thoughts" (2:2). The king was "in a more pleasant mood than usual" when he saw that Nehemiah was downcast,[15] and he was concerned for Nehemiah, who clearly was a favorite. Nevertheless, depressed and worried as he was, Nehemiah was terrified by the king's remark. He feared the king might suspect him of sedition[16] and of trying to poison him.[17]

It is possible that Nehemiah deliberately chose this moment to drop the jovial mask he had worn since receiving Hanani's report. The date of the events appears to have been the first of Nisan, the beginning of the new year for the Persians (and the first Jewish month) at which a feast may have been held. Herodotus reports that the king granted requests that were made to him at his birthday feast.[18] The same custom may also have been practiced at other feasts. In any event, whether by inadvertence or design, Nehemiah now had no choice but to tell the king what was on his mind.[19]

The conversation took place behind a curtain that separated the two men from the rest of the court.[20] The queen appears to have been

13. For a discussion, see Rabbi Yehuda Zoldan, "*Heteirei Halakha Shenitnu LeKrovim LeMalkhut*," *Teḥumin* 21 (5761/2001): 171–79.
14. Rashi, Neh. 2:1, s.v. *velo*.
15. Josephus, *Antiquities*, XI:164. Though his comment implies that the king was moody, in contrast to what Plutarch later wrote, it may simply be that Artaxerxes was in a particularly good mood that day.
16. Similar language on the Behistun Rock connotes a seditious nature.
17. Rashi, Neh. 2:2, s.v. *ein*.
18. Herodotus, *Persian Wars*, IX:110.
19. Perhaps his having drunk some of the wine prior to handing it to the king stiffened his spine when responding.
20. Zer-Kavod, *Ezra UNeḥemia*, 70. Yamauchi (*Persia and the Bible*, 260) points out that the cupbearer was the king's confidant in a palace that witnessed the assassination of four, possibly five, of the thirteen Achaemenid rulers.

the only other person behind the curtain. Still, despite the near privacy that prevailed, and the queen's presence, Nehemiah was exceedingly circumspect as he replied to the king. He chose to frame the state of Jerusalem in general in terms of its impact upon him personally rather than to cast the issue as a Jewish one. Esther had done much the same in her day, when she accused Haman of planning genocide against her people. As Nehemiah put it, "How should I not look bad, when the city of the graveyard of my ancestors lies in ruins, and its gates have been consumed by fire?" (Neh. 2:3).

Nehemiah's reluctance to mention Jerusalem, despite his favored position with both the king and the queen, reflects his uncertainty about the royal attitude toward the notion of a Jewish polity. This might have remained hostile even if the Jews in Persia itself, or for that matter those in Judah, were not suffering from oppressive discrimination. While Artaxerxes tolerated the Temple as a purely religious symbol, he might not have been equally accepting of an emergent Jewish national entity. Nehemiah concluded that it was safer to avoid any language that smacked of Jewish nationalism.[21] Indeed, not long before Nehemiah made his appeal, Artaxerxes had put down a revolt by a local satrap named Megabyzus in which some Jews may have participated.[22] By framing his reply in terms of the condition of his ancestors' graves, Nehemiah played upon the sympathy and respect for ancestral tombs that was universal in the Middle East at the time.[23]

---

21. That was very much the situation in Britain in the 1930s and 1940s, when Jews were a tolerated minority but hostility to Jewish immigration to Palestine was government policy, to the point where Emmanuel Shinwell, the Jewish secretary of state for war, was kept in the dark about various aspects of British policy in Palestine. Arguably the situation today in much of Europe is not dissimilar: Jews have full rights as citizens, but Israel is constantly the subject of withering criticism and, in some cases, boycotts. In some respects, the early Zionists debated the question of nationalism as well. Cultural Zionists like Ahad Ha'am downplayed its nationalistic aspects; Jabotinsky's followers highlighted Jewish nationalism. Herzl and those who followed him fell somewhere in between.
22. Joseph Blenkinsopp, "The Mission of Udjahorresnet and Those of Ezra and Nehemiah," *Journal of Biblical Literature* 103 (September 1987): 416.
23. Williamson, *Ezra, Nehemiah*, 179.

Nehemiah's response to Artaxerxes has been described as "a master stroke of diplomacy in view of the manifestly high standing of the cupbearer."[24] Nehemiah's challenge, like Esther's before him, was to reverse a royal edict. Changing a long-standing policy was no small matter, in those days as in ours – though today it is bureaucracies, rather than absolute monarchs, that continually pose major stumbling blocks to reform or change of any kind – regardless of whether the policy in question is obsolete, invalid, or irrelevant.

Artaxerxes recognized immediately that Nehemiah was about to petition for something, although Nehemiah had not yet indicated what he had in mind. He asked his cupbearer, "What is your request?" indicating, perhaps, that it would be granted.[25] Nehemiah hesitated for a moment, so that he could utter one last, silent prayer; he does not record this appeal for posterity, perhaps because he had already demonstrated his religious credentials when he outlined his earlier prayer.

Having been given an opening, Nehemiah then pressed his advantage. He not only asked for a leave of absence, but also requested permission to rebuild "the city of my ancestors' graves" (Neh. 2:5). It was the latter objective that lay at the heart of Nehemiah's request, and he wanted to oversee the project himself.

It was not unusual in ancient times, or today either, for policy advocates to so position themselves as to be put in charge of implementing the policy advocated. Pharaoh had promoted Joseph to oversee the gathering of grain in the seven good years and its distribution in the lean years that followed. Ahasuerus had given Esther the authority to protect her community and to retaliate against its opponents. Similarly, in modern times, the advocates of particular policies, notably in the field of foreign and national security affairs, have sometimes been delegated, usually at their own instigation, to implement the policy abroad, even if the advocate is not part of the official foreign-policy apparatus.[26]

---

24. Myers, *Ezra/Nehemiah*, 99.
25. Rashi, Neh. 2:4, s.v. *al*.
26. To some extent, this observation derives from my own experience. As a result of my request to join an official delegation to Israel, I was assigned by the US Department

Nehemiah made no bones about his objective. But, given his position in court, he was also very much aware of the fact that his request dovetailed with Achaemenid strategic policy. In the aftermath of multiple revolts in Egypt, and the revolt of Megabyzus, as well as the constant threat of Greek encroachments, the king had embarked upon the policy of fortifying towns at the western extremes of the empire.[27] While not near the sea or a river, Jerusalem was an ideal locale for fortification because it was set on hills, enabling it to dominate the surrounding region, and would not easily be conquered – assuming its loyalty could be assured. Nehemiah, as a Persian official whose loyalty to the king was unquestioned, but also as a Jew who could maintain order among his often unruly coreligionists, seemed the perfect candidate to implement the policy in Jerusalem without any unwanted consequences for Persian control.

Nehemiah may also have been aware of the successful plea that the Egyptian notable Udjahorresnet had made to Cambyses, whom he served as master of protocol, another position of power in the king's inner court. Udjahorresnet "petitioned… Cambyses, concerning all the foreigners who had settled in the sanctuary of Neith [an Egyptian goddess], that they be expelled from it, so that the sanctuary of Neith be restored to all its former splendor."[28] In fact, "the central government tended to support local priesthoods and to take a detailed interest in the proper carrying out of local cults."[29] And it was to ensure that the government pursued its usual policies that Nehemiah petitioned in the way that he did.

PLANNING FOR THE MISSION

Artaxerxes, while sympathetic, was not ready to grant so valuable a counselor a blank check. He asked Nehemiah the obvious question: "How long will you be gone and when will you return?" (Neh. 2:6). Artaxerxes was not prepared to have his trusted assistant take an indefinite leave of absence.

---

of Defense to undertake a review of a major Israeli weapons program that the department had for some time opposed. Dov S. Zakheim, *Flight of the Lavi: Inside a U.S.-Israeli Crisis* (Washington, DC: Brassey's, 1996), 4.

27. Hoglund, *Achaemenid Imperial Administration*, 270ff.

28. Cited in Blenkinsopp, "Mission," 410.

29. Ibid., 413.

He wanted the mission to have a specific timetable, which Nehemiah, who still required official authorization for his mission, promptly gave him.

It is unlikely that Nehemiah had not thought the mission through carefully, including the required length of his leave of absence, prior to broaching the matter with the king. He may have needed the time between Kislev, when he heard the news, and Nisan, when he spoke to Artaxerxes, to carry out sufficient research so as to be ready to answer whatever questions the king might put to him when the issue finally surfaced.

Unfortunately, Nehemiah did not record for posterity just what date he gave the king for his return. Perhaps Nehemiah worried that future readers of his memoirs might misunderstand. If he wrote that he had asked for a relatively brief leave, which was likely the case, future generations might conclude that he had no intention of doing anything other than what he told the king he would do, namely, ensuring that his family's graves were intact and well cared for. In light of the events that followed, Nehemiah may have judged that it was best for the image he wished posterity to have of him not to record much more about his original intentions when requesting the king's leave.

Having been granted that leave, Nehemiah then asked for official letters to the governors of the provinces of Abar Nahara granting him laissez-passer: Nehemiah was critically dependent upon a royal grant of safe conduct. In fact, the ancient diplomatic practice of providing a series of escorts through different provinces is still in force among some desert tribes.[30] Then, as today, official writ was crucial. Without it, the provincial authorities, who after Darius's administrative reorganization of the empire were under tight central control, would question and probably obstruct Nehemiah's mission.[31] In addition, Nehemiah had to reckon with the fact that once the Samaritans learned of his plans, they would do everything they could to abort the mission prior to his arrival in Judah.

Nehemiah, sensing that he was "on a roll," added a further request. He sought "a letter to Asaph, the keeper of the king's park, directing him to give me timber for roofing the gatehouses of the Temple fortress

30. Zer-Kavod, *Ezra UNeḥemia*, 72n25; see also Galil, *Daniel, Ezra UNeḥemia*, 208.
31. For a discussion of Darius's reforms as viewed from the provinces, see Roux, *Ancient Iraq*, 408–10.

and the city walls and for the house I shall occupy" (Neh. 2:8). Asaph happens to be a Hebrew name; it was the name of a leading psalmist.

It should come as no surprise that Nehemiah was not the only senior Jewish official in the king's retinue.[32] Persian Jewry had assimilated well, even as the community strongly maintained its Jewish identity, and, like Jews in more recent years, must have displayed a talent for public administration. In fact, Josephus states that Addaios – probably a corruption of the Greek version of Asaph – was governor of Syria, Phoenicia, and Samaria.[33] In that case, Asaph's role as keeper of the forest was in addition to his governorship; nobles in later times, too, often held more than one official position at the monarch's behest.[34]

What was special about Nehemiah was not that he was alone in being a Jew who rose to great power in the empire. Rather it was that he, and he alone, was ready to employ his political influence for the betterment of the Judean community. Others, like Asaph, were prepared to follow his lead and play a supporting role, but not themselves to lead.

It is not clear what Nehemiah meant when he referred to the gatehouses of the Temple fortress. It may have been the one on the northwestern part of the Temple Mount, in which case it would appear that Nehemiah had very precise, detailed knowledge of the situation in Jerusalem.[35] On the other hand, he may simply have been referring to the assembly hall before the Temple courtyard.[36]

When speaking of his own house, it likewise appears that he had a specific place in mind. Nehemiah may have been referring to a new

---

32. Slotki, *Daniel, Ezra, Nehemiah*, 189.

33. Josephus, *Antiquities*, XI:6; Myers, *Ezra/Nehemiah*, 98, citing J. B. Bewer.

34. Such, for example, was the case in Elizabethan England, where various officials in the queen's household held multiple offices. For example, the Earl of Essex was master of the horse, Earl Marshal of England, chancellor of Oxford University, and lord deputy of Ireland; see Alison Weir, *The Life of Elizabeth I* (New York, Ballantine, 1998), 430, 432, 438, and 439. Similarly, William Cecil was a member of Elizabeth's Privy Council, "which wielded vast and real executive and judicial powers," and was also her chief secretary; other colleagues on the council also held important state offices, such as lord treasurer and lord chancellor. See Stephen Budiansky, *Her Majesty's Spymaster: Elizabeth I, Sir Francis Walsingham and the Birth of Modern Espionage* (New York: Plume, 2006), 89–90.

35. Zer-Kavod, *Ezra UNeḥemia*, 72.

36. Ralbag, Neh. 2:8, s.v. *lekarot*.

governor's residence,[37] especially if it is assumed that the seat of government had not previously been Jerusalem. On the other hand, he may simply have meant that he wished to build a house in which to reside during his stay in the province.[38]

It is also possible that Nehemiah was requesting timber to expand an existing king's house,[39] perhaps to add a wing in which he would reside and, as befitting a governor, entertain large numbers of guests. This royal palace may have been a smaller, rebuilt version of the one that had existed prior to the exile. It had subsequently served as a royal guest house for visiting officials and now needed to be expanded to accommodate Nehemiah's needs.

The Talmud arrives at an interesting ruling on the basis of Nehemiah's request for timber. The ruling appears in the course of a discussion about whether or not one may accept a gift for Temple repairs from an idol-worshipper, the concern being that there may be nefarious ulterior motives behind a seeming act of goodwill.[40] R. Yosef observes that, on the contrary, such a gift must be acceptable, because not only did Nehemiah accept the timber from Cyrus (whom the Talmud identifies as Artaxerxes), in whose park the trees were located, but he actually requested the gift. Abaye demurs, however, noting that gifts from a government are a special case: sovereign commitments are always binding and no ulterior motives may be ascribed to such gifts.[41] The principle is one that contemporary major Western governments, as well as the State of Israel, subscribe to when offering aid to needy countries; if there is a motive, it is to obtain goodwill, rather than to subvert the governments of the aid recipients.[42] In the same vein, Artaxerxes had no negative intentions when he granted Nehemiah's request; to the extent that his motives were mixed, they were driven by a desire to establish a powerful and loyal satrapy in Judah.

37. Myers, *Ezra/Nehemiah*, 98.
38. Rashi, Neh. 2:8, s.v. *velabayit*.
39. Ibn Ezra, Neh. 2:8, s.v. *velabayit*.
40. See Rashi, Arakhin 6a, s.v. *betḥila*; see also Rashi ad loc., s.v. *delo*.
41. Arakhin 6a.
42. It is arguable that German reparations to Israel in the early 1950s were likewise motivated by a desire, driven by guilt over the Holocaust, to foster goodwill with the new Jewish state.

Nehemiah 2:9–20

Arrival in Jerusalem

JOURNEY TO JERUSALEM

Nehemiah had now been granted everything he requested. Artaxerxes shrewdly recognized that granting his cupbearer's wish would serve Persian national security interests – and probably also saw in Nehemiah a potential for strong leadership that would be critical to the success of his proposed enterprise. Much in the same way that American support for Israel, especially during the Cold War, stemmed from the belief that Israel was a regional bulwark against Soviet predations, a fortified Jerusalem, from the king's perspective – a city under the rule of a loyal, competent, and tough courtier – could serve as useful outpost for helping to maintain order in Persia's unruly western provinces. It was no doubt for this reason that the king provided Nehemiah with something he had not asked for: a military escort consisting of army officers and cavalry, in addition to the local escorts providing him with safe conduct through the provinces he traversed on his journey to Jerusalem.

The armed retinue accompanying Nehemiah had a twofold role. It was certainly a symbol of his official status and royal support, though he had yet to mention the fact in his memoir.[1] In addition, however,

1. The text at this stage bears no indication of a permanent royal appointment, since the king demanded to know when Nehemiah was planning to return to Persia.

and of greater long-term consequence to Artaxerxes, the armed guard constituted the backbone of any force that Nehemiah would organize to ensure the province's loyalty to the Persian royal house (Neh. 2:9).

Josephus asserts that Nehemiah also took with him "many of his countrymen who followed him voluntarily."[2] While it is possible that the armed force that accompanied him was Nehemiah's "small private army,"[3] it is far more likely that Jews constituted some portion of the armed escort. Since Jews served in the Persian army, some may have requested permission from their commanding officers to accompany Nehemiah. In addition, a powerful man like Nehemiah no doubt had his own personal following within the Jewish community, and some of them may have joined the Persian force on the occasion of his departure for Judah. Finally, other hangers-on may have hoped to benefit from their association with him on his journey to Judah.

THE OPPOSITION

News of Nehemiah's journey spread quickly, no doubt because of his official status and his interactions with leading Persian officials along his route to Jerusalem. The local authorities in Judah were none too pleased by what they clearly perceived as a threat to their power and privilege. Foremost among those who rightly felt threatened was one Sanballat the Horonite, the local provincial governor, who was based in Samaria. Sanballat, as has been noted, is the leading villain of Nehemiah's memoir.

Sanballat's origins are unclear. Jewish tradition, and some modern scholars, considers him to have been descended from the mixed group that the Assyrians settled in Samaria, although there is some speculation that he was of Ephraimite extraction.[4] The Book of Kings records that an unnamed Assyrian king, in accord with his country's usual practice, transferred several nations to the territory of

2. Josephus, *Antiquities*, XI:168.
3. Steinsaltz, *Biblical Images*, 209 (see chap. 1, n. 3).
4. Cross, *From Epic to Canon*, 189–90 (see chap. 1, n. 16), points out that "Persian policy… ordinarily favored persons or families of native stock for appointment to local, provincial governorships. Cf. Tobiah of Ammon and Gashmu of Arabia, among others." He could have added Nehemiah of Judah.

the Northern Kingdom when he exiled its Jewish population. When the new arrivals retained their idolatrous beliefs, God sent lions to attack them. They protested to the Assyrian king that they were being attacked because of their unfamiliarity with local religious custom, and he ordered one of the exiled Jewish priests to be sent to them to instruct them in his religion. The newcomers proceeded to adopt Jewish beliefs while retaining their original customs, resulting in a syncretistic form of worship that they continued to practice for centuries (II Kings 17:24–41).

If he was descended from these people, Sanballat would have had more than a passing understanding of the Jewish religion.[5] Nehemiah, on the other hand, like many of the Jews who preceded him and those who followed, considered the Samaritans to be virtual heathens. While Sanballat's name was Babylonian (*sin-uballit*, meaning "the moon god gives life"), the term Horonite may connote that he was a native of one of the Beit-Horon towns (about eighteen miles northwest of Jerusalem). There is uncertainty about this as well, since, as is sometimes the case with biblical names, Horonite may have been a pejorative term reflecting his association with a syncretic religion that combined worship of the god Horon with adapted aspects of the Jewish faith.[6] Despite his association with pagan gods, Sanballat's sons bore Jewish names. It is noteworthy that the condemnation of Sanballat "never refers to religious practice,"[7] though at least one medieval rabbinic commentator called him "an apostate."[8] He nevertheless may have seen himself as an adherent of the Jewish religion.[9]

The sages of the Talmud codified what had long been the standard Jewish view, namely, that the Samaritans were not to be considered Jews,

5. Bright, *History*, 382 (see chap. 1, n. 27).
6. Myers, *Ezra/Nehemiah*, 100–101, citing J. Gray; see also Galil, *Daniel, Ezra UNeḥemia*, 210; Cross, *From Epic to Canon*, 189.
7. Coggins, *Ezra and Nehemiah*, 74.
8. Mathews, *Commentary*, 23.
9. Bright notes that while Sanballat surely saw himself as an Israelite, "more Orthodox Jews like Nehemiah found [the Samaritans'] (surely somewhat syncretistic) religion unacceptable and regarded them no better than heathen" (Bright, *History*, 382). Shaver likewise asserts that Sanballat was a "Yahwist"; Shaver, *Torah*, 39.

even if they viewed themselves as such.[10] A midrash provides a fanciful but fascinating elaboration of the scriptural account that highlights later rabbinic antagonism toward the Samaritans:

> When the Israelites were exiled from their homeland in Samaria, the king [of Assyria] sent his servants and settled them in Samaria to raise taxes for his kingdom. The Holy One, Blessed Be He, inflicted lions upon them who were killing them. So they sent and informed the king, "The land that you asked us to settle rejects us, because our numbers have declined from many to few." So the king sent for all the elders of Israel and told them, "All the years that you were in your land, you were never decimated by the beasts of the field, and now what is happening?" So they said, hoping that they would be restored to their land, "Our lord king, the Holy One, Blessed Be He, refuses to accept gentiles who do not study Torah and are not circumcised." But [instead] he said to them: "Nominate two from among you who will go there to teach them [the Torah]; and the royal command cannot be withdrawn." So they sent R. Dustai b. Yannai and R. Sevaiah, who taught them the Torah in its original script even as they cried. And still these people followed both the precepts of the Torah and that of their gods … until Ezra came from Babylon together with Zerubbabel and Joshua the son of Jehozadak and began to build the Sanctuary. At that point the Samaritans – who were really Cuthites but were called Samaritans to connote the city of Samaria [where they now resided] – threatened to attack them with 180,000 [soldiers] and they also tried to kill Nehemiah through trickery … and they delayed the holy work for two years until the second year of Darius's rule. How did Ezra, Zerubbabel, and Joshua respond? They gathered the entire populace into the Sanctuary and brought three hundred priests, three hundred shofars, three hundred Torah scrolls, and three hundred infants and they blew the shofars while the Levites sang and played their

10. See, for example, Shabbat 17b, where the sages ruled that a Samaritan girl should be considered ritually impure from birth.

> instruments and they banned, cursed, and excommunicated the Cuthites, using the secret formula of the Tetragrammaton and with the script written on the Tablets of the Law and with the ban from the heavenly court and the terrestrial court that no man should eat the bread of a Cuthite.[11]

There can be little doubt that Nehemiah and his supporters viewed Sanballat in much the same fashion as this midrash.

Whatever his origins and beliefs, Sanballat evidently was the founder of the dynasty that bore his name and ruled Samaria until Hellenistic times.[12] He was likely to have been especially sensitive to threats of any kind, since his claim to rule was of recent vintage. Nehemiah's mission and his appointment as governor meant that Judah would become a separate Persian province again, and no longer incorporated into the province of Samaria. Nehemiah, therefore, represented more than a threat to the political status quo and to the local political elites. Sanballat may well have viewed Judah as a "breakaway" province that posed a danger to the integrity of his regime and of the Samarian entity.[13]

Sanballat was not alone in opposing Nehemiah. His closest collaborator was one Tobiah, whom Nehemiah describes as "the Ammonite servant" (Neh. 2:10). Tobiah was far from being a slave, however. If anything, his pedigree was superior to Sanballat's. The name Tobiah is a Hebrew one; he was a scion of an old, illustrious family and may have been descended from the Davidic household.[14] The term "servant" in

11. *Midrash Tanḥuma, Vayeishev* 2. *Pirkei DeRabbi Eliezer*, 38, has a nearly identical version, although it identifies the second rabbi as R. Zechariah rather than R. Sevaiah.
12. The Egyptian Elephantine papyri of 408 BCE refer to Sanballat as governor of Samaria. Since he must have been quite old by that time, his sons were presumably ruling in his name.
13. In much the same way as the People's Republic of China fears the potential independence of Taiwan as a catalyst for upheavals that might terminate the Communist regime and fracture the integrity of the Chinese state.
14. There are conflicting views about Tobiah's origins, but most scholars identify him with the prominent Tobiad family. Williamson argues that the term "Ammonite"

this context indicates that he was a servant of the king, or a royal official.[15] Some scholars posit that he was governor of Ammon, but this is highly unlikely. If Tobiah had been a rival Jewish official, he would have protested directly to the Persian king in a way that Sanballat, a non-Jew, simply could not. Nehemiah's case before the king was predicated upon his concern for the "city of the graveyard of [his] ancestors" (Neh. 2:3). Tobiah could equally strongly have claimed, as a Jew, that Nehemiah's assertions were exaggerated – the modus operandi of renegade Jews throughout the centuries, including the modern State of Israel's most vocal critics.

That Tobiah did not approach the king directly appears to indicate either that he was a Jew with no formal office or that he was a non-Jewish aristocrat and governor who, through marriage, had undergone a form of conversion and had aligned himself with the Judean upper classes. Tobiah may have been Sanballat's scribe, itself a position of some importance, but not important enough to justify an independent approach to the court in Susa. In contemptuously labeling Tobiah a servant, Nehemiah was indicating that he was a renegade who practiced a syncretic form of Judaism that incorporated idolatrous practices. Syncretism, even more than pure idolatry, was the bugbear of Jewish religious leadership virtually from the time the Israelites entered Canaan, being practiced not only by those who had superficially converted to Judaism, but by many whose Jewish pedigrees were beyond dispute.

The talmudic view identifies Sanballat and his coconspirators as the "adversaries of Judah and Benjamin" who opposed Zerubbabel.[16] As noted, the Talmud places all of the events in Nehemiah's memoir much earlier than the mid-fifth century BCE. Still, it is to be expected that Sanballat had his agents in Susa, from whom he must have learned the details of Nehemiah's mission. There was little he, or Tobiah, or their henchmen could do to stop Nehemiah, however, because of the armed escort that accompanied him.[17]

---

refers to his actual ancestry; Williamson, *Ezra, Nehemiah*, 183. He may have married a Jewish woman; in that case, her marriage to him would have been in defiance of the biblical injunction against marrying an Ammonite.

15. Myers, *Ezra/Nehemiah*, 98.
16. Ezra 4:1ff. See Rashi ad loc., s.v. *tzarei*.
17. Cross, *From Epic to Canon*, 190.

NEHEMIAH'S FIRST ACTS IN JERUSALEM

No one challenged Nehemiah's credentials anywhere along the journey. The presence of the armed escort confirmed to local governors the legitimacy of his mission; they might otherwise have questioned the authenticity of the king's letter of safe conduct. Instead, the local governors probably fell over themselves to provide this obviously powerful Persian official with food and logistical support; Nehemiah does not record having to request anything along the way. He arrived safely on the first day of the month of Av – the same date that Ezra had first appeared in Jerusalem – several months after his departure from Susa.[18] The preparations for his journey clearly had taken some time; in particular the timber he had requested from Asaph must have come from the mountains of Lebanon and been transported to him somewhere along his route to Judah.[19]

Though Sanballat knew of the mission to Jerusalem, Nehemiah appears to have successfully kept secret the actual day of his arrival. This served him in good stead, as he was determined to map out a plan of action before anyone could mount a coordinated resistance to his efforts.

The city that Nehemiah entered was a shadow of its former self. It was not merely that its walls were in disrepair, or even that it had been subject to occasional raids by marauding tribes. Despite its potential as a strategic location from a military perspective, it was in actuality simply a backwater, set in the brown Judean hill country with no outlet to any body of water, not situated along a major trade route. And it was a small place, with a circumference of just over a mile.[20] It was unattractive to all except the most devout. Even the Temple, the heart of the city and its only real attraction, was a pale replica of its pre-exilic predecessor. The new edifice was smaller and less imposing in every respect than the First Temple. No wonder the prophet Haggai had to reassure the people that this Temple would eventually outshine the one it had replaced (Hag. 2:9).

---

18. Zer-Kavod, *Ezra UNeḥemia*, 74. See Ezra 7:9.

19. Myers, *Ezra/Nehemiah*, 100.

20. Kathleen Kenyon, *Jerusalem: New Aspects of Antiquity* (London: Thames & Hudson, 1967), 110.

The city of Jerusalem was underpopulated. It was really a very small town, with fewer than two thousand inhabitants.[21] Other than the Temple, there was no significant source of economic activity. The society was agrarian, and most of the earlier returnees from the exile had preferred to resettle on their families' former homesteads, where they raised their crops and herded their sheep. The rich were able to buy up land from the poor, who, like small-holders everywhere, were often in debt and, as was – and would be – the case for centuries, were forced to mortgage their fields, ultimately becoming sharecroppers. When there was nothing left to mortgage, the poor sold off their children into slavery. This, too, was a long-standing practice, as it still is in parts of the non-Western world, though these days it is known formally as "trafficking in persons." The prophets had inveighed against this practice before the exile. As Amos put it: "Hear this, you who trample upon the needy… saying: When will the new moon be over that we may sell grain? And the Sabbath… that we may buy the poor for silver and the needy for a pair of sandals, and sell the refuse of the wheat?" (Amos 8:4–6).[22] Jewish law expressly forbade such behavior.[23] Few had paid attention to the preaching of the prophets in the past, and it seems that just as few paid attention once Jews began returning to their native land.[24]

While they maintained the trappings of their religion, many of the local populace were not particularly strict about its details. Non-Jewish merchants had no difficulty selling their wares inside the city walls on the Sabbath. Even more troubling, and of far greater consequence, the

---

21. Bright, *History*, 377, notes that "numerous towns in Judah were now inhabited…. Still the land was not thickly populated; Jerusalem itself had very few inhabitants." Bolin states that "the most recent population estimates claim that the city was no larger than 1,500 people at this time" (*Ezra, Nehemiah*, 91).
22. For a discussion of the prophets' call for social justice, see Abraham J. Heschel, *The Prophets: An Introduction* (New York: Harper, 1969), notably 81–82, 104–105, 202–203.
23. For a discussion of the limits to the laws of expropriation as they related to the post-exilic period, see Rabbi Isaac Halevi Herzog, "*Batei Din BeYisrael*" (Jewish Courts in Israel), *Teḥumin* 7 (5746/1985): 281–82.
24. Rabbi Herzog speculates that the rich Jews of Nehemiah's day were not as evil as those during the First Temple era, but they certainly did exploit the poor to the point that children were sold into slavery. See Herzog, "*Batei Din BeYisrael*," 282, but see Neh. 5:2.

people, both rich and poor, were hardly averse to intermarrying with the indigenous population despite the presence of the Temple in their midst. Even the Temple priests – and the High Priest himself – were prone to marrying non-Jews. They, and the rich more generally, married into the local aristocracy. Intermarriage had become so pervasive among the people that any attempt to eliminate it by force threatened to rip the entire society apart and ignite a civil war between those who had married out of the faith and those who resisted doing so.

In his zeal to extirpate what he rightly considered the primary threat to Jewish identity and posterity, Ezra had confronted a challenge of massive proportions when he arrived in Judah just over a decade before Nehemiah. In choosing to fast, pray, and sway the public with reproofs and admonitions, Ezra attempted to maintain communal cohesion.[25] His efforts secured him promises of good behavior, but, ultimately, nothing more. The promises were not kept, and Ezra was reduced to tearing out his hair (Ezra 9:3).

Well before he arrived in Jerusalem, no doubt, Nehemiah must have heard from Hanani and his colleagues that the Jewish elite in Judah was divided between a faction that was likely to support him and others who had come to terms with the Samaritans and other non-Jewish inhabitants of the province, were benefiting from these connections, and often were married to non-Jews. Not surprisingly, therefore, upon arriving in Jerusalem, and not knowing whom to trust, Nehemiah temporized for three days and kept his own counsel. There was no point stirring up opposition before he knew what he was going to do.

There were some men Nehemiah knew he could trust; possibly they were members of the armed guard that had accompanied him from Susa. With these men, none of whom he names in his memoir, he "got up at night... and telling no one what my God had put in my mind to do for Jerusalem, and taking no other beast than the one on which I was riding, I surveyed the walls of Jerusalem that were breached and its gates, consumed by fire" (Neh. 2:12–13). Only Nehemiah was mounted; his men walked on foot, so as not to arouse the sleeping inhabitants of the town.

25. Herzog, "*Batei Din BeYisrael*," 283.

It is unclear where Nehemiah began his stealthy nighttime survey; moreover, it is difficult to identify the details of his route even though Nehemiah gives the specific locations he passed along the way. Some say that his route started somewhere near what is today the Jaffa Gate; others argue that it began northwest of what is now the City of David, near what is believed to have been the location of his house.[26]

In any event, Nehemiah attempted to circumnavigate the city's perimeter. He reached a point, however, where, he later recalled, "there was no room for the beast under me to continue" (Neh. 2:14). He could not get through all the gaps,[27] either because they were too small, or because of the debris and rocks piled high along the wall.[28] The damage to the walls clearly was of major proportions if there was no room even for a single mount to pass forward. Accordingly, Nehemiah turned back, having surveyed two sides, possibly three, of the walls surrounding the city.

Though Nehemiah failed to reconnoiter the entire wall, or what was left of it, he did succeed in keeping his mission a secret. As he recounts, "The prefects knew nothing of where I had gone or what I had done, since I had not yet divulged it to the Jews – the priests, the nobles, the prefects, or the rest of the officials" (Neh. 2:16). No doubt Nehemiah knew he had some support among the populace. Nevertheless, he had yet to establish whom exactly he could count on. Even those who might have been expected to support him – for example the priests, because they were religious functionaries – still might not favor an interloper from the Persian capital. Nehemiah could not be certain of support from the prefects – the assistant governors – or the lower-ranking officials, all of whom likely had been chosen by Tobiah, if not by Sanballat himself; they doubtless gave their allegiance to his enemies. In initially being secretive as a result of anticipating possible resentment from the locals, Nehemiah foreshadowed the behavior of

26. Cf. Zer-Kavod, *Ezra UNeḥemia*, 74; Slotki, *Daniel, Ezra, Nehemiah*, 190; Myers, *Ezra/Nehemiah*, 104.
27. Rashi. s.v. *va'e'evor*.
28. Myers, *Ezra/Nehemiah*, 105, citing Kathleen Kenyon's archaeological findings in the 1960s.

an array of political leaders upon returning from residence or service abroad with aspirations of leading their nations – from Julius Caesar to Napoleon to Lenin to Mohandas Gandhi.

Of the various groups that Nehemiah initially kept in the dark about his doings, the nobles were likely to be the center of any opposition to his plans, since they benefited most from the status quo. They had made their peace with the local powers that be and had married into the local aristocracy, as Tobiah appears to have done. They paid their taxes by soaking the poor. They paid lip service to their religion but no more than that – crying with Ezra when he chastised them, ignoring him afterwards. They were unlikely to be sympathetic to the intervention of an outsider who could threaten their position, privileges, and prerogatives. Members of an ethnic aristocracy under a foreign ruler have always found themselves torn between nationalism and membership in the establishment. Modern examples include the Scottish clan chieftains who undermined Scottish nationalism in the eighteenth century, the Hungarian nobles who opposed Kossuth in the nineteenth, and, most recently, the Zulu leadership that worked hand in glove with the Afrikaner establishment virtually until the collapse of apartheid in South Africa.

ASSEMBLING THE PEOPLE

Nevertheless, the time had come for Nehemiah to explain his presence to the populace, no matter how suspicious they might be of his motives or skeptical about whatever he might say. Before doing so, he may have added to the wreckage so as to impress upon the people the urgency for restoration to begin.[29] He then assembled the people – most likely, as Josephus asserts,[30] in the Temple court (the *azara*), where, from the height of the Temple Mount, they would have been able to see the extent of the damaged wall in every direction.

Nehemiah understood that the wall fulfilled several different functions, none of which was acceptable to his opponents. It ensured the city's centrality to the life of the nation by affording protection to the Temple. It represented a place of refuge for the population in the

29. Ibn Yahia, Neh. 2:13, s.v. *hayiti*.

30. Josephus, *Antiquities*, XI:168.

countryside in the event of attack by domestic or foreign marauders. Finally, it established the city as an important element in the Persian Empire's western defenses, with the concomitant economic benefits that accrued to such outposts. His challenge was to convince the Jewish community of its importance.

With the panorama of the wreckage as a backdrop, Nehemiah called upon the people to join him in rebuilding the city and its wall. To win them over, he first appealed to their native pride: he asserted that by reconstructing Jerusalem they would "suffer no more disgrace" (Neh. 2:17). In so doing he implied that the sorry state of Jerusalem caused their neighbors to heap scorn upon their religion.[31] Moreover, he conveyed a more subtle message, namely, that the disorder in the capital would be interpreted both by their enemies in the region and the court in Susa as a political statement of their weakness. Nehemiah knew very well that the people were aware that such a perception embodied great danger: they had only to think back to Haman's argument to Ahasuerus that it was not worth tolerating the continued existence of their dispersed and disloyal community.

Nehemiah went on to tell his listeners that he was the beneficiary "of my God's benevolent care" (Neh. 2:18). But he was shrewd enough to realize that simply invoking God's name would not necessarily convince a skeptical and potentially hostile people. This was especially the case with the community's leaders, given their vested interest in the status quo. In consequence, he immediately turned to "the things that the king had said" (ibid.). He knew full well that by stressing that he was not some interloper, but rather enjoyed royal support and spoke with official authority, he was sure to get their attention.[32]

Nehemiah appears to have been a convincing, if not a charismatic, speaker. His oration prompted an enthusiastic response from the people. Their enthusiasm recalled the way the Israelites had first greeted Moses when he reemerged in Egypt to announce that God would free them (Ex. 4:31). Nehemiah's challenge was to ensure that this support

31. See Zer-Kavod, *Ezra UNeḥemia*, 75; Myers, *Ezra/Nehemiah*, 105.

32. Compare Moses's initial experience with the leaders of Israel in Ex. 4:29–31; 5:20–21.

did not wane as soon as it confronted opposition – much as Moses had quickly discovered.

THE OPPOSITION MOUNTS

The resistance was not long in coming. Sanballat and Tobiah soon learned of Nehemiah's plans; they probably had some agents planted among his audience.[33] They were joined by a third local leader, Geshem the Arab. Geshem was the powerful ruler of the Qedarites (an inscription describes him as their king). Qedar, located to the south and east of Judah, was nominally under Persian control but in practice was essentially an independent entity.[34] It is possible that Geshem may also have held an official position at the Persian court while ruling over his domains.[35]

Geshem's opposition was a major strategic challenge for Nehemiah. The threat Geshem posed to Jerusalem from the south and east, when combined with Sanballat's power in the north, meant that Nehemiah could not rule out the possibility of a two-front conflict. In this regard, Nehemiah's situation was not unlike the challenge the State of Israel has faced since its creation. Geshem's rejection of Nehemiah's plans marks the first recorded instance of tension between Jews and Arabs over Jerusalem – which has not subsided for two millennia.

Sanballat and his allies mocked Nehemiah's plans and contemptuously asserted that his real intention in building the wall was to enable him to lead a revolt against the king.[36] Their reference to rebellion was a veiled threat to take the matter to the Persian government, as they had done earlier in Artaxerxes's reign.[37] This was precisely the allegation that opponents of Jewish migration to Palestine hurled at the leaders of the Zionist Yishuv and their overseas supporters; the tactics were likewise similar. By applying pressure on the Foreign

33. Williamson, *Ezra, Nehemiah*, 191–92; see also Galil, *Daniel, Ezra UNeḥemia*, 218.
34. Williamson, *Ezra, Nehemiah*, 192.
35. Coggins, *Ezra and Nehemiah*, 77.
36. Rashi, Neh. 2:19, s.v. *haal*. Ralbag ad loc., s.v. *haal*.
37. Cf. Zer-Kavod, *Ezra UNeḥemia*, 75–76, and Ezra 4:7.

Office, the Arab leadership was able to reverse British immigration policy to Palestine.[38]

Nehemiah did not directly address the threats leveled against him, since he was confident of his authority. Instead he told his three antagonists, and presumably, their henchmen, "The God of heaven will grant us success, and we, His servants, will start building. But you have no share (*ḥelek*) or claim (*tzedaka*) or stake (*zikaron*) in Jerusalem!" (Neh. 2:20). In effect he was challenging them to try to make their case at Susa, where he was sure to prevail.

The very nature of his response made something else clear: like Zerubbabel before him, Nehemiah had absolutely no intention of accepting any offer that might be forthcoming from Sanballat and his ilk to join the Jews in the construction of the walls (Ezra 4:1–3). The Hebrew words *ḥelek, tzedaka,* and *zikaron* respectively connote a share in the construction work, the provision of financial support, and the sanctification of materials for the effort. Each of these expedients was intended to achieve the objective of claiming some degree of sovereignty over the city, and all three were unacceptable to Nehemiah.[39] As he was to demonstrate continually over the next few months, Nehemiah was wise to the intrigues and prevarications of his opponents, and at no point was he prepared to have anything to do with them. Instead, he focused squarely on his mission – to rebuild the city and restore the nation's sense of identity – and to overcome whatever opposition he faced in doing so.

---

38. With the publication of the 1939 White Paper and its enactment into law, immigration above strictly controlled limits (which could only be set with Arab acquiescence) and the expansion of Jewish territorial holdings were both construed as, in effect, rebellion against His Majesty's Government.

39. The Talmud concludes from this verse that gentile donations for the construction of Jerusalem are unacceptable; Y. Shekalim 5b.

Nehemiah 3 and 4
The Wall Is Almost Complete

STRATEGIC ASSIGNMENTS FOR BUILDING THE WALL

Nehemiah found himself faced with the vocal opposition of the local non-Jewish population, represented by Sanballat and Geshem, as well as by men like Tobiah, wealthy assimilated Jews who were satisfied with the status quo. He went to great lengths to ensure that the reconstruction project had the broadest possible base of support within the population. Nehemiah recognized that the community as a whole was internally riven over the entire project; some of its leaders were even linked by marriage to Sanballat's party. Like any good politician, Nehemiah allocated the work on the walls in a strategic fashion, matching tasks to the self-interest of the people to whom they were assigned. He successfully coped with the need to cater to the self-images of those involved, many of whom were drawn from the resident nobility. He often appealed to their self-interest by assigning construction near their homes or their market stalls.

Nehemiah left behind a highly detailed roster of those who participated in the wall's reconstruction. It is clear from the list that they represented the germ of the coalition upon whose support Nehemiah relied. In addition to recruiting priests and nobles, whose loyalty and reliability remained uncertain, Nehemiah was able to call upon numerous officials of varying ranks, the Levites, and ordinary citizens.

The text does not indicate how assignments were made. There were forty sections of wall that required rebuilding or repair. Assigning them to different work units called for considerable planning and negotiation,[1] all within a constrained time frame so as to catch Sanballat off-guard.

Nehemiah's political acumen was evident throughout. He accorded the leading priests, foremost amongst them Eliashiv the High Priest, their due respect by linking their task to their religious stature. They were the first to begin the work, and they were assigned the construction of the Sheep Gate.[2] Eliashiv apparently supported the construction despite also consorting with Nehemiah's enemy, Tobiah (Neh. 13:4). The two issues were not necessarily linked, however: Eliashiv may have disapproved of Nehemiah's policy of excluding the Samaritans, even as he supported the reconstruction policy.[3]

The Sheep Gate was located toward the northeastern portion of the city and was possibly part of the Temple Mount wall; it was certainly the gate nearest the Temple.[4] The offering of the firstborn was brought through this gate.[5] Other sacrifices may have been brought through it as well: according to a medieval commentator, it was "the Gate of God through which all holy sheep [presumably for sacrifices] entered."[6] The

1. Myers, *Ezra/Nehemiah*, 112.
2. Much of the description of the wall's reconstruction, which is outlined in Neh. 3:1–32, deals with the names of places whose location is uncertain, and is the subject of considerable speculation and disagreement. For an in-depth discussion of these locales, see especially Malbim on Neh. 3; Myers, *Ezra/Nehemiah*; and Zer-Kavod, *Ezra UNeḥemia*. Coggins, *Ezra and Nehemiah*, 79, observes that Nehemiah is not named in this account and that there are no references to "the people or incidents from the Nehemiah tradition." He concludes that this section of chapter 3 was not part of the "original block of Nehemiah material." In fact, the description of the rebuilding underscores Nehemiah's political acumen; there is simply no need to mention him, since his role is self-evident. Moreover, the rebuilding is itself a critical event in Nehemiah's tenure, and there is no plausible reason why other events, such as his later administrative decisions, should be cited in this chapter.
3. Slotki, *Daniel, Ezra, Nehemiah*, 193.
4. Zer-Kavod, *Ezra UNeḥemia*, 76; Myers, *Ezra/Nehemiah*, 113.
5. Mathews, *Commentary*, 24.
6. Ibn Yahia, Neh. 3:1, s.v. *vayivnu*.

Talmud[7] cites a statement by Abba Saul that "there were two districts [or meadows] on the Mount of Olives, the lower and the upper; the lower was consecrated with all these [i.e., the king, High Priest, and Urim and Thummim];[8] the upper was not consecrated with all these, but by the returned exiles,[9] without king and without Urim and Thummim." Given the status of the Sheep Gate, it was natural for the High Priest and his colleagues to be tasked with its reconstruction.

The Sheep Gate was the only one of the city's gates to be sanctified; it required consecration because the area had been incorporated into the old city limits as they had stood during the First Temple.[10] The precincts were sanctified despite the dangers that could arise from confusion about the different states of holiness, because imparting them with a sense of holiness would encourage a stronger degree of commitment from the returning exiles.[11]

Though the Sheep Gate had a special status, many, though not all, of the gates appear to have been reserved for prominent citizens. In fact, most of the gates had been virtually destroyed, indicating that the city had been subject to one or more raids, with marauders charging through gates that were forced open. Only the wealthier members of the community were in a position to repair them. Repairing gates, therefore, involved a degree of prestige; Nehemiah seems to have capitalized upon this fact, essentially treating the repair of gates as a form of patronage.

The portion of the wall whose construction was assigned to Eliashiv and the senior priests extended to the Tower of the Hundred and the Tower of Hananel. The Tower of the Hundred was located just north of the Sheep Gate, providing it with protection.[12] It has been called "the great synagogue of Jerusalem where, in accordance with rabbinic

7. Tosefta Sanhedrin 3; Shavuot 16a.
8. Rashi (Shavuot 16a, s.v. *taḥtona nitkadsha bekhol elu*) comments on the passage: "During the First Temple era it was incorporated within the city boundary and joined by a wall."
9. Rashi (Shavuot 16a, s.v. *ela beolei gola*) states: "They added to the city and built a surrounding outer wall."
10. Zer-Kavod. *Ezra UNeḥemia*, 76.
11. See *Tosafot*, Shavuot 16a, s.v. *ela*.
12. Zer-Kavod. *Ezra UNeḥemia*, 76.

dicta regarding the requirement to utter one hundred daily blessings (Menaḥot 43b), one hundred 'Amen's were voiced in response."[13] It was for this reason that the area was consecrated together with the Sheep Gate. The exact location of the Tower of Hananel has not been identified, though it must have been along the northern wall.

It appears that the wall extended beyond the city limits that obtained during the First Temple era. The portion assigned to the priests had to be completely rebuilt, as all of it had collapsed.[14] Interestingly, despite local opposition to reconstruction of the wall, the expansion of Jerusalem per se does not appear to have aroused the same sentiments. It is not clear why this was the case. Perhaps the locals saw economic opportunity as distinct from a political threat. Later in his memoir Nehemiah recounts that the level of trade between Jews and non-Jews was so extensive that it even took place on the Sabbath (Neh. 13:15) – much to his annoyance, as we will see. An expanding Jewish population in an enlarged Jerusalem meant more business for all.[15]

Nehemiah appears to have instructed the builders to work westward along the northern side of the wall. The northern wall was perhaps the most important part of the city's exterior defenses, because of its terrain and the fact that it faced Samaria, the ground zero of local opposition to the Jews in general and Nehemiah in particular.[16] Not surprisingly, those working on this side were among the province of Judah's most prominent people and families, fitting "neighbors" to toil alongside Eliashiv the High Priest.

The composition of the group building the northern wall is worthy of mention; Nehemiah would need their support, or at least the support of most of them, if he were to implement the reforms that he must have already planned during the course of his journey to Judah.

13. See Mathews, *Commentary*, 24.

14. Malbim, Neh. 3:2, s.v. *ve'et*.

15. Such an attitude stands in marked contrast to the current Palestinian leadership's opposition to any expansion of modern Jerusalem, which it views only in political terms.

16. Malbim (Neh. 3:1, s.v. *vayivnu*) asserts, however, that construction began on the eastern wall and the teams worked northward, the eastern wall being opposite the Temple.

Among those undertaking repairs near Eliashiv and his crew were the residents of the ancient city of Jericho, which had been inhabited by the tribe of Benjamin in the era before the destruction of the Temple. Next to them was a group led by a prominent scion of the tribe of Judah, Zacur the son of Imri. Zacur was a direct descendant of Peretz son of Judah; as such he was a member of the royal line, though perhaps a distant one, because Peretz had been an ancestor of King David.

The builders of the next major gate along the northern wall, the Fish Gate, were other prominent members of the tribe of Benjamin. Unlike the Sheep Gate, which is not mentioned in other biblical books, the Fish Gate was reportedly built by King Menashe; it received its name from the nearby fish market.[17] Menashe, the son of the saintly Hezekiah, was very much the antithesis of his father. He was a great sinner, to the point that a later rabbinic tradition held that he had no place in the World to Come, in contrast to virtually every other Jew – and many non-Jews (Sanhedrin 90a). The Fish Gate appears to have been in an exceedingly serious state of disrepair, even when compared to other portions of the wall. Nehemiah recounts that the Benjamites "roofed it and set up the doors, locks, and bars" (Neh. 3:3). It was critical that the gates be fully repaired; attackers would seek to breach a city's gates, if possible, rather than attempt to scale its walls.

Two other prominent men led the construction in the sections of the northern wall adjacent to the Fish Gate. Meremoth son of Uriah was the Temple treasurer and, because of the major revenues that passed through his hands, one of the most powerful men in the province. The passage of centuries has not altered the truism that he who controls funds controls policy. Alongside Meremoth was a team led by Meshullam son of Berechiah. Meshullam's son had married into Tobiah's clan, so his loyalty to Nehemiah was suspect. But, as in the case of Eliashiv, he too may have supported the need to rebuild the city walls even as he opposed Nehemiah as an interloper. In any event, Nehemiah could not exclude him from the construction any more than he could exclude Eliashiv, whatever his suspicions. Meshullam was too prominent to be ignored; discounting him would guarantee his enmity.

17. Zeph. 1:10; II Chr. 33:14 and *Targum Rav Yosef* ad loc.

Once Meshullam was accepted as part of the reconstruction team, his prominence ensured that he would be included among those granted the honor of rebuilding the northern wall.

If Meshullam's connections might raise Nehemiah's suspicions, the people of Tekoa, a town southeast of Bethlehem, certainly did not. Tekoa was the birthplace of Amos, one of the most outspoken of the Temple-era prophets on matters of social justice. It was a relatively impoverished agricultural community, and the Tekoans, like farmers to this day, were conservative religiously and nationalist politically. As such, they represented a significant part of Nehemiah's political base. Perhaps that is why he had them working on the section that was separated from Meshullam's by just one other segment, one headed by a priest named Zadok. Despite his clear preference for assigning work on the northern wall to the rich and famous, Nehemiah also needed reliable people to keep an eye on workers whose loyalties were suspect. Meshullam certainly fit into this category – hence the placement of the Tekoans nearby.

It is noteworthy, but perhaps not at all surprising, that while the people of Tekoa joined in the construction, the town's *adirim* – which literally means "mighty men" but is often translated as "nobles" – "would not take upon their shoulders the work of their lord" (Neh. 3:5). Some classical commentators, focusing on the phrase "*their* lord," argue that the leaders neglected their duties of fealty to the provincial governor in order to participate in the repair of the walls.[18] This interpretation is questionable, however, since the leaders of Tekoa were not the only prominent men with obligations to the authorities; the fact that Nehemiah spoke only of them in these terms indicates that there was something unique about their behavior.

Instead, it is possible, as some modern commentators contend, that the town's leaders considered it beneath their dignity to undertake manual labor.[19] The nobles may have been the owners of the livestock that the younger Tekoans tended. They could not see themselves working alongside mere shepherds and cowherds. On the other hand, they must have seen that Eliashiv the High Priest and other notables were

18. Ralbag, Neh. 3:5, s.v. *vaadireihem*.
19. Williamson, *Ezra, Nehemiah*, 196.

doing exactly that. If the High Priest could soil his hands in support of a worthy cause, surely so could they. That they did not do so indicates, again, that other factors were involved.

It is far more likely that the Tekoan nobles simply did not want to associate themselves with Nehemiah's project. As one medieval commentator observes, the nobles "did not want to expend as much as a *pruta* for the reconstruction, but the poor, even in their poverty, undertook the repairs."[20] In contrast to the destitute ordinary townsfolk, the nobles of Tekoa had a vested interest in a politically weak Jewish leadership, and more generally, in the preservation of the status quo, of which they were the prime beneficiaries. It is probable that political prudence, in the face of Nehemiah's authoritative royal writ – especially given that he had the support of the Persian provincial authorities, indicating that the writ was very much in force – led them to temper their open opposition to his plans. While they would not participate in the reconstruction of the city walls, they did not dare prevent their tenants and villagers from doing so. Whatever the nobles' motivations, Nehemiah clearly took notice of their abstention from the common enterprise.

The next section of the wall also involved a gate, the Jeshanah Gate. Its precise location is unknown, as is the source of its name. The gate probably was located in the western portion of the wall, near its northwestern corner. Those in charge of its construction, Joiada son of Paseah and Meshullam son of Besodeiah, were not as prominent as the others who worked on the northern wall.[21]

Two sections of the wall, also probably in its western portion, were built by people from Gibeon and Mitzpah. What is noteworthy about them, as Nehemiah recounts, is that they were "under the jurisdiction of the governor of the province of Abar Nahara" (Neh. 3:7).

20. Ibn Yahia, Neh. 3:5, s.v. *vaadireihem*.

21. Some commentators believe that the gate's name was simply Jeshanah, possibly after a town of the same name (II Chr. 13:19 and Josephus, *Antiquities*, XV:12; see also Rashi, Neh. 3:6, s.v. *hayeshana*; Myers, *Ezra/Nehemiah*, 110; Williamson, *Ezra, Nehemiah*, 196). Others say that the name connotes "the old gate," that is, a gate from the original city wall that predated the destruction and exile (Ralbag ad loc., s.v. *ve'et*). Whatever its location or origins, it was, like the Fish Gate, in a serious state of disrepair, and its beams, doors, locks, and bolts all had to be rebuilt and retooled.

Mitzpah was only about three and a half miles north of Jerusalem, but it may have been outside Judah's boundaries, as was Gibeon. As a result, they were under the direct control of the satrap. Nevertheless, the residents of both towns lent their assistance to the reconstruction of the capital.[22] The involvement of Diaspora Jewry in the activities of the state is a constant in Jewish history. Jews from abroad participated in Temple ceremonies during the three pilgrimage holidays of Passover, Shavuot, and Sukkot (*aliya laregel*). More recently, Diaspora Jews have been involved in Israel's political and military affairs, including the establishment of the military services during the state's early years, and political campaigns and the expansion of housing and settlements in Jerusalem and elsewhere since the late 1970s.

The construction of the remaining walls featured contributions from city officials, from various guilds, and from some who made a second contribution to the reconstruction effort. Among the city officers repairing the wall was one Rephaiah son of Hur, whom Nehemiah describes as "chief of half of the district of Jerusalem" (Neh. 3:9). Judah was divided into a number of administrative districts, which were further subdivided; the administrator of each subdistrict was termed "chief of half the district."[23] The term for district, *pelekh*, appears only in chapter 3 of Nehemiah's memoir, but nowhere else in Scripture. On the other hand, it is used frequently in tannaitic sources as an administrative term relating to the creation of district courts with capital jurisdiction. These were the courts of twenty-three judges that functioned outside Jerusalem, the seat of the Sanhedrin, the supreme court of seventy-one judges.[24]

Another official who led the repair of a section of the wall was also named Nehemiah; he was the son of Azbuk. Like Rephaiah, he was in charge of a half-district, in this case that of Bet-Zur. He led the team that repaired the portion of the wall that fronted the royal Davidic burial grounds and extended as far as the section that faced "the House

22. Ralbag, Neh. 3:7, s.v. *anshei*.

23. Zer-Kavod, *Ezra UNeḥemia*, 80.

24. For a discussion, see Ephraim E. Urbach, *The Halakhah: Its Sources and Development*, trans. Raphael Posner (Tel Aviv: Yad LaTalmud/Modan, 1996), 63.

of the Warriors." No doubt this was a military barracks, presumably for the kings' personal guard.

Interestingly, one medieval commentator, eager to make a point about the importance of Torah study, seized upon Nehemiah's descriptive term as an indication that it was a beit midrash, or house of study, wherein the students, or "warriors," engaged in discussions that constituted the "battles of Torah."[25] In so redefining the plain meaning of the text, the commentator foreshadowed one of the major arguments that modern-day *ḥaredim* have articulated in their opposition to military service for yeshiva students: namely, that the students are already engaged in combat, albeit of a different kind that consists of Torah study and exegesis. Many *ḥaredim* argue that this is as crucial to the survival of the Jewish state as is the might of the Israel Defense Forces – if not more so.

Rephaiah and Nehemiah son of Azbuk were not the only officials to participate in the wall's reconstruction. More senior officials were involved as well. Shallun son of Col-Hozeh was the lord of the entire district of Mitzpah (Neh. 3:15) and a member of one of the first families to return to Judah from Babylonia (Neh. 11:3, 5).[26] A rabbinic commentator posits that Shallun's father was a scholar, although there is no evidence other than the fact that Col-Hozeh literally means "sees all."[27] More likely, however, is another commentator's assumption that Shallun's title was equivalent to "duke," reflecting the highest level of nobility, just below the monarchy.[28] Like the other senior officials and Eliashiv the High Priest, Shallun took the lead in repairing one of the city's gates, in this case the Fountain Gate.

Malchijah son of Rechab, likewise in charge of an entire district, that of Beit HaKerem (not to be confused with the neighborhood of the same name in modern Jerusalem), led the reconstruction of the Dung Gate, which was along the southern portion of the wall. Malchijah was an aristocrat, scion of the prominent pre-exilic family of Rechab that, the Talmud recounts, had the honor of providing wood for the altar in the

25. Mathews, *Commentary*, 24.
26. See Zer-Kavod, *Ezra UNeḥemia*, 82.
27. Mathews, Commentary, 24.
28. Rashi, Neh. 3:9, s.v. *sar*.

rebuilt Second Temple.[29] Despite his prominence, Malchijah's commitment to the reconstruction project was so strong that it appears from the text (*hu yivnenu* – "he would build it"; Neh. 3:14) that he personally repaired the gate rather than relying upon a team of hired hands.[30] Finally, Ezer son of Jeshua was yet another district governor – in this case of another district named Mitzpah – who participated in the reconstruction effort.

The fact that Shallun, Malchijah, Ezer, Nehemiah son of Abzuk, and Rephaiah all supported Nehemiah's project could indicate their dissatisfaction with the Samaritan hierarchy. As nobles themselves, they may well have seen the Samaritans as parvenus. Though they may have viewed Nehemiah in similar fashion, he was, at least, one of their own nation. They may have calculated that, given the Persian king's support for his mission, Nehemiah was likely to prevail over any opposition, and that siding with him was an act of prudence that would enable them to maintain their privileged position within Judah's society.

The Levites, whose work appears to have been concentrated on the southern and eastern walls, tended to be among the underprivileged in Judahite society. Nevertheless, over the centuries, there were times when less fortunate minorities, including Jews in Christian and Muslim lands, achieved some degree of prominence; the Levites, notably scions of important families, did so, serving as chiefs of half-districts. Among these were Hashabiah and Bavvai son of Henadad, who were each in charge of half of the district of Keilah. Hashabiah was among the leaders of the Levites who had returned with Ezra thirteen years earlier. He is identified there as descended from the Levite Merari, Aaron's great-uncle. Bavvai's forebears had been active in the construction of the Second Temple under Zerubbabel. In any event, their status does not appear to have prevented them from throwing in their lot with Nehemiah.

With respect to the guilds, the smiths contributed as a group, and perhaps as a family – not an unusual circumstance, since artisans normally trained their children to follow in their calling – as did the perfumers, who completed the restoration as far as what Nehemiah

29. II Kings 10:15; see also Zer-Kavod, *Ezra UNeḥemia,* 81 and Mishna Taanit 4:5.
30. Zer-Kavod, Ezra UNeḥemia, 81.

termed the Broad Wall (and were next to the abovementioned Rephaiah son of Hur). The artisans' guilds played a critical role in Nehemiah's project. They probably had their markets near the portion of the wall that they repaired and thus had a vested interest in its fortification. On the other hand, they risked the wrath of Nehemiah's opponents, and a consequent loss of income, by supporting the reconstruction of the city. More likely, the artisan guilds were simply very nationalistic, and as a political and economic pillar of the community, they elected to throw their considerable weight behind the project.

Just as the priests repaired the wall near their place of service in the Temple, and the artisans near their workplaces, so too did several citizens repair the wall nearest to their own homes. In every case, Nehemiah shrewdly manipulated the assignments so as to appeal to the self-interest of those being recruited for the construction project. Of course, as people identified Nehemiah's project with their own interests, they were more likely to align themselves with other projects and policies that he would undertake in the future.

There was one other group that participated in repairing the walls, a group that might not have been expected to take part in Nehemiah's project – and, in fact, a group that in later times would probably have been banned from any activity relating to it. That group was the women of the community. Nehemiah relates that among the builders was one Shallum son of Hallohesh, like Rephaiah, chief of the half-district of Jerusalem. Nehemiah adds, "he and his daughters" (*benotav* in Hebrew; Neh. 3:12). While some commentators, not surprisingly perhaps, prefer to interpret the word *benotav* as "settlements" or "suburbs" attached to the half-district from which Shallum recruited workers, others, more realistically, translate it in its usual sense, since the word is translated as "suburbs" only when directly relating to a city, not, as in this case, to a person.

In general, women do not figure prominently in Nehemiah's memoir. Nevertheless, Israelite women's tradition of fierce nationalism is well documented – Miriam, Deborah, Yael, and, of course, Esther, are among the scriptural examples. The unnamed daughters of Shallum, who were obviously highborn, appear to have followed in the wake of their illustrious forebears. One Modern Orthodox commentator, writing just after the founding of the State of Israel, adds: "The modern *ḥalutzot* in

Israel are following an ancient precedent."[31] And foreshadowing the women pioneers who helped rebuild modern Israel, the daughters of Shallum had no problem taking on physical labor, and doing so shoulder to shoulder with the menfolk.

In the midst of describing the rebuilding of the wall, Nehemiah interposed in his memoir a brief reference to the Temple servants who lived in the Ophel. These servants, in Hebrew *netinim*, were descended from the Gibeonites that Joshua had forced to become "hewers of wood and drawers of water" (Josh. 9:21). They had their own residences near the Temple. The Ophel was a tower south of the Temple Mount where a portion of the *netinim* lived; they repaired the wall near where they lived until opposite the Water Gate,[32] which was located between the Horse and Sheep Gates.[33] According to a midrash, Ezra maintained the long-standing physical separation between the *netinim* and the rest of the populace by settling them in the Ophel.[34] The reference to physical separation is reminiscent of the Israelites' enclave in Goshen.[35]

The Temple servants lived in an area that abutted the Water Gate, which the Mishna appears to indicate was one of four gates along the southern entrances to the Temple compound.[36] According to the above-mentioned mishna, there were two possible reasons for its name: either because the water for the Sukkot libation was brought through it or, as R. Eliezer b. Yaakov argues, because (in accordance with Ezekiel's prophecy; Ezek. 47:1–2), water trickled through it and will someday issue forth beneath the Temple threshold.

Both traditional commentators and non-traditional scholarship have posited a variety of theories about the gate's location: some scholars argue that it was not a gate at all; others place it south of the Ophel

31. Slotki, *Daniel, Ezra, Nehemiah*, 97.
32. Rashi, Neh. 3:26, s.v. *vehanetinim*.
33. Zer-Kavod, *Ezra UNeḥemia*, 85.
34. *Midrash Shoḥer Tov*, 64.
35. Such enclaves are not unique to the Jews; modern southeastern Europe and the Caucasus region have been enmeshed in conflicts stemming from the existence of similar ethnic enclaves.
36. Mishna Middot 2:6 and Mishna Sukka 4:9; see also *Tosafot*, Sukka 48a, s.v. *shaar hamayim*.

(and the Temple) at the northeastern corner of the City of David.[37] In any event, the servants do not seem to have participated in the wall's reconstruction, though they did not impede it either. Perhaps it was for that very reason that Nehemiah saw fit to mention them when he did.

THE ENEMY'S RESPONSE TO THE CONSTRUCTION

Sanballat, on the other hand, displayed none of the servants' passivity. He recognized that the wall was a threat to his authority and, as Nehemiah puts it, "was extremely vexed" (Neh. 3:33). His problem, however, was that Nehemiah was a royal official who was ostensibly on a mission from the king. For that reason, he could not openly take up arms against Nehemiah. Instead, Sanballat initially resorted to a form of psychological warfare: "He mocked the Jews, saying in the presence of his brothers and the Samarian force, 'What are the miserable Jews doing? Will they restore, offer sacrifice, and finish one day? Can they revive those stones out of dust heaps, burned as they are?'" (3:33–34). Sanballat delivered this address to his followers – the "force" being a body of irregular troops – within earshot of the Jewish workers in order both to intimidate them and to arouse doubts about the likelihood that the wall could be completed in a timely fashion. This was not a trivial concern; the Jews' prior efforts to rebuild the Temple had foundered as a result of interminable delays, postponements, and royal cancellations. Sanballat and his mob, in effect, conducted a loud and noisy rally, complete with taunts and epithets.[38]

Tobiah the Ammonite then chimed in with a taunt of his own: "That stone wall they are building – if a fox climbed it he would breach it!" (Neh. 3:35). His point, which no doubt was not lost upon the Jewish workers, was that even if the construction were somehow completed, it would never be sufficiently fortified. Foxes would continue to dig breaches in the walls. Tobiah's metaphor echoes the passage at the close of Lamentations: "Because of these our eyes are dimmed: Because of

37. Myers, *Ezra/Nehemiah*, 115.

38. Sanballat's behavior is not dissimilar to that which at times marked Palestinian rallies near Israeli construction sites in East Jerusalem throughout the 1990s.

Mount Zion, which lies desolate; jackals prowl over it" (Lam. 5:17–18).[39] Tobiah might well have been familiar with Jeremiah's lament and the likely psychological impact it would have on the construction crews.

Faced with this concerted effort to undermine his followers' morale, Nehemiah once again prayed: "Hear, our God, how we have become a mockery, and return their taunts upon their heads! Let them be taken as a spoil to a land of captivity!" (Neh. 3:36). He looked to God for vindication, and cursed his opponents with the wish that they suffer in exile as the Jews had suffered.

Nehemiah did not limit himself to prayer, however. While he certainly sought divine assistance, he was, at bottom, a man of action, and he forged ahead with the wall's construction. He rallied the workers and continued to stoke their enthusiasm, so that fairly quickly the wall was rebuilt "till it was continuous all around to half its height" (Neh. 3:38). The success that had so far been achieved fed on itself: the more the work on the wall progressed, the more eager were the workers to finish the job.

Nehemiah's enemies were far from ready to concede defeat, however. Sanballat and Tobiah recruited other indigenous peoples to their cause: Scripture lists "Arabs, Ammonites, and Ashdodites" (Neh. 4:1); Josephus adds "Moabites, Samaritans, and all those living in Coele-Syria [i.e., the Bekaa Valley region]"[40] for good measure. Certainly, the Jews were surrounded by enemies on all sides: the Samaritans to the north, the Arabs to the south, the Ammonites to the east, and a mix of nations (or Philistines) in the province of Ashdod to the west. Whatever the composition of the opposition, "one way or another all four Persian provinces participated in attempts to thwart the reconstruction of Jerusalem."[41]

The members of the anti-Jewish alliance pledged to come together and fight to prevent the completion of Nehemiah's project. In this respect, they foreshadowed the events that took place immediately upon the creation of the State of Israel, though in the latter case more than threats were involved. As Chaim Herzog, historian, general, and sixth president

39. See Slotki, *Daniel, Ezra, Nehemiah*, 202.

40. Josephus, *Antiquities*, XI:174.

41. Myers, *Ezra/Nehemiah*, 125.

of Israel, records: "On the night of 14/15 May [1948], the armies of five Arab states (Egypt, Jordan, Syria, Lebanon, and Iraq) crossed the borders and began the invasion of Palestine."[42] Yet the parallels do not end there. It is truly amazing how little changes in the Middle East over the span of the centuries – indeed, millennia. The world continues to refuse to recognize the sovereignty of the Jews over Jerusalem. Israel's neighbors in the Middle East, even those prepared to live with it in peace, cannot come to terms with its right to Jerusalem as its capital, or with the very notion of a Jewish state. Moreover, like the enemies who confronted Nehemiah, some would almost seem to prefer a Jerusalem that is desolate to one that is developed and beautiful, as long as the Jews cannot call the city their own.

Sanballat urged upon his supporters a plan to "fight against Jerusalem and to throw it into confusion" (Neh. 4:2). Since he was outnumbered by the Jews, who also had royal support, Sanballat recognized that he had to resort to stratagems in order to lull Nehemiah's builders into a false sense of security. He assumed that the Judahites would not realize that he and his supporters intended to wage war against them and thus would not be sufficiently mindful of their enemies' preparations for an assault.[43] The plan had the force of logic behind it: all too often, in ancient, modern, and contemporary history – and as recently as the Yom Kippur War – states with strong defenses have nevertheless found themselves at a military disadvantage because they were slow to perceive an imminent threat.

NEHEMIAH'S DEFENSIVE TACTICS

Nehemiah, however, recognized what Sanballat was up to, and responded accordingly. Though he and his cohorts prayed to God for assistance, they also prepared themselves for an assault by establishing a twenty-four-hour watch on the walls.[44] Nevertheless, not everyone among the

42. Chaim Herzog, *The Arab-Israeli Wars: War and Peace in the Middle East from the War of Independence Through Lebanon* (New York: Vintage Books, 1984), 47.
43. Ralbag, Neh. 4:2, s.v. *velaasot*.
44. The Midrash relates that Jacob behaved in a similar fashion in anticipation of his meeting with Esau; see Rashi, Gen. 32:9, s.v. *vehaya*.

builders was willing to take up arms. It was one thing to ignore taunts; it was quite another to engage in military combat. Some people clearly were frightened, worried that Sanballat, with his own powerful connections, not only would triumph but would exact retribution from those who sided with Nehemiah. As is often the case when cowardice shows itself, they tried to persuade others to quit working by arguing that "the strength of the basket-carrier has failed, and there is so much rubble; we are not able ourselves to rebuild the wall" (Neh. 4:4).[45]

This was exactly the reaction that Sanballat hoped to prompt. Nevertheless, the malingerers were in the minority, though Sanballat did not realize it. For his part, he urged his supporters on by asserting that "before they know or see it, we shall be in among them and kill them, and put a stop to the work" (Neh. 4:5).

Nehemiah had his own sources of intelligence, however. Jews who resided outside areas under Nehemiah's immediate authority were forced to serve in his enemies' armies. They acted as a fifth column, providing Nehemiah with information about troop movements that enabled him to organize his defenses in the most efficient manner.[46] Their basic message was that "from all those places where you will be scattered in the course of construction, take heed that you gather together so as to be in a position to fight us as a unified force."[47]

The Jews were undoubtedly disloyal to their gentile commanders, and such "dual loyalty" in the military has been grist for anti-Semitic diatribes over the centuries. In fact, in this case, the Jews never professed to be loyal to anyone but their coreligionists; they had been drafted against their will. Later accusations of dual loyalty among

45. Lamentations Rabba I:43 quotes R. Tanḥum b. R. Yirmeyahu that oppressive government "robs a man's strength."

46. Ralbag (Neh. 4:6, s.v. *mikol*) postulates that the Jews mentioned in the verse were to report back on troop movements or planned ambushes by Nehemiah's enemies. In Rashi's view (ad loc., s.v. *vayehi*), the Jews who lived among the gentiles and were serving in their forces were able to betray their plans when they met with Nehemiah's troops in the military parleys that often preceded actual combat in the Middle Ages. Ibn Yahia's approach (ad loc., s.v. *HaYehudim*) is similar, and he, like Metzudat David (ad loc., s.v. *hayoshvim*), also believes that the Jews outside Nehemiah's domain had no choice but to serve in the local militias.

47. Rashi, Neh. 4:6, s.v. *vayomru*.

Jews serving in gentile armies also did not reflect reality – but for a different reason. Whenever given the opportunity to serve their rulers, the Jews did so with honor and heroism – whether the rulers were Muslim caliphs in medieval Spain, or (beginning in the nineteenth century) the monarchies of Europe, or the forces of the United States ever since the American Revolution. Jews also did not hesitate to serve on fronts where they confronted the possibility of shooting at other Jews; this was most notably the case during World War I, when Jews were to be found in both the officer corps and enlisted ranks of virtually every major combatant, as well as during the American Civil War, when Jews fought for both the Union and the Confederacy.

Nevertheless, the role of the Jews as intelligence agents for Nehemiah certainly has contemporary echoes. During the early years of the State of Israel's existence, when it benefited from an influx of Jews from Arab lands and did not have the technical means that prevail in modern intelligence structures, Israel relied heavily upon its "Oriental" Jews. They served as agents and critical sources of strategic and tactical intelligence on the capabilities, intentions, plans, and operations of Israel's Arab enemies. And they performed as well as their ancient ancestors whose information enabled Nehemiah to cope with any attack.

Nehemiah recognized that, although he was governor, he did not necessarily have the authority to preempt his enemies. Accordingly, while preparing for a defensive battle, he also sought to adopt a deterrent posture that maximized the effectiveness of the forces at his disposal while signaling to the enemy the futility of any attack they might be contemplating. He placed his troops at strategic locations behind the wall and was able to move them rapidly to positions where he anticipated enemy attacks based on the intelligence he had been provided. Generally this meant moving forces from lower, more vulnerable positions to the higher rocks, so as to have early warning of troop movements and repel the invaders.

Nehemiah also deployed his forces in family units, possibly even including the women who had worked on the wall, so as to ensure the highest level of morale, cohesion, and dedication to the cause. Morale and cohesion continue to be critical yet overlooked factors in modern warfare;[48] they compensate for disadvantages in the balance of opposing forces.

Having organized and inspected his defenses, Nehemiah then did what every military leader has done from time immemorial: he gave a rousing motivational speech to his troops, "the nobles, the prefects, and the rest of the people, 'Do not be afraid of them! Think of the great and awesome Lord, and fight for your brothers, your sons and daughters, your wives and homes!'" (Neh. 4:8).

His address was noteworthy on several counts. To begin with, the prefects were part of both his defense force and his target audience. Their participation was important not merely because of their seniority in Judah's society, but also because they were Jewish officials of the Persian administration. By including them among his forces, Nehemiah made it doubly difficult for Sanballat to attack; to do so would have meant assaulting officials of the Persian crown.

Second, Nehemiah's theme was one that was certain to arouse the passions and the determination of his followers: protecting one's loved ones and dearest possessions. It is a theme that has recurred in similar morale-boosting speeches throughout history.

Finally, as with his earlier address to the people at the start of his project, Nehemiah began with references to the deity before he proceeded to deal with more temporal factors. His use of the phrase "Do not be afraid" was quite deliberate. It harked back to the priest who was anointed to accompany the troops into battle (*mashuaḥ milḥama*), as outlined in Deuteronomy 20:3. It thus recalled the glorious battles of yesteryear, when God had enabled Israel's heroes to outsmart, outmaneuver, and ultimately defeat the people's enemies.

Not surprisingly, Nehemiah's creation of a militia to guard the walls, and his speech to his followers, soon became known to Sanballat. Nehemiah intended as much. Rather than await an attack and then ambush the enemy, Nehemiah chose to husband his resources by

48. For a discussion, see William Darryl Henderson, *Cohesion: The Human Element in Combat* (Washington, DC: National Defense University Press, 1985), and Jon W. Blades, *Rules for Leadership: Improving Unit Performance* (Washington, DC: National Defense University Press, 1986).

marshaling his own psychological warfare assets. By ensuring that they knew he was aware of their plans, as well as by his inclusion of royal officials among his forces, Nehemiah effectively foreclosed an immediate military option for Sanballat and his colleagues. His strategy mirrored that of the great Chinese general and theorist of war Sun Tzu: "To win every battle by actual fighting before a war is won, it is not the most desirable. To conquer the enemy without resorting to war is the most desirable.... The adepts in warfare are those who can conquer the enemy without fighting battles."[49]

Nehemiah's defensive activities naturally had been a diversion from the frenzied effort to finish the wall and thereby present the Samaritans, Ammonites, and anyone else with a fait accompli. Nehemiah had to recommence work on the walls, but at the same time had to ensure their protection. He recognized that it was not enough to foil Sanballat's plan; he needed to create a standing deterrent to any threat of attack. To this end he altered his operational posture by dividing his human resources: "From that day on, half my servants did work and half held lances and shields, bows and armor. And the officers stood behind the whole house of Judah" (Neh. 4:10). The armed men included the royal escort that had accompanied him from Susa[50] and whatever local people could afford to equip themselves with military paraphernalia, since Nehemiah did not himself distribute any weapons.

Nehemiah's division of his forces between those bearing arms and those rebuilding the city exemplifies the classic trade-off between "guns and butter." Deterrents are expensive because they presuppose a defensive posture. To be effective, deterrent forces must be well armed, well trained, and dedicated to their purpose. They must also be able to absorb an attack and retaliate with decisive force. Such forces are not cost free. The "opportunity cost" of these men was their unavailability to carry on the task of reconstruction. It was a price that Nehemiah had no choice but to pay.

---

49. Sun Tzu, *On the Art of War*, ed. Lo Shun-te, trans. Cheng-Lin (Taipei: n.p., 1991), 67–68.

50. Zer-Kavod, *Ezra UNeḥemia*, 91.

The workers on the walls were also armed, but unlike the designated guard, they did not have their weapons at the ready; they needed both hands to do the work of building. Likewise, the porters who loaded the construction materials from baskets onto the animals that carried it to the builders needed both hands free. On the other hand, the basket carriers who transferred the materials for the walls to the porters were able to do so with one hand, and held their weapons in the other.[51]

Like any good military leader, Nehemiah was ever present with his troops. He served as a rallying point; having exhorted his supporters, he needed to be visible so as to ensure that the workers and troops did not panic. Nehemiah also appears to have had a personal armed escort, much as he had when he arrived in Jerusalem. He knew full well that he was a constant target for assassination. If he were to be killed, there was little doubt that the project would come to a crashing halt.

Nehemiah recognized that his decision to proceed with the construction at a pace as close as possible to what had prevailed prior to the perceived emergence of a military threat meant that the builders would be dispersed from one another as they worked on the walls, unable to hear or see signals from the adjacent areas. This circumstance naturally posed a problem in the event that Sanballat tried to mount a surprise attack. Accordingly, Nehemiah kept a trumpeter near him to sound the alarm, and instructed all the officials who led the work teams, as well as the workers themselves, who would be the foot soldiers in any military confrontation and needed to be fully aware of the plan for defending the walls: "There is much work and it is spread out; we are scattered over the wall, far from one another. When you hear a trumpet call, gather yourselves to me at that place; our God will fight for us!" (Neh. 4:13–14).

Nehemiah's instructions and his invocation of God both made good military sense. Having his troops coalesce at a single location represented the most effective way to mount a defense along a long line with thinly scattered troops. In fact, the mobile strategy of NATO's forces along the Central European front (known as the Inner German Border) during much of the Cold War was virtually identical in principle. In addition, Nehemiah recognized the possibility that his forces would

51. Malbim, Neh. 4:11, s.v. *hanose'im*.

be outnumbered. While an unfavorable force ratio did not necessarily mean defeat (NATO planners assumed that a 1:3 ratio was sufficient to stop attacking Warsaw Pact forces), the disparity might frighten Nehemiah's forces. He wisely invoked God, whose help was, in any event, both a necessary and sufficient condition for victory.

His instructions having been issued, Nehemiah led the teams back to work, while the guards remained on duty. Their day was a long one, from before sunrise (*alot hashaḥar*) until it was night (*tzet hakokhavim*).[52] In such circumstances, it was impractical, if not dangerous, for workers who had come in from the surrounding villages to return home every night. Nehemiah wanted to prevent any further loss of construction time due to his workers having to commute each day from outside the city walls. Time was already being lost because a portion of his work force had to stand guard, while those who labored while armed could not proceed with their work at a normal pace and no doubt tired more easily. And, of course, the men who were on nocturnal guard duty could not possibly return home. Accordingly, Nehemiah ordered "that every man with his servant lodge in Jerusalem" (Neh. 4:16). As a result, people slept in shifts, much as they have always done in military and work units that are expected to be active around the clock. The force was thus "a kind of national guard."[53]

Moreover, Nehemiah, his senior officers, and the troops went even further, no doubt to inspire and reassure the workers: "Nor did I, my brothers, my servants, or the guards following me ever take off our clothes, [or] each his weapon, even at the water" (Neh. 4:17). They had to wash their clothes and bathe in shifts, the only exception being for the purpose of ritual purification. They were thus constantly on "alert

52. Neh. 4:15. Both *alot hashaḥar* and *tzet hakokhavim* have halakhic connotations: the related term *amud hashaḥar* indicates seventy-two minutes before sunrise. For a discussion, see Rabbi Steinsaltz's commentary on the Talmud, Berakhot 8a (see chap. 3, n. 15). *Tzet hakokhavim* is also a technical term in both Talmud and halakha. It connotes the appearance of three stars, and marks the official onset of "night." The Talmud cites this verse, as well as the phrase "use the night" in the following verse, as the basis for calculating when the nightly *Shema* prayer may first be recited (Berakhot 2b).

53. Elie Wiesel, *Sages and Dreamers: Biblical, Talmudic, and Hasidic Portraits and Legends* (New York and London: Summit, 1991), 129.

status," much like contemporary air force pilots or paratroop units that expect to be called into action at any time. Nehemiah's strategy succeeded; Sanballat and his allies were deterred, at least for the moment.

In his magnum opus, *Emunot VeDeot* (The Book of Beliefs and Opinions), the great medieval philosopher Rabbi Saadia Gaon contrasts Nehemiah's strategy for constructing the walls under the protection of an armed guard with the vision of Isaiah, who foresaw that "aliens shall build up your walls."[54] Nehemiah had no choice but to provide an armed guard while the Jews rebuilt Jerusalem's walls under threat from a coterie of enemies. Isaiah, on the other hand, foretold a time when the redemption would be complete, and Israel's adversaries would be transformed into Jerusalem's handmaidens. Current circumstances in the Middle East demonstrate that there are many bridges yet to cross before any peace process will even come close to yielding the results that Isaiah envisaged and Rabbi Saadia yearned for.[55]

---

54. Interestingly, today a significant percentage, perhaps a majority, of construction workers in Israel are non-Jews.

55. Saadia Gaon, *Emunot VeDeot* 8:6.

Nehemiah 5
Social and Economic Strains

ECONOMIC CRISIS

With the threat of attack no longer immediate, the social and economic strains that the crisis, as well as the poor harvests, had created within the community burst into the open.

> There was a great outcry by the common folk and their wives against their brother Jews. Some said, "Our sons and daughters are numerous; we must get grain to eat in order that we may live!" Others said, "We must pawn our fields, our vineyards, and our homes to get grain to stave off hunger." Yet others said, "We have borrowed money against our fields and vineyards to pay the king's tax." (Neh. 5:1–4)

It was no accident that Nehemiah was forced to address the economic and social schisms within Judean society once the challenge from Sanballat and his henchmen appeared to have subsided. History demonstrates that communal strains long buried beneath a united front toward an external foe often surface once that foe no longer looms large. In the immediate aftermath of World War II, for instance, British voters overwhelmingly voted for the new economic and social order that the socialist Labour Party represented, rejecting the Conservative leadership – in the person of none other than Winston Churchill – that had won the war. Economic and social resentments of Israel's have-nots, particularly among Jews of Sephardi origin, likewise propelled long-time opposition leader Menachem Begin to power in May 1977, just a few years after the state had successfully withstood the existential threat posed by the Yom Kippur War. Long-simmering disputes among disparate religious and ideological elements of Israeli society once again burst into the open in the aftermath of Israel's signing of the Oslo Accords in September 1993. The bitterness seemed at times to threaten the state's political stability, notably when Prime Minister Yitzhak Rabin was assassinated in November 1995. Again, in 2011, with the relative relaxation of the security threat to Israel from its immediate neighbors, and with a growing economic gap between rich and poor, there erupted demonstrations involving hundreds of thousands of protesters from a variety of socio-economic and religious backgrounds opposing the continuing rise in the cost of living (particularly housing) and the deterioration of public services such as health and education. In this case, the rallying cry echoed the protesters who had appealed to Nehemiah: "The people demand social justice." Truly, "there are few issues so divisive of a harmonious community as extreme disparity in personal wealth and income."[1]

The protests that confronted Nehemiah were certainly not unique to Judah. Some eight decades earlier, the Egyptian governor Udjahorresnet experienced almost identical challenges in his own country. What was unique was the circumstance that led to the protests, and particularly the role of women in the protests.[2] In traditional societies, then as now, women are responsible for feeding their families. Yet because the men of Judah had been forced to remain in Jerusalem to manage and undertake the construction, the women not only had to feed their families, but had to work to acquire provisions, rendering their situation

1. Williamson, *Ezra, Nehemiah*, 245.
2. In a noteworthy parallel, women activists were crucial players in the 1888 protests in New York against the imposition of a tax on kosher poultry (a lead seal, termed a *plumbe*, was attached to each chicken for which the tax had been paid). For a discussion, see Abraham J. Karp, "New York Chooses a Chief Rabbi," *Publications of the American Jewish Historical Society* 44 (March 1955): 161–64.

even more tenuous. In addition, with the impending harvest would come demands from creditors for the repayment of loans. The specter of further expropriations only added to the protesters' panic.[3] Finally, the ongoing presence of enemies outside the precincts of Jerusalem made it more difficult to carry out normal agricultural activities.

Such a situation could not be sustained indefinitely. Nehemiah was confronted with a mob that was not only bitter, but on the verge of hysteria. He had to act if he wished to complete the construction of the wall; otherwise it was clear that the workers, aware of the strains on their families and feeling pressure from their spouses, would return to their farms.

The protesters fell into three distinct groups. The poorest tended not to have land of their own. They desperately needed grain to survive. They were finding themselves forced to sell their children into slavery, since their fields had already been mortgaged. Yet selling off family members was as much a personal as an economic disaster for these people. To this day, poorer elements of society tend to have larger families; it is the family unit that provides the ultimate security for its members, late in life as in early life, and children often are an essential part of the family's labor force. Not surprisingly, given their desperate straits, they threatened Nehemiah that if he did not act, they would do so on their own, seizing food wherever it might be found.

A tradition among the rabbis of North Africa states that this poorest group of protesters included the leading sages of the time, the Men of the Great Assembly. In this tradition, these rabbis, "who [had] established statutes for Israel when they returned from the exile," were totally destitute. The effort to relate biblical circumstance to contemporary times no doubt reflected the poverty-stricken state of many, though certainly not all, Jewish communities under Muslim rule. This was particularly true of the rabbinic class, whose penury dated back to the storied poverty of Hillel the Elder.[4]

3. For a brief discussion, see Williamson, *Ezra, Nehemiah*, 236.
4. The poverty of the Men of the Great Assembly was related by the great fourteenth-century decisor Rabbi Isaac bar Sheshet Perfet, known as Rivash. See *She'eilot*

The second group of protesters was slightly better off. These people at least had property against which they could borrow. They too were starving, however, and in the end were not much more fortunate than those who had no fields in the first place.

The third group appealed to Nehemiah in his capacity as a representative of the king. They appear to have been in a somewhat better position than those who had pawned their fields. In the end, however, they too found themselves without the means to acquire food, having used the produce of the fields and then mortgages against the fields to pay the king's levy upon small landholders to fund local projects.

In all three cases, the poor looked in vain for assistance or debt relief from their wealthier brethren. In fact, however, the rich had connived, through intermarriage with local elements, to feather their own nests, often at the expense of their poor compatriots. They were unlikely to volunteer any meaningful assistance to fellow Jews who were starving. The poor bitterly resented the wealth of the rich, even as they were forced to struggle for survival.

The Jews had never accepted the notion of a nobility divinely placed to lord over the rest of society. The Torah specifically bequeathed the land to all, thereby providing that a small sector of society could not aggrandize itself at the expense of everyone else; under Torah law, land could not be mortgaged in perpetuity (Lev. 25:23), but at most for fifty years. The Torah also explicitly forbade exploiting those who were forced to borrow funds: "You shall not behave toward him as a creditor" (Ex. 22:24).

The economic exploitation of the poor by the wealthy thus clearly violated biblical commandments that were the essence of Jewish autonomy. Nehemiah was furious at the rich, both for their indifference toward those who were penniless to begin with and for their exploitation

---

UTeshuvot HaRav Yitzḥak bar Sheshet, ed. David Metzger, vol. 1 (Jerusalem: Machon Yerushalayim, 5753/1993), nos. 153, 158. Rabbi Isaac knew whereof he spoke. Himself a refugee, having escaped Valencia, Spain, after the attacks on Jews in 1391, and settled in Algiers, he lived in extreme poverty, though at the same time he tried to help those even less fortunate than he was. The story of Hillel's poverty is related in Yoma 35b.

of those who had lost their possessions through mortgages, taxes, and, implicitly, usury.

Earlier prophets had complained loudly and bitterly about similar exploitation of the poor by the rich. So did Malachi, who may have been a near-contemporary of Nehemiah. The protesters thus reflected traditional Jewish values when they shouted at Nehemiah, "Our flesh is as good as our brothers', and our children as good as theirs; yet here we are subjecting our sons and daughters to slavery – some of our daughters are already subjected – and we are powerless, while our fields and vineyards belong to others" (Neh. 5:5).

NEHEMIAH RESPONDS

Facing the protesters, Nehemiah recognized that he could not pursue his vision of a rebuilt Jerusalem and a vibrant Jewish commonwealth without the support of a united polity. Yet he found himself in an awkward position. He needed to soothe public anger, something he could do only by reducing the financial burdens that were crippling the poor. Yet, as the appointed royal governor, he was part of – indeed, a representative of – the system that had created that burden in the first place.

Having determined that the economic chasm within the community threatened his agenda, Nehemiah had to decide upon a plan of action. To do so he consulted no one but, as he put it, his "heart" (Neh. 5:7). He did not act emotionally, neither fasting nor tearing out his hair, as Ezra, the community's religious leader, had done upon learning of Judah's intermarriage crisis (Ezra 9:3). Nor did he hurl verbal fire and brimstone at the nobles, as the great prophets would have done. Instead, he drew upon his powers of persuasion, backed by his secular stature as a senior Persian official. He privately censured the local nobles and officials on the basis of what was religiously right and proper, demanding of them, "Are you pressing claims on loans made to your brothers?" (Neh. 5:7).

In rebuking the nobility, Nehemiah offered no preliminary parables, as did Nathan, for example, when rebuking David for his affair with Bathsheba (II Sam. 12:1–6). Nehemiah's basic point was that the nobles should have been dispensing charity, not foreclosing mortgages on loans that should never have been made in the first place – the subprime toxic assets of the day.[5] But his appeal to the nobles did not succeed; they appear to have ignored him.

Nehemiah was not a man to be brushed aside, however. Once again unlike Ezra, he did not torture himself for the misdeeds of others. Instead, he opted for the role of populist rabble-rouser. If inciting a mob was required to pressure the nobility, restore communal harmony, and proceed with the reconstruction of Jerusalem, Nehemiah was prepared to do so. As he recounts, he "raised a large crowd against them" (Neh. 5:7). His example has been followed time and again by men of noble birth who broke ranks with their own class to rally the poor against their overlords. As the great Liberal prime minister William Gladstone famously averred: "All the world over, I will back the masses against the classes."[6]

Now, with the angry crowd looking on, Nehemiah told the nobles, "We have done our best to buy back our Jewish brothers who were sold to the nations; will you now sell your brothers so that they must be sold [back] to us?" (Neh. 5:8). Nehemiah focused on the redemption of captives (*pidyon shvuyim*) for a good reason: one by-product of the Babylonian exile had been the selling of Jews into captivity. Strenuous efforts had been made to redeem as many of these Jews as possible, and Nehemiah wanted to stress an activity that already had become a major communal priority. When addressing the nobles, Nehemiah may have used the word "we" because he had been personally involved in redeeming captives.

Over the centuries that followed Nehemiah's emphasis on the redemption of captives, the practice continued to command the highest priority. During the Middle Ages, Christian overlords frequently imprisoned Jewish communal and religious leaders, confident that the communities, however economically hard-pressed they might be, would nevertheless find the exorbitant resources demanded of them to free their brothers. The sixteenth-century *Shulḥan Arukh*, the authoritative Code of Jewish Law, states unequivocally that redemption of captives takes precedence over supporting the poor: "There is no greater mitzva

5. For similar sentiments see Is. 58:6–10.
6. William Gladstone, Speech at Liverpool, June 28, 1886.

than redemption of prisoners."[7] Perhaps Rabbi Yosef Caro, author of the Code, derived this conclusion from Nehemiah's public argument to the nobles, which initially focused on prisoner redemption rather than feeding the poor. During the nineteenth century, in fact, Sir Moses Montefiore achieved widespread recognition for his efforts to obtain the release of Jews imprisoned in Syria and elsewhere; more recently, *pidyon shvuyim* motivated international Jewish movements to free Soviet, Ethiopian, and Syrian Jewry. It continues to underpin the unceasing efforts of the world Jewish community to redeem Israeli prisoners of war.[8]

Nehemiah evoked the redemption of captives not only because some of the crowd he was addressing might well in the past have helped redeem captives,[9] but also because some of those captives might have been in the crowd, listening to his words. His argument to the nobles held that their behavior would lead to the creation of new captives who would then have to be redeemed. His point was that such behavior simply made no sense. Why expend valuable resources to redeem a new set of captives, this time sold into slavery by their Jewish mortgagees?

Nehemiah went on to say that the actions of the wealthy made them the subject of reproach in the non-Jewish world. He asserted that they were sowing the seeds of *ḥillul Hashem*, the desecration of God's name, which takes place when Jews fail to live up to the standards that are set by their faith and that they have advertised to the world. To this day, *ḥillul Hashem* is a concern for Jews; news that individual religious Jews have been found guilty of crimes, often of a financial variety, invariably causes fear within the community that all Jews will be tarred by the non-Jewish world with the shortcomings of their compatriots and, as a result, that the Jewish faith itself will be besmirched.

---

7. *Shulḥan Arukh, Yoreh De'ah* 252:1.
8. In this regard, the European practice of paying ransoms for kidnapped hostages closely parallels Jewish law, in contrast to the American policy of refusing to submit to extortion by hostage-takers.
9. Malbim, Neh. 5:8, s.v. *et*.

LEADING BY EXAMPLE

Nehemiah continued with a revelation of his own: he too was a creditor! "I, my brothers, and my servants also, have claims of money and grain against them; let us now abandon those claims!" (Neh. 5:10).

He seems, in fact, to have been a foreign investor, with long-standing economic interests in Judah. He probably relied on his family and associates to look after his investments in the province. Although he is unlikely to have lent his money at interest, and certainly does not appear to have foreclosed on the borrowers' land or forced them to sell their children into slavery, his representatives may have done so. He admitted that he too, at least indirectly, was part of the problem, as opposed to simply blaming others or employing the ancient version of the contemporary technique of avoiding blame by admitting that "mistakes were made" without stating by whom. Thus Nehemiah significantly enhanced his credibility with the protesters.

Having indicated that he had as much to lose as the others in forgiving the debts of the poor, he proceeded to forgo his claims. No doubt he recognized that in so doing he was establishing himself as an "enemy of his own class" and potentially compounding his already serious political difficulties with the establishment elites. In this, he was much like certain later leaders: Gladstone, Theodore Roosevelt in the early twentieth century, and his cousin Franklin Roosevelt in the 1930s all evoked the deep and undying hatred of the upper classes precisely because they were traitors to their "own kind."

Nehemiah had little time to reflect on such considerations, however. He had to settle the economic mess immediately so that the work on Jerusalem could proceed. He issued a peremptory order and left no doubt that it had to be obeyed: "Give back at once their fields, their vineyards, their olive trees, and their homes, and [abandon] the claims for the hundred pieces of silver, the grain, the wine, and the oil that you have been pressing against them!" (Neh. 5:11). What he demanded was no different from what the prophets had sought in earlier times; the difference was that as governor, he could apply secular muscle to religious motivation.

The elites understood the situation: they were cornered by Nehemiah, on the one hand, and the mob, on the other. They had no option but to give in to Nehemiah's demands. Their advantage over the poor had come to an end. Like it or not, they agreed to return all the mortgaged properties and renounce their claims on their debtors. But Nehemiah did not trust them; after all, the rich had made such promises in the past, only to renege at the first opportunity.

The historical record of the elites was dismal. As Jeremiah recounts, the nobles had released their bondmen and bondwomen in accordance with a covenant they had made with King Zedekiah, only to recapture and enslave them once more (Jer. 34:9–11). Since Nehemiah's agenda could not tolerate such socially disruptive behavior, he employed the device of a solemn oath, administered by the priests, to ensure compliance. The priests, of course, had every interest in seeing the construction continue, since a strengthened city promised the prosperity that was required to sustain the Temple's – and their – financial requirements. But they too were required to forgive their loans to the poor.[10]

Nehemiah then made a gesture that he knew would cause unease among the already traumatized wealthy, especially among the superstitious, who no doubt constituted the majority of them. He shook out the bosom of his garment, uttered a curse that God would "shake free of his household and property" anyone who reneged on the promise that Nehemiah had just extracted, and caused them all to answer "Amen" and praise God (Neh. 5:13).

The elites most certainly must have recalled that Moses used similar language, if not imagery, when he required six of the tribes, standing on Mount Eival in Shechem, to answer "Amen" to the curses that would befall them if they failed to keep the laws of the Torah (Deut. 27:12–26). No doubt, too, they recognized that their reply of "Amen" not only evoked the "Amen" of those on Mount Eival, but also the "Amen" of the *sota,* the woman accused by her husband of infidelity; she was subjected to the test of the bitter waters and accepted the priest's curse if she failed the test (Num. 5:19–27). Finally, Nehemiah's demonstrative use of clothing evoked yet another curse from Israel's pre-exilic past: King Saul, upon tearing the corner of Samuel's garment, was told by the prophet that God had torn away his throne and passed it to another (I Sam. 15:27–28).

10. Rashi, Neh. 5:12, s.v. *laasot.*

The curses and the gesture, coming on the heels of pressure from the riotous mob that could explode again at any time, proved too much for the wealthy. As Nehemiah put it, in the height of understatement, "the people kept this promise" (Neh. 5:13).

Having successfully removed the threat of class warfare, which would have rent the Jewish body politic asunder, and presumably forgiven the debts owed personally to him, Nehemiah looked for other ways to demonstrate to all concerned that he would not exploit his position, unlike so many others before him. Beginning with his very first day as governor, and throughout his twelve-year tenure, Nehemiah never drew upon the daily food allowance of forty silver shekels to which his rank entitled him. Nor did he tax the people for bread and wine, which he was also authorized to do.

Nehemiah's forty-shekel allowance represented the equivalent of $3,000 per diem, or over a million dollars annually. Such an amount is far in excess of what American ambassadors receive in what are termed annual "representation funds," though it falls far short of what is granted to Britain's royal family each year. Still, Nehemiah's allowance was hardly an insignificant sum, and the fact that it did not have to be supported from public accounts meant a considerable easing of the burden on a populace that still had to pay other taxes that were transferred to the Persian treasury.

As governor, Nehemiah also had to support a large number of retainers, as well as foreign guests. He states that he provided for some 150 "Jews and prefects" (Neh. 5:17). In addition, in conducting affairs of state, the governor had to entertain visiting delegations of all kinds, "who came to us from surrounding nations" (5:17). These delegations, like those of modern heads of state, could be very large. Scripture recounts that the Queen of Sheba was accompanied by an exceedingly large retinue (*ḥayil kaved meod*; I Kings 10:2) when she visited King Solomon. In modern times, state visits by American presidents can involve dozens upon dozens of personnel; those by heads of state visiting Washington often are nearly as large, even if the state in question is rather small. While Nehemiah was not a head of state, he represented the power of the Persian Empire; that would have been enough to attract the attention and presence of local, lesser potentates. The entertainment costs involved in hosting these visits in addition to supporting those who regularly ate at his expense were daunting, as they can still be for ambassadors today,[11] yet these too Nehemiah covered out of his own pocket. Other than receiving tax relief, however, none of the local gentry appears to have benefited from his largesse.

That Nehemiah was apparently independently wealthy may have eased his ability to forgo the usual perquisites of power. Nevertheless, rarely have such considerations prevented greedy tyrants and dictators, from Nehemiah's day to our own, from adding to their already overflowing coffers by taxing their subjects to cover, if not more than cover, their own lavish outlays. Greed has no limits, whether in ancient times or in the cases of Imelda Marcos of the Philippines, Saddam Hussein of Iraq, or Viktor Yanukovych of Ukraine, to name some famous contemporary exemplars. It is the nature of greed that it feeds on itself, with each dose of lucre adding to the appetite for more.

Ever the politician, Nehemiah did not hesitate not only to outline in general terms the financial burden that he bore, but to publicize specifics of the personal allotment to which, by right, he was eligible. He was entitled to reimbursement for the daily consumption of "one ox, six select sheep, and fowl… and at ten-day intervals all sorts of wine in abundance," the daily wine allotment being the equivalent of ten days' consumption (Neh. 5:18).[12] His objective was to underscore further how he had eased the yoke of taxes weighing heavily on the shoulders of the common people. In doing so he was not merely seeking their support, but also seeking to deflect popular jealousy of his lifestyle as governor. He recognized full well that he had no shortage of enemies who would stop at nothing to sully his reputation. Nehemiah wanted both his contemporaries and posterity to know that the people's tax money was not used to cover his expenses. In this regard his behavior contrasted sharply with that of King Rehoboam son of Solomon, who increased the already onerous tax burden his father had imposed on the people,

11. Today, US government funds to cover what are termed "representation costs" for hosting dinners and the like often fall short of the actual expenses that ambassadors incur in capitals with a high cost of living, such as London, Paris, Brussels, and Rome.
12. On the daily wine allotment, see Rashi ad loc.

prompting the northern tribes to rebel and the kingdom to split into two states (I Kings 12:3–16, 19–20).

It is significant that Nehemiah not only refrained from dipping into the public exchequer, but restrained his associates from doing so as well. In this regard, Nehemiah departed from the practices of politicians and officials both ancient and modern. Even those who themselves have never exploited their positions often – indeed, usually – permit their associates to do so. It is as common today, as it was in ancient times, for those in subordinate but powerful positions to abuse their power beyond that of their principal. To some extent, such behavior is a function of insecurity; a subordinate holds office at the master's whim, and thus is never sure how long his or her tenure will last. The incentive to grab as much as possible, as quickly as possible, tests even the most ethical of officials.

Like all great leaders, Nehemiah was setting an example. If he could forgo his legitimate privileges, the elites could do without the resources they tended so often to acquire by methods of dubious legitimacy. Moreover, Nehemiah's decision not to draw upon the fund meant to cover his expenses represented a savings to the rich as well as the poor, since they too had to pay the taxes that supported that fund. The tax relief for the rich partially offset the financial burden Nehemiah had imposed upon them by forcing them to forgive the debts owed to them. No doubt Nehemiah's efforts to mitigate the impact of his policies on the rich enabled him to secure the support of at least some of their number.

Nehemiah went further still. Neither he nor his colleagues engaged in any form of land speculation. Naturally, the value of land in Jerusalem was likely to rise considerably once the wall was erected and the city fully protected. In particular Nehemiah refrained from purchasing the fields of the workers who labored on the walls; no doubt those fields could have been acquired for a fraction of their value. He also contributed financially to the construction of the wall and covered the expenses of the workers, since they could not earn their livelihoods from their fields and farms. Finally, he seconded his own servants to the workforce.

Nehemiah was fully aware of the significance of his social reforms; he wanted posterity to be aware of them, too. In an act that annoyed the rabbis of later generations, Nehemiah pointed out in his memoir that "the former governors who preceded me laid heavy burdens on the people, and took from them for bread and wine more than forty shekels of silver. Their servants also tyrannized over the people. But I, out of the fear of God, did not do so" (Neh. 5:15). The Talmud cites R. Yosef's opinion that as a rebuke to Nehemiah for disparaging his predecessors, his memoir had not been treated as a separate book of Scripture, nor was it named after him. R. Yosef focuses on the belittling of Daniel, who he claims also served as governor of Judah and was a greater man than Nehemiah.[13] This view would be consistent with that of some traditional scholars who believed that some Jews lived under gentile rule, presumably Sanballat's, while others lived under a Jewish governor in Yehud.[14] Recent archaeological findings indicate that all the governors of the Persian province of Yehud were Jewish.[15]

This last hypothesis begs the question of who ruled over Jerusalem, however. While the history of the city between 1948 and 1967 indicates that non-Jews could control Judaism's holiest sites even as Jews were sovereign in their own state, it is nevertheless unlikely that this was the situation during the seventy-five years between Zerubbabel's rule and that of Nehemiah. Certainly, if that had been the case, Nehemiah would somewhere have mentioned it in his memoir, if only to demonstrate that, in contrast to his Jewish predecessors, it was he who restored Jewish rule over Jerusalem. It remains unclear whether all of Nehemiah's predecessors were Jewish.

Nehemiah also annoyed the sages because of his plea that "God remember to my credit all that I have done for this people!" (Neh. 5:19).[16]

---

13. Sanhedrin 93b. Rabbi Judah the Hasid cites the Talmud's statement when he advises, "If a man sees that people have wronged him, if one of them is righteous, he should not blame them all, because he includes the righteous man among them .... Nehemiah criticized the governors [who had preceded him] of whom Daniel, who was perfectly righteous, was one; and the Book of Ezra was not designated in Nehemiah's name"; Rabbi Judah the Hasid, *Sefer Ḥasidim*, no. 482. See also Rashi on Ezra 5:14, s.v. *di peḥa sameh*.
14. This is Malbim's view, Neh. 1:2, s.v. *hapleita*.
15. Zer-Kavod, *Ezra UNeḥemia*, 94.
16. See also Sanhedrin 93b.

Nehemiah was not acting differently from other officials of his era. The inscription of Udjahorresnet the Egyptian had similar language,[17] and, in fact, it was "a standard formula... to extol a person's good deeds as ruler."[18] Nehemiah might even have intended that his plea to God be set up in a public place as a sort of memorial.

Yet it was precisely the fact that Nehemiah was aping the practices of heathen rulers that no doubt further enraged the rabbis. Nehemiah was no Udjahorresnet, and the rabbis felt he was out of line. Though the Talmud notes that David had made a similar request for credit in God's eyes, it argues that Nehemiah's plea was not phrased properly. Whereas David recognized that he did not merit any reward, yet asked God's mercy in granting him favor, Nehemiah based his appeal on his own merits. This was a difference that Nehemiah, according to the sages, simply failed to perceive. Thus, even as Nehemiah went to great lengths to claim credit for his actions,[19] as a result of his doing so, centuries passed before he received the encomia he so manifestly and desperately craved.

17. Blenkinsopp, "Mission," 415 (see chap. 4, n. 22).

18. Bolin, *Ezra, Nehemiah*, 73.

19. See *Margaliot Hayam* (see chap. 2, n. 2) on Sanhedrin 93b, citing *Yaarot Dvash*.

Nehemiah 6
New Threats Emerge

A NEW TACK: SANBALLAT RESURFACES

Having managed to maintain communal cohesion by pressuring the wealthy to ease the financial strains on the poor, Nehemiah was able to turn his attention back to the completion of the wall. The actual walls had been fully repaired, but there was still a need to set up doors in the gateways to ensure the security of the town. His enemies, however, still sought to undermine the project. They had access to Nehemiah's plans because of men like Eliashiv and Meshullam. Eliashiv, though working on the wall, nevertheless had little sympathy for Nehemiah and was related by marriage to Tobiah; Meshullam likewise helped repair the wall but was related by marriage to Sanballat. Thus the Samaritan and his henchmen knew that Nehemiah planned to install the doors as the final step in securing the city, which would render an attack exceedingly problematic, if not impossible. In any event, even without the doors, any attack would have to be channeled through the wall's gates, creating easy targets for defenders who had a clear field of fire for their lances and spears from their positions at the top of the walls.

Sanballat and his colleagues now realized that their only hope was to eliminate Nehemiah himself, thereby depriving the Jewish community of its inspirational and effective leader.[1] Sanballat and Geshem invited

1. See *Pirkei DeRabbi Eliezer*, 38.

Nehemiah to a meet them at Kephirim in the Ono Valley. Located northwest of Lod, possibly with a mixed population of Jews and gentiles, the city was on the border of Judah, in a relatively remote area. The choice of this place was intended to lull Nehemiah into a false sense of security; it was, after all, within his jurisdiction.[2] In fact, because it had a non-Jewish population that was unlikely to be sympathetic to Nehemiah, the town was better suited to covering up the crime. The plotters wanted to minimize any chance that the murder would arouse the suspicions of the Persian authorities, who might not take kindly to the unauthorized assassination of one of their officials.

The plotters were exceedingly cautious. Even had the authorities become aware that foul play was involved, they might still not have reacted in any meaningful way. The Persian court was itself the scene of intrigue and murder, and Nehemiah must have had powerful enemies at court; after all, the indigenous peoples living in Judah had hired lobbyists against the Jews several decades earlier, in Haman's time. Sanballat had surely worked with these lobbyists or their successors, people who no doubt capitalized on the resentment of the Persians and Medes toward an upstart Jew who first was royal cupbearer and had now been elevated to provincial governor. In truth, his rival governors had every incentive to get him out of the way, especially since, as has been noted, his fortifying of Jerusalem signified that it would be the linchpin of the Persian Empire's western defenses and would accordingly benefit economically, to the detriment of other seats of provincial governance.

Significantly, Tobiah did not join in the invitation to Nehemiah. He may have shrunk from the idea of murdering a fellow Jew. He may also have been assigned to attack the city while Nehemiah was at Kephirim. Leaderless, the Jews might have been expected to panic and, heeding the voices of the likes of Tobiah's kinsman Eliashiv, who after all wielded considerable authority as High Priest, to surrender without a fight.

Nehemiah, however, immediately sensed that he was being set up and would likely be ambushed. He replied with a message that has

2. Ono is nowhere else mentioned in Scripture. For a discussion of conflicting views regarding its location, see Williamson, *Ezra, Nehemiah*, 254–55.

had its echoes throughout the centuries, whenever a government official has politely and diplomatically declined an invitation to an event that he or she never intended to attend: "I am engaged in a great work and cannot come down, for the work will stop if I leave it in order to come down to you" (Neh. 6:3). Nehemiah was, in fact, telling the truth – a rarity for a politician. His repairing the wall was only the first of many projects that Nehemiah intended to launch in order to transform the province into a thriving religious and national polity.

Sanballat and his associates were not to be denied so easily, however. They reissued the invitation three more times. They were desperate; they still hoped to forestall, at the eleventh hour, the overturning of the old order under which they benefited. They may have repeated the message to ensure that Nehemiah himself saw it, or to be certain that he fully comprehended it. For his part, Nehemiah was as unimpressed by the last message as he was by the first; each time he declined in the same manner.

Sanballat then sent Nehemiah the same message a fifth time, this time as an open letter carried by his servant. Some symbolism was attached to the fact that the letter was an open one; such a letter was a sign of disrespect to Nehemiah and his office.[3]

The letter read as follows:

> Word has reached the nations, and Geshem too says that you and the Jews are planning to rebel – for which reason you are building the wall – and that you are to be their king. Such is the word. You have also set up prophets in Jerusalem to proclaim about you, "There is a king in Judah!" Word of these things will surely reach the king; so come, let us confer together. (Neh. 6:6–7)

The letter represented a significant threat to Nehemiah. "Treachery on the part of satraps and governors was a commonplace in the Persian Empire,"[4] and the charge was one that the king would take seriously. At a minimum, if word of the allegation reached Persia,

3. Zer-Kavod, *Ezra UNeḥemia*, 96.
4. Bolin, *Ezra, Nehemiah*, 74.

Nehemiah would be recalled to explain himself to the king, who would feel doubly betrayed because Nehemiah had been his trusted cupbearer. Should Nehemiah's explanation to the Persian king fail to convince, death was a certainty. Even were Nehemiah able to defend himself successfully, his absence from Jerusalem during a critical phase of its reconstruction would probably have brought the entire enterprise to a screeching halt.

There were, of course, no prophets, at least no legitimate ones, calling for Nehemiah to be king. Prophecy had ended with Malachi, whose lifespan may have overlapped with Nehemiah's (R. Joshua b. Korḥa asserts that Malachi was Ezra) and who, in any event, would not have prophesied in the manner that the letter described.[5] That, of course, did not prevent Sanballat from hiring false prophets as provocateurs. They could stir up the population, especially the poorer classes who supported Nehemiah, on one hand, and, on the other, could add credence to Sanballat's allegations and provide the basis for complaints to the Persian court that Nehemiah was a rebel. In addition, while, as noted, the letter was a sign of disrespect to Nehemiah and his office, it would have been deemed appropriate if Nehemiah was viewed as nothing more than a rebel against Persian authority.

No doubt at the same time Sanballat was hoping to win public support by means of the letter. It was intended to put Nehemiah on the spot by intimating to the populace that he was an unbending extremist who refused to enter into a reasonable discussion that could lead to a compromise between the conflicting parties. After all, Sanballat's use of the phrase "come, let us confer together" was certain to evoke in the minds of the people Isaiah's virtually identical phrase (Is. 1:18).

This time Nehemiah replied, stating that the allegations were false, the product of Sanballat's imagination. He added that he was surprised that, after the outright enmity that Sanballat had displayed, the Samaritan was now prepared to confer with him. Clearly, he asserted, the letter represented just another attempt to get the people to desist from their work.

5. R. Joshua's view is a minority opinion, though he is not alone. See *Aggadat Esther* 5:28.

Having issued his reply, Nehemiah decided to confront one of the false prophets whom he suspected of being on Sanballat's payroll. The man in question was one Shemaiah son of Delaiah son of Mehetabel. Under normal circumstances, Nehemiah would have summoned Shemaiah to his palace, but the "prophet" was ill, so Nehemiah instead went to the man's home. Undeterred by the governor's presence, Shemaiah brazenly suggested, "Let us meet in the House of God, inside the sanctuary, and let us shut the doors of the sanctuary, for... by night they are coming to kill you" (Neh. 6:10).

On its face, Shemaiah's suggestion was one that should have appealed to Nehemiah. With the doors to the gates of the city wall yet to be built, the Temple was the only place safe from assassins. Shemaiah's warning of a likely attack on Nehemiah, which he knew Nehemiah feared, only added credibility to his advice. Delilah did the same thing to Samson on more than one occasion (Judges 16:9, 14).

But Nehemiah quickly realized that Shemaiah was a false prophet and his offer was meaningless. How did Nehemiah conclude that Shemaiah was a fraud? Several indicators gave him away. Shemaiah did not identify who was coming to murder Nehemiah, but it was not difficult for Nehemiah to infer that the reference was to Sanballat or his men. After all, Sanballat was his nemesis. Having been highly sensitized to claims inspired by Sanballat, and articulated through false prophets, that he was planning to rebel against the Persian monarchy and establish himself as king, Nehemiah recognized that an "escape" to the Temple would lend credence to the accusations being leveled against him. In seeking the protection that the Temple might afford – such protection was common from ancient times through the late Middle Ages in Europe – Nehemiah would, in effect, be admitting that he had planned a rebellion, per Sanballat's allegation, but had now realized that it would not succeed. Such an implied admission was nothing less than a death sentence. Thus, were he to accept Shemaiah's offer in order to escape death, Nehemiah would instead bring death upon himself. Nehemiah, ever suspicious, quickly concluded that Shemaiah could not be trusted and was neither ally nor prophet.[6]

---

6. A variation of this argument is made by David Shepherd, "Prophetaphobia: Fear and False Prophecy in Nehemiah VI," *Vetus Testamentum* 55 (April 2005): 232–50, especially 233, 237–38, 243, 248–49.

There was another reason why Nehemiah quickly concluded that Shemaiah was an imposter. Shemaiah's proposal that they meet in the Sanctuary, in particular, only served to confirm Nehemiah's conclusions about his real character and motives. Nehemiah had no qualms about entering the general Temple precincts – he would later recall in his memoir that he entered the Temple during his second tour of duty in Judah. But Shemaiah was not merely suggesting that they meet in the Temple; he specified that they meet in the *Hekhal*, the Sanctuary. This term has two meanings: while it can signify the entire Temple area, in the Torah it stands for the Temple's inner sanctum, adjacent to the Holy of Holies. That was how Nehemiah interpreted the term, as his immediate reaction – "Who such as I can go into the Sanctuary and live?" – clearly indicated.[7] Shemaiah's suggestion clearly belied his intentions: the Sanctuary was forbidden territory to all but the priests; anyone else entering it was guilty of a capital crime.[8] In other words, in order to enable Nehemiah to avoid death by assassination, supposedly, Shemaiah was setting him up for death by divine, if not human, judgment.

Nehemiah immediately saw through Shemaiah's proposal and rejected it outright, both because he had no intention of fleeing from anyone and because he was ineligible to enter the Temple. As he recounted, "Then I realized that it was not God who sent him, but that he uttered that prophecy about me – Tobiah and Sanballat having hired him – because he was a hireling, that I might be intimidated and act thus and commit a sin, and so provide them a scandal with which to reproach me" (Neh. 6:12–13).

There is, however, something peculiar about Nehemiah's phraseology. Surely he knew that Shemaiah was a false prophet; as noted above, prophecy had terminated with Malachi. What, then, was the realization that came upon him when he spoke to the man? Perhaps Nehemiah was not certain that Shemaiah was a false prophet and fantasized about becoming the new king of Israel.[9] After all, his references

7. For a discussion, see *Encyclopedia Talmudit*, s.v. *Hekhal*.
8. Malbim, Neh. 6:11, s.v. *umi*.
9. See Malbim, Neh. 6:12, s.v. *ki*.

to all the good things he had done for the people, as well as his less than flattering comparison of his predecessors' actions to his own, indicate that he was a man with a not inconsiderable ego. Only when Shemaiah proposed that he do something he knew to be contrary to an explicit commandment in the Torah did Nehemiah recognize the man for what he really was, a paid toady of Sanballat and Tobiah, one who was trying to enmesh him in scandal. The scandal would not only result from the obvious violation of biblical law. It would also arise from the likely allegation that it was Nehemiah who had hired the false prophets to trumpet his claim to Judah's throne, precisely what Sanballat had alleged in his open letter.

In recalling these events, Nehemiah asked God to remember what Tobiah and Sanballat had attempted to do to him. It is fairly certain that Sanballat still held office when Nehemiah wrote his memoir. Tobiah may also still have been living. Nehemiah not only would have wished to bring God's wrath upon them, but also to have God avenge him by punishing their descendants, who continued to maintain a prominent position in politics and society. He also asked God to act against "Noadiah the prophetess, and against the other prophets that they wished to intimidate me!" (Neh. 6:14).

Nehemiah had not previously mentioned Noadiah, nor would he mention her again. It is unclear why he singled her out for condemnation. Perhaps it was because, unlike the other false prophets, who simply predicted that his supposed rebellion against Persia would succeed, she may also have predicted that he would become king of Israel.[10] Yet Shemaiah had implied the same, and although Nehemiah had just written about their meeting (he never mentions a meeting with Noadiah), he did not identify him by name again. One lesser-known midrash resolves the absence of any further mention of Shemaiah by arguing that he and Noadiah were one and the same person. It asserts that his name was changed to Noadiah after he suggested that Nehemiah meet him in the Temple, the name reflecting Shemaiah's suggestion to meet (in Hebrew *niva'ed*), having the same root as *no'ad*, with the name alluding

10. Malbim (Neh. 6:14, s.v. *vegam*) speculates that Noadiah predicted that Nehemiah would be king, and also avers that Shemaiah had issued an identical prediction.

to "a meeting before God."[11] The midrash adds that the prophecy was couched in the feminine form because Shemaiah's suggestion was "the advice typical of women." No other talmudic or midrashic source supports this interpretation, however.

The Scripture mentions few prophetesses,[12] and even fewer false ones. The Torah does speak of the female prophetesses of Ov, and Scripture recounts that King Saul visited one such woman to make contact with the deceased prophet Samuel. This form of soothsaying had long since died out, being last mentioned in Kings as existing during the reign of Josiah, more than a century before Nehemiah arrived in Judah.[13]

The fact that Noadiah was identified by name indicates that she must have had some communal stature and influence; if she had been a total unknown, there would have been no point in Nehemiah's mentioning her. In contrast to Shemaiah, whom Nehemiah calls a hireling, Noadiah was the subject of no such accusation, though she and any associates she may have had, might, like Shemaiah, have been on Sanballat's or Tobiah's payroll.[14]

Alternatively, Noadiah may have been closely tied to the local aristocracy that so resented Nehemiah's efforts. This would explain her being singled out by Nehemiah. On the other hand, the unnamed prophets that he mentioned along with her may have been her associates, if not her followers, and certainly did not cut the same figure in elite circles.

---

11. *Aggadat Esther* 5:51. Ibn Ezra (Neh. 6:14, s.v. *vegam*) cites a number of unnamed commentators who argued that Noadiah was a man and not a prophetess at all. They emend the text by dropping the final *heh* in the Hebrew word *nevia* (prophetess), thereby rendering the noun masculine instead of feminine. Ibn Ezra's reference may have been to the Septuagint, which likewise applies the masculine noun form to the Hebrew term for prophet. Alternatively, his source may have been *Aggadat Esther*.
12. *Aggadat Esther* (5:13) cites seven prophetesses: Sarah, Miriam, Deborah, Hannah, Abigail, Hulda, and Esther.
13. Rabbi Saadia claims that Noadiah was a prophetess of Ov, in other words, a necromancer, but offers no basis for this assertion. Nor does he appear to be drawing from a midrash, as is often the case with his commentary. See Mathews, *Commentary*, 26.
14. Rashi, Neh. 6:14, s.v. *vegam*.

THE TENSION SUBSIDES

At the end of the day, neither Sanballat's letters, nor Shemaiah's proposals, nor Noadiah's prophecies were sufficient to deflect Nehemiah from his determination to complete the construction of the doors to the gates and thereby secure the wall. And so it was that a mere fifty-two days after the reconstruction project began, the wall was finished. The date was the twenty-fifth of Elul, just days before Rosh HaShana. The work must therefore have begun on the fourth of Av; Nehemiah would have arrived on the first of Av and then taken three days to settle in and reconnoiter the city. As noted earlier, Ezra had arrived in the city on exactly the same day thirteen years earlier. Both men may have timed their arrival on the first of the nine days leading to the anniversary of the first Temple's destruction on Tisha B'Av to validate the prophecy of Zechariah that, "As I proposed to do evil unto you, when your fathers provoked Me… so again I propose in these days to do good unto Jerusalem and to the house of Judah."[15] The contrast with the gloomy forebodings of the false prophets could not have been greater.

At this point it appeared to Nehemiah that his adversaries had finally come to terms with the reality of a self-contained Jewish province. He felt that they were intimidated, that they realized that "this work had been accomplished by the help of our God" (Neh. 6:16). It was not at all clear that the nations surrounding Judah ascribed Nehemiah's success to divine support, nor was it the case that they had given up all hope of returning to the status quo that had prevailed prior to Nehemiah's arrival on the scene. However, the fact that Nehemiah saw God's hand in support of his actions underscored not only his deeply felt beliefs but also his self-assurance that he would continue to prevail over his enemies.

As it happened, both Nehemiah's overt enemies and the reprobate Judahite nobility continued to plot their return to power. The nobility, publicly cowed but privately resentful over their loss of status and perquisites, "kept up a brisk correspondence with Tobiah, and Tobiah with them" (Neh. 6:17). They may well have been Tobiah's vassals and

15. See Zer-Kavod, *Ezra UNeḥemia*, 97–98, citing Zech. 8:14–15.

continued to view themselves as obligated to support him.[16] Even if they had had no formal relationship with him, they were certainly close to him – Nehemiah called them Tobiah's confederates. Some, like Meshullam son of Berechiah – as we saw earlier – were related to Tobiah by marriage (6:18). The nobles did not necessarily wish to depose Nehemiah, as Tobiah most certainly did. Instead, as Nehemiah records, "They would… speak well of him to me" (6:19). Unlike Tobiah, they wanted a more balanced relationship with the Persian-appointed governor, one that would allow them to resume their predatory practices while he continued to rule the province. Such relationships were not uncommon in the ancient world, and persist to this day in many countries, notably in the Developing World and in the former Soviet bloc.

Whatever their motives, the nobles' attempt at mediation reflects the danger that can sometimes arise when non-official intermediaries insert themselves into relations between governmental entities. While such "Track II" efforts at diplomacy, as they are currently termed, may often bring about understandings that might otherwise not be reached between suspicious adversaries, this is not always the case – especially when, as with Tobiah's interlocutors, their motives are definitely mixed.[17]

Even if the motives of the nobles were not entirely hostile to Nehemiah, Tobiah exploited them to undermine his authority. Nehemiah recorded that nobles passed on details of his affairs to Tobiah, perhaps in order to show that a compromise was possible, perhaps in order to strengthen Tobiah's bargaining position. Tobiah responded by sending further missives designed, as Nehemiah put it, "to intimidate

---

16. Reflecting the practices that governed feudal politics in his day, Rashi (Neh. 6:18, s.v. *ki*) observes that the Judahite aristocracy had sworn oaths of fealty to Tobiah.
17. The problem of mixed motives and crossed signals was illustrated during the 1996 crisis between the United States and China over Taiwan. A senior Chinese general, who doubled as an official of a think-tank, asked a former American diplomat in his "non-governmental" capacity whether the United States was willing to trade Taipei for Los Angeles, implying a nuclear threat of sorts. Obviously, it was impossible to separate the think-tanker from the general, or to establish whether his question was meant as the musings of an objective analyst or a thinly veiled military threat. The interchange did little to calm relations between the two countries.

me" (Neh. 6:19). Of course, Tobiah got nowhere. It is hard to intimidate a man who believes he has the force of God behind him.

Having been so thoroughly outmaneuvered by Nehemiah, Sanballat and Tobiah appear to have quietly nursed their political wounds. Although they explicitly threatened to apprise the royal court that Nehemiah was a rebel, it is clear that they never carried out that threat. Had they done so, Nehemiah surely would have recorded their action, if only to demonstrate his having prevailed over them.

Why Sanballat and Tobiah did not try to make their case at the court in Susa or one of the three other imperial capitals is something of a mystery. Both men were individuals of consequence, with records of loyalty to their Persian overlords. Sanballat, no less than Nehemiah, was a royal governor, presumably appointed by the king, as Nehemiah had been. Tobiah, too, may have been a governor. Even as Sanballat's secretary, or right-hand man, he would have had contacts among his counterparts in the Persian bureaucracy, who could then have influenced their superiors to counter Nehemiah's plans.

Moreover, the blatant lobbying at the Persian court decades earlier against the construction of the Temple had successfully delayed the project for some twenty years. Sanballat's forebears, and perhaps he himself in a youthful incarnation, clearly were not innocents when it came to political intrigue. Surely, they should have at least attempted to undermine Nehemiah. The fact that he was a royal governor would not have deterred them, as the court, like so many royal courts, was a hotbed of backstabbing, both metaphorical and literal.

In the absence of any evidence from Nehemiah, or any other source, one can only speculate as to the reasons why Nehemiah's adversaries chose not to carry out their threat even though they must have realized that by not doing so, they damaged their credibility with their supporters, of which there still were many. These men were certainly not fools. They had employed a host of stratagems to undermine Nehemiah. They were experienced leaders and, as noted, wise to the ways of the Persian court.

Most likely, they feared that Nehemiah would prevail in any showdown at court. He was, after all, not only a governor, but still the king's cupbearer, and, if he fit the pattern of most holders of that office, a trusted royal confidant. He had never relinquished that role; he was on what would today be called a leave of absence, and could be recalled at any time. Furthermore, he seems to have had the queen's support as well; the fall of Haman was emblematic of the power that a favorite from the harem wielded in the king's court.

Sanballat, and to a lesser extent Tobiah, had much to lose if Nehemiah prevailed in a confrontation before the king. At a minimum, they would be stripped of their official positions. Maximally, they, and their families – like Haman's sons – would be put to death. The cost of carrying the fight to the Persian capital was not worth the risk of losing it.

LESSONS IN LEADERSHIP

The great medieval scholar Levi ben Gershon (1288–1344), known both by his Hebrew acronym, Ralbag, and his Latin name, Gersonides, interrupts his commentary on Nehemiah at this point in the text. Drawing upon Nehemiah's experience from his initial request to the king, to the successful completion of the wall, to his outmaneuvering his enemies, Ralbag outlines a series of ethical, religious, and political guidelines gleaned from the story. The latter are worthy of a Machiavelli, though, of course, Ralbag preceded him by a few centuries. They are as follows:

- One should make close inquiries regarding the attitudes of purported friends.
- Prayer and fasting help avert evil decrees.
- If granted royal leave to undertake a project, one should not refrain from requesting the widest possible assistance to ensure its success.
- It is important to scope out a task before it is undertaken. (Ralbag is referring to Nehemiah's nighttime reconnaissance upon his arrival in Jerusalem.)
- If one anticipates opposition to a project, one should initiate it in secrecy.
- God intervenes to support the objectives of His servants.
- Those who receive financial support must act in a generous manner themselves.

- One should press an advantage when obtaining a positive outcome, so as to ensure guarantees of its permanence, just as Nehemiah elicited a vow from those who relieved the poor of their debts.[18]

Such guidelines, notably the political and administrative ones, would be of value to any putative leader operating in a difficult political environment, regardless of time and place. Circumstances may change, but human nature remains the same.

18. Ralbag, Neh. 6:19, s.v. *gam.*

Nehemiah 7
Consolidating Power

ASSIGNING NEW ROLES TO LOYALISTS

With the walls rebuilt, the doors in place, the community's external enemies in disarray, and internal opposition at least temporarily dormant, Nehemiah might have been expected to return to Persia, or at least seek further guidance regarding his term of office.[1] After all, he had accomplished the mission for which he had requested leave from Artaxerxes, namely, to rebuild the city. He did not contact the royal palace, however, nor did he receive any further direction from the king. Instead, he set about solidifying his control over Judah and Jerusalem.

Nehemiah was faced with a dilemma. He could not rely on the loyalty of the priests, since many of their leaders had ties by marriage to his opponents. Yet he also could not displace the priests. His religious commitment forced him to support priestly activities in the Temple.

His solution was quite clever; without derogating from the duties of the priests, he diluted their power by lifting the Levites from the underclass and giving them a stake in the Temple apparatus. The Levites had already indicated a willingness to align themselves with Nehemiah

1. It is possible that there were communications between Nehemiah and the royal palace, but that Nehemiah chose not to include them in his memoir, for reasons best known to himself. See Galil, *Daniel, Ezra UNeḥemia*, 310 (see chap. 1, n. 35).

when they contributed to his efforts to repair the wall. By enhancing their economic prospects, as well as their social stature, Nehemiah guaranteed himself the solid support of a class that could legitimately claim a leadership role within the ritual framework alongside that of the priests.

In particular, in addition to restoring their traditional role as singers in the Temple services and guardians of the Temple entrances, he organized them into a new security force. The Levites were to work alongside the lookouts who were posted on the towers set into the walls. The lookouts had been designated during the rebuilding process and continued to function even after the walls were complete. By serving in the new amalgamated force, the Levites not only were armed, but for the first time functioned as state auxiliaries, with all the power and prestige that such positions entailed.

Nehemiah also appointed his brother Hanani, as well as another man with a similar name, Hananiah, to lead the military contingent.[2] These appointments further strengthened Nehemiah's hand, since he could be sure of the loyalty of his top lieutenants. There already were two civil governors of Jerusalem, both of whom had worked on the walls, and there was no need to replace them. On the other hand, Hananiah clearly had some military background – perhaps he had served in some capacity in the Persian army, as other Jews had – and he was already "the captain of the fortress" (Neh. 7:2). Moreover, Nehemiah considered that Hananiah was "a more trustworthy and God-fearing man than most" (ibid.). No doubt Hananiah's religious outlook played an important role in his appointment, but by mentioning his trustworthiness first, Nehemiah indicated where his priorities lay.

Nehemiah had no need to justify Hanani's appointment; it was understood that the brother who had first enmeshed him in Judah's difficulties could be relied upon to carry out his wishes. Hanani may not have had any military experience. Perhaps it was for this reason that

2. Some medieval Jewish commentators read the passage as referring to two men, since the text mentions "Hanani and Hananiah" (*Ḥanani veḤananiah*). Others, as well as some modern commentators, are of the view that Hanani and Hananiah are one and the same. They argue that the *vav* that links the two names, and has been translated as "and," appears in the Scripture as an occasional superfluity (viz. Gen. 36:24: *Aiah* and *Ana*).

Nehemiah made a dual appointment: Hananiah would serve as the military man, while Hanani was, in effect, an ancient version of a Soviet military commissar, whose role it was both to ensure that the loyalty of the military personnel never wavered and to enforce all the governor's objectives faithfully.

The fact that Hanani's appointment was blatant nepotism mattered little in ancient times. Nepotism did not have the same stigma then as it does today, and even today it bears a stigma primarily in Western societies, particularly in government.[3] Much like John Kennedy's appointment of his brother Robert to be attorney general, Nehemiah's choice of Hanani demonstrated the degree to which he considered his brother his closest political confidant. In that sense, political behavior has remained constant over the centuries and millennia.

Nehemiah's orders to both men were explicit, and designed to ensure the security of the city:[4] "The gates of Jerusalem are not to be opened until the heat of the day, and – before you leave your posts – let the doors be closed and barred. And assign the inhabitants of Jerusalem to watches, each man to his watch, and each in front of his own house" (Neh. 7:3). Nehemiah's injunction reflected the fact that the town was most vulnerable in the hours after midday, when the Mediterranean climate fosters lethargy and the guards might be expected to doze off. This was exactly what enabled Alaric and the Visigoths to break through Rome's Salarian Gate at noon in 410 CE. As the Roman historian Procopius records, the guards "were, as usual, dozing after a midday meal."[5]

Nehemiah's orders also emphasized the importance of having the members of the city's security force posted before their homes. As when he oversaw the repairing of the wall, Nehemiah understood that the morale of defenders was highest when they were protecting their

3. Nepotism is not an insurmountable barrier to promotion in private firms.
4. The text (*ktiv*) actually states "he said" (*vayomer*), but the word is traditionally read (*kri*) as "I said" (*vaomar*). As written, the text would be referring to Hananiah, who transmitted Nehemiah's orders. For a discussion, see Zer-Kavod, *Ezra UNeḥemia*, 100.
5. Procopius, *History of the Wars*, trans. H. B. Dewing, vol. 2 (Cambridge, MA: Harvard University Press, 1916), III:17.

own property. He could be certain that there would be no slackening of the watch at any time, even when the sun was at its hottest.

AUGMENTING THE CITY'S POPULATION: THE CENSUS

Having arranged for the city's physical security to his satisfaction, Nehemiah now turned to the need to populate it. While Nehemiah described Jerusalem as "broad and large" (Neh. 7:4), it was really neither. It was, moreover, seriously underpopulated, with far fewer households than Nehemiah felt the city – now safe from predation – should have. Moreover, its economic success was central to the economic success of the province as a whole – and to flourish, it needed people. For these reasons Nehemiah decided, or as he put it, "my God put it into my mind" (7:5), to repopulate the city on the basis of a register of the returning exiles, though many of their offspring had intermarried and were presumably aligned with the assimilationist camp.

Nehemiah assembled the entire populace, from the most prominent to the most humble, and asked them to review their genealogical records. Nehemiah's gathering of all the people reflected his predilection for public spectacle, as well as his need for a unified approach to the challenge he faced. His populism previously had permitted him to rally the masses against the community's leaders; by assembling the hoi polloi with the elites, he ensured the latter's cooperation in the effort to populate Jerusalem, though any check of the records carried the risk for the rich that they might have to cede some of their property to poorer claimants.

Nehemiah's census stood in contrast to the one conducted by King David hundreds of years earlier. Whereas Nehemiah claimed divine inspiration, David acted in defiance of both the law and his chief general and adviser, Joab. He soon regretted his decision; he was chastised by the prophet Gad, and the Angel of Death killed seventy thousand people. Nehemiah had no second thoughts about what he was doing, perhaps because he was simply basing himself on the details laid out in "the genealogical register of those who were the first to come up" (Neh. 7:5). In any event, no divine punishment was inflicted on the Judahites.

The list of families produced by the census was made up of the people who had returned with Zerubbabel; it is nearly identical to a list of returning exiles that appears in the Book of Ezra.[6] While Nehemiah's list was ostensibly compiled in order to provide a demographic basis for the relocation of the population to Jerusalem, it was also of theological significance. In the aftermath of Nehemiah's security and social policies, it outlined, as one scholar has put it, the

> entire community in its divinely ordained divisions...which obediently attends to the law and observes the festivals. It is a community which claims legitimacy on the basis of links with the past, and one to which one can adhere, or from which one can be excluded, on the basis of a profession of faith and a level of moral performance consistent with it.[7]

The census was only one of several lists of names that Nehemiah included in his memoir and, presumably, publicized throughout the province (the twelfth chapter of his memoir is devoted to another such list). These lists, apart from their theological importance, were also integral to Nehemiah's effort to provide the people with a sense of historical legitimacy and national cohesion by linking his activities to the past. He had, after all, undertaken to reconstruct the social order.

---

6. See Ezra 2. In commenting on Nehemiah's list in chapter 7, Rashi (Neh. 7:7, s.v. *Yeshua*) acknowledges that its numbers are not identical with those in Ezra. He reasons that the author simply wished to signify the degree of communal commitment to the return from exile and did not trouble himself with numerical details. Ibn Ezra (Neh. 7:6, s.v. *bnei*) ascribes the discrepancies to one of two things: either the list is rounded out or it indicates that certain clans had increased or decreased in size since the list was first compiled. The list of those returning to their homes also appears later in Neh. (11:3–19), as well as in I Chr. (9:2–34). Still another list appears in Ezra (8:1–14). It is all terribly confusing, and does seem to indicate multiple sources, combined, perhaps, with a sloppy editing process. Perhaps as a result, different commentators identify parts of the list with different eras. On the other hand, a strong case has been made that when Ezra and Nehemiah are viewed as a structural whole, the appearance of the lists in different portions of the books is both consistent and makes sense. See Tamar Cohn Eskenazi, *In an Age of Prose: A Literary Approach to Ezra-Nehemiah* (Atlanta: Scholars Press, 1988), 88–96.
7. Blenkinsopp, *Ezra-Nehemiah*, 281–82. Blenkinsopp sees this progression as part of the Chronicler's editorial purpose. One need not accept the theory of a "Chronicler" to appreciate Blenkinsopp's logic and insight into this section of the book.

He had instilled a new national pride in the people, not least by providing them with a viable capital city as a focus of their religious and civic lives. He had imposed social reforms to ease the burdens of the poor. He had upgraded the status of the Levites. He would soon provide the society with a constitution, something he no doubt had been planning for some time before it was unveiled. His lists added to the overall effect of nation-building; they demonstrated that his activities were part of, and culminated in, the process of return from exile.

Nehemiah introduced his outline of the census by asserting that "These are the people of the province who came up from among the captive exiles that Nebuchadnezzar, king of Babylonia, had deported, and who returned to Jerusalem and to Judah, each to his own city" (Neh. 7:6). His emphasis was on the last part of the passage: the return to ancestral homes and villages is the yearning of all exiles. Refugee populations displaced early in the twentieth century, for example, have retained their nostalgia for their patrimony even though the passage of time has erased all resemblance between the homes they left and the places to which they might (or might not) return.[8] Such yearnings can last centuries, or even millennia, as in the case of Jews after the Roman exile. The return of the Judahite exiles to their homes, particularly in an era when so many other captive nations – including the northern tribes of Israel – were unable to do so, underscored the miraculous nature of the return from Babylon.

The list begins with the most prominent men who returned with Zerubbabel and Jeshua the High Priest, namely "Nehemiah, Azariah, Raamiah, Nahamani, Mordekhai, Bilshan, Mispereth, Bigvai, Nehum, Baanah" (Neh. 7:7). Of these men, the first listed, Nehemiah, may or may not have been the protagonist of the book that bears the same name; the name was not uncommon among Jews of that period. On the other hand, it is possible that the Nehemiah on the list is the same Nehemiah whose memoir we are studying in this volume. If so, his name was included on the list as a sign of respect, even though he did not arrive in Judah until

8. The experiences of minorities "ethnically cleansed" in Bosnia and Kosovo, in various African states, and in Syria are only among the more recent of a long line of such disappointed longings.

long after the initial return under Zerubbabel, to indicate that he was one of the leading figures of the revived polity of Judah.[9]

Some modern scholars identify Azariah, the second of those listed, with Ezra, just as the rabbis of the Talmud did. They assert that the name is the Hebrew version of the Aramaic name Ezra, presumably meaning "God's help."[10] To the moderns, however, mention of Ezra is proof that the list in this chapter is of later origin than the text, an opinion shared by many academic scholars.[11] On the other hand, the Aramaic name Ezra is missing the letter *yod,* which signifies the name of God. That letter always is part of the name Azariah, including its Hebrew diminutive, Uzziah. Azariah was the name of Ezra's grandfather; since Zerubbabel preceded Ezra by several decades, it is highly likely that the Azariah who appears in the census was Ezra's grandfather. In fact, the presence of his grandfather in Judah may well have spurred Ezra to leave Babylonia. Scripture provides no other motivation for him to organize an *aliya,* much less depart his native country (Ezra 7:1).

Finally, it is possible, though not terribly likely, that the Mordekhai of the list is none other than the hero of the Book of Esther. He may have been a young boy who was part of the *aliya* led by Zerubbabel sometime after 538 BCE. In that case, he would have been well past middle age in the early years of Xerxes's reign, which began in 486 BCE; the events of Esther could have taken place three years later.[12]

Rabbinic tradition states that the Mordekhai listed here is indeed the Mordekhai of the Esther story. The rabbis seized on his being listed

9. See Zer-Kavod, *Ezra UNeḥemia,* 9.

10. See, for example, Zeitlin, *Rise and Fall,* 24 (see chap. 1, n. 2); Bolin, *Ezra, Nehemiah,* 96.

11. Grabbe, *Ezra-Nehemiah,* 156.

12. A midrash asserts that Mordekhai originally was raised in Judea, where he reached adulthood. He chose to be exiled with King Jeconiah, then returned to Judea on his own, only to be exiled again with King Zedekiah (cited in *Yalkut Shimoni* II:1054). Rabbi Elijah of Vilna (1720–1797, also known as the Gra or the Gaon of Vilna) conjectures that he was exiled three times, the third time being after the murder of Gedaliah son of Ahikam (cited in Eliezer Ginzburg, *Naḥalei Mayim* [Brooklyn, NY: n.p., 5761/2001], 110). There was obviously a tradition that Mordekhai had lived in Judea prior to his returning with Zerubbabel's *aliya.*

later in Nehemiah's version of the genealogical register than in Ezra's version, one of several minor discrepancies between the two lists, to emphasize that the study and teaching of Torah is the highest priority even when life is endangered. According to rabbinic legend, Mordekhai confronted Haman's threat during the time of Ezra, since, in their view, Ahasuerus was the son of Cyrus, and Ezra was Mordekhai's contemporary, as was Nehemiah. Once Mordekhai had defeated Haman, he should have resigned his position and returned to the study house. Since he did not, Nehemiah's list downgraded him.[13] Nehemiah himself was not, however, manifestly superior to Mordekhai in this regard. His position at the Persian court was attained prior to his knowledge of the problems in Judah; in theory, he should have spent his time in study rather than as a courtier. Nor did he indicate any commitment to study during the intervening years between his first and second tours of duty in Judah. Perhaps his behavior furnished the rabbis with yet another reason not to be enamored of the cupbearer-turned-governor.

The sages also assert that Mordekhai and Bilshan were a single individual. The Talmud plays on the root of the word that signifies language (*lashon*) to assert that Mordekhai spoke seventy languages, the number representing the rabbinic version of the sum total of spoken languages worldwide (Menaḥot 65a). Knowledge of languages was, according to the rabbis, a prerequisite for membership in the Sanhedrin – tradition also has Mordekhai as a member of that august legal body.[14] Nehemiah, of course, must have been conversant in both Aramaic and Persian in order to communicate effectively with the king whom he served.

13. Megilla 16b and Rashi ad loc., s.v. *me'ikara*.

14. Menaḥot 65a and Megilla 13b. It is a pity that there are elements in the contemporary Orthodox world that reject the need for knowledge of languages other than Yiddish, and, in extremis, not more than the bare essentials of the language of the country in which they reside. Indeed, as recently as 1939, Rabbi Chaim Ozer Grodzinski, at the time the acknowledged leader of Ashkenazic *ḥaredi* Orthodoxy, proclaimed that the knowledge of languages was essential – "*Shprachen darf man kennen*" were Rabbi Grodzinski's exact words. See Rabbi Zvi H. Zakheim, "*Kuntres Vilna Lifnei HaShoah*" (Treatise on pre-Holocaust Vilna), in *Zvi HaSanhedrin*, vol. 1 (Brooklyn, NY: Simcha-Graphic, 1976), 21.

Nehemiah's detailed list included many families and clans that had returned from the exile but had then intermarried with the local population. Among them was Jeshua the High Priest, four of whose descendants intermarried. Other descendants of those who returned under Zerubbabel also married non-Jewish spouses.

At first blush it seems surprising that successor generations of the returnees under Zerubbabel subsequently married local gentile spouses. One might expect that those who left Babylonia for an unknown fate in Judah would have been especially concerned with preserving their national identity, and would have imbued succeeding generations with that sense of identity. Clearly, whatever religious zeal and degree of religious practice may have colored the generation of returnees did not extend much beyond many of their children.

Moreover, having reestablished themselves in their "old-new land," many members of the successor generations of the early returnees, who now comprised the local elite, appear to have quickly forgotten their own recent immigrant status and looked down upon the new immigrants. In particular, they bitterly resented the interference of the later arrivals, whose religious commitment had remained strong in Babylonian exile. The attitudes of Israel's once-dominant Ashkenazic elite, not only toward the Sephardic *olim* from Yemen and North Africa in the 1950s, but especially toward the Religious Nationalist immigrants from North America in the aftermath of the Six-Day War and to the Ethiopian immigrants of the 1980s and 1990s, mirror those of their ancient predecessors. As in ancient days, the fault-lines between older returnees and later immigrants have been both political and social. As a result, many well-established Israelis resent the more recent arrivals, almost wishing that they would stay in their countries of origin.[15] Similar feelings colored

15. The literature on Israeli immigration continues to expand. For a range of Israeli views on issues relating to immigration, religion, and intermarriage, see Dan Urian and Efraim Karsh, eds., "In Search of Identity: Jewish Aspects in Israeli Culture," a special issue of *Israel Affairs* 4 (Spring/Summer 1998), especially Urian and Karsh, "Introduction"; Eliezer Schweid, "Judaism in Israeli Culture"; Charles S. Liebman, "Secular Judaism and Its Prospects"; Baruch Kimmerling, "Between Hegemony and Dormant *Kulturkampf* in Israel"; and Gershon Shaked, "Shall We Find Sufficient Strength? On Behalf of Israeli Secularism."

the attitudes of early Jewish arrivals to the United States, primarily German, toward later East European immigrants who likewise were more wedded to tradition.[16]

Most of the people named in Nehemiah's census are listed by their clans and as "the sons of" a given individual, similar to the Arab use of the word *al-*, meaning "the house of." Some of the clans were descended from men who were prominent during the earliest days of the First Temple. One such family was that of Pachat-Moab. In Hebrew, the name means "governor of Moab"; presumably, the family's eponym was governor of that region when it was under the domination of the Kingdom of Judah.[17] But the sages of the Talmud were convinced that the family tree reached even further back. Indeed, the *Tanna* R. Meir insisted that they were descended from King David himself; R. Yose, however, argued that they were descended from David's commander-in-chief, Joab son of Zeruiah. Both made their cases from the same source – the reference to Moab – since both King David and Joab were descended from Ruth the Moabitess (Taanit 28a). In other words, this was a family of nobles who had survived the exile and returned to their homeland.

Many of the families that Nehemiah listed later were responsible for bringing the wood offering to the Temple. The woodpile was replenished nine times a year, and the offering rotated among nine families. The family of Pachat-Moab was one of these, as were the families of Arah, Parosh, Zattu, and Adin, all from the tribe of Judah, as well as the Benjamite family of Senaah (Taanit 26a). Like the family of Pachat-Moab, the family of Adin had royal blood. R. Judah claims that, like Pachat-Moab, the Adin clan was composed of direct descendants of King David; once again, R. Yose disagrees, arguing that they, too, were descended from Joab (Taanit 28a).

Not every group on the list represented a family unit. In a number of cases the returnees were listed as "the men of" a given town – such

16. The tension between older and newer immigrants has a parallel in a completely different context: the resentment the Taiwanese have toward Chinese immigrants who arrived on the island of Taiwan after the fall of the Nationalist government on the mainland in 1949. Many Taiwanese are themselves actually descendants of mainlanders who arrived on the island in the nineteenth century.

17. Zer-Kavod, *Ezra UNeḥemia*, 10.

as the "The men of Bethlehem.... The men of Anathoth.... The men of Michmas" (Neh. 7:26–33 passim) among others – most were from the territory of Benjamin. The exiles in Babylonia manifested romantic longings for their hometowns and villages; mention of the towns reflected the above noted phenomenon, still prevalent today, of exiles retaining memories of, and pining for a return to, their ancestral villages.

Anathoth was a city of priests, the birthplace of the prophet Jeremiah. That its townspeople returned home is considered by the rabbis of the Talmud to be of special significance. It is from the mention of the people of Anathoth that R. Joshua b. Levi postulates that "repentance effects complete atonement."[18] As the Book of Jeremiah records, the people of Anathoth had so strongly rejected Jeremiah's prophecy that they ordered him to cease and desist or else face death at their hands. God responded by telling the prophet: "Behold, I will punish them; the young men shall die by the sword, their sons and their daughters shall die by famine; and there shall be no remnant unto them; for I will bring evil on the men of Anathoth" (Jer. 11:22–23). Still, avers R. Joshua b. Levi, despite God's commitment to eradicate the town's populace, "because they repented, they were privileged to be mentioned in the genealogical record."[19]

Jeremiah has another unfortunate connection with a different group listed in the record. Among the returnees were the sons of Pashhur, an old established family that had long been opposed to stricter interpretations of the religion. Pashhur the son of Immer was a senior Temple official, a "warden of decorum... [and] chief disciplinarian"[20] who, upon hearing Jeremiah's prophecies about the imminent fall of Judea resulting from the people's sins, physically struck him and had him placed in the stocks that were in the Temple's upper Gate of Benjamin (Jer. 20:1–2).[21] When Pashhur released Jeremiah, the prophet hurled a series of imprecations at him, foretelling his death and burial in captivity in Babylonia. Not surprisingly, perhaps, six clan members later intermarried (Jer. 20:3–6; Ezra 10:22).

18. Leviticus Rabba 10:5.

19. Ibid.

20. Lau, *Jeremiah*, 96 (see chap. 1, n. 33).

21. See also ibid.

Pashhur's family was one of four surviving priestly *mishmarot*, or rotations for Temple service, to return from Babylonia. Prior to the Temple's destruction there had been twenty-four of these units, consisting of both priests and Levites; they had a long pedigree, having been established by King David.[22] Apart from Pashhur's family, the others were the sons of Jedaiah, Harim, and Immer. The Talmud relates that "the prophets among them" subdivided each of the families into six groups to achieve the original number of twenty-four.[23] Jedaiah's family, which was second in rank among the *mishmarot* during the First Temple era, was given pride of place in the Second. The family it replaced in the priestly order of precedence, that of Jehoiarib, was downgraded because Jehoiarib had hesitated to return from Babylonia.[24] Nevertheless, despite the honor bestowed upon them, several of Jedaiah's descendants, like those of Pashhur, married non-Jewish women.[25]

After naming the priestly families, the genealogical record lists those of the Levites. Of these, the most prominent was the family of Asaph – no relation to the keeper of the Persian king's forest – twelve of whose compositions are included in the Book of Psalms. Chronicles records that Asaph was descended from Gershom son of Levi and was the leader of the singers in David's day (I Chr. 6:16–17, 24–28). His offspring sang in the Temple, and his psalms were recited by King Hezekiah (II Chr. 29:30). Chronicles also relates that he was a prophet (ibid.).

It appears that the family of Asaph was the only one of the Levitical guilds of singers that returned to Judah from Babylonia.[26] On the other hand, the returnees included a larger number of Levites who

---

22. I Chr. 23:1ff., 24–26; II Chr. 8:14; see also Neh. 12. The Talmud (Taanit 2a) asserts that Moses initially organized eight teams of priests and Levites to rotate over the course of a year; Samuel doubled the number to sixteen, and David increased it to twenty-four.
23. Taanit 27a–b.
24. Ibid. 27a; see also Rashi, Taanit 27b, s.v. *lo*.
25. The contrast with the Jews who remained in Babylonia is striking; intermarriage there appears to have been non-existent. See Peter R. Bedford, "Diaspora: Homeland Relations in Ezra-Nehemiah," *Vetus Testamentum* 52 (April 2002): 155.
26. Slotki, *Daniel, Ezra, Nehemiah*, 121 (see chap. 1, n. 34).

had served as gatekeepers during the First Temple era. They were not as prominent as the singers, however.[27]

It is possible that because they were relatively impoverished, many Levites never left Judah in the first place, but remained behind with the other more destitute classes. Even those who were exiled appear to have suffered from so great a decline in their importance after the Temple was destroyed that they chose to make their future in Babylonia – where Jews had easily assimilated and many prospered – rather than return to Judah with Zerubbabel.[28]

The genealogical record also includes the names of thirty-six families of Temple servants, the *netinim,* as well as the descendants of ten of Solomon's slaves, who accompanied the returnees. The *netinim,* as we saw earlier, were originally captives. They had been assigned support duties in the First Temple, and were reassigned to these duties in the new Temple. They lived in the Ophel, near the Temple Mount. It appears that with time, the descendants of Solomon's slaves blended into the *netinim* and no longer maintained a separate identity.[29]

Virtually all the *netinim* and the sons of Solomon's slaves had non-Jewish names. One name in particular stands out – Soferet, listed among the sons of Solomon's slaves. There is some speculation that Soferet was a woman.[30] It would have been unusual for a clan or family to derive its name from a woman and to be listed as such. Nevertheless, as Nehemiah's assignment of women to the construction of the wall indicates, at least some women held positions of importance in the community, and thus it was no insult to a family if its name derived from a female ancestor.

The origins of the *netinim* are shrouded in mystery. The talmudic view, as we noted, is that they were the descendants of the Gibeonites, who tricked Joshua into signing a peace treaty and in consequence forced to become "hewers of wood and drawers of water" (Josh. 9:21). A closer look at the individual names reveals a variety of ethnic origins,

27. Galil, *Daniel, Ezra UNeḥemia,* 138.
28. Williamson, *Ezra, Nehemiah,* 35, basing himself in part on Ezek. 44:10–14.
29. For a discussion, see Galil, *Daniel, Ezra UNeḥemia,* 139.
30. Ibn Ezra, Ezra 2:55, s.v. *bnei.*

however. Indeed, there is some speculation that many of these people were captured at other times – for example, in Moses's war with the Midianites – and assigned to serve the Levites.[31]

Whatever their origins, by the time of the exile and Zerubbabel's return to Judah, the *netinim* and the sons of Solomon's slaves appear to have become completely absorbed into Jewish society. Ezra seems not to have viewed them as anything other than Jews; there is no indication that he pressed the returnees to separate themselves from spouses who were *netinim*, as he did with respect to marriages that he considered to be mixed with people outside the faith. In any event, the *netinim*, like the sons of Solomon's slaves, nevertheless continued to constitute the lowest echelon of the Jewish social order.[32]

THE QUANDARY OF THE UNDOCUMENTED RETURNEES

There was another not insubstantial group of returnees whose names did not appear on the genealogical register. These people, especially those who claimed to be priests, posed a special problem for Nehemiah. Were they to be taken at their word, and restored to the responsibilities and privileges they claimed their families had held during the First Temple era? Or should they be disqualified from the priesthood or from membership in the Levitical clans, the priestly families being subclans of the tribe of Levi? Or, for that matter, should they even be counted as Jews? Their case was not all that different from that of present-day immigrants to Israel who for some reason, often because of the loss of records in the Holocaust, are unable to document their Jewish origins.[33]

31. Galil, *Daniel, Ezra UNeḥemia*, 139.
32. Ibid., 139–40.
33. The challenges arising from lack of documentation are not confined to the offspring of those who perished in the Holocaust. See, for example, Rabbi Moshe Shternbuch's ruling that a woman who was listed in Israeli documents as a convert, but insisted that she had never converted because she was born Jewish, should nevertheless undergo a conversion. Rabbi Shternbuch asserted that without the conversion that he was mandating she could not be accepted as a Jewess. He reasoned, in what was a classic "catch-22" situation, that on the one hand, she could not document her Jewishness, while, on the other, she was to be believed that she had never undergone a conversion; Rabbi Moshe Shternbuch, *She'eilot UTeshuvot Teshuvot VeHanhagot HaShalem*, vol. 2 (Jerusalem: n.p., 5754/1994), no. 514, 420.

Some of the undocumented returnees from Babylonia claimed a quite distinguished lineage. For example, a priestly family called the sons of Barzillai claimed that it was descended from a man who had married a daughter of Barzillai the Gileadite and had taken his name. Barzillai was famed for having received David with food and drink when he fled Absalom. David commanded that Solomon elevate his descendants to royal retainers ("They should be among those who eat at your table"; I Kings 2:7). Those who married into the family no doubt changed their names in order to benefit from its status in the royal household.

Nehemiah resolved the matter both as a religious leader, since the issue involved religious privileges, and as a Persian official – the *tirshata,* the Persian word for "excellency."[34] In a ruling that reflected a remarkable degree of political realism, no doubt driven by the desire to preserve the fragile communal unity he had worked so hard to achieve, Nehemiah did not disqualify these families from the priesthood, despite their lack of documentation. Instead, he barred them from eating "of the most holy things until a priest with Urim and Thummim should appear" (Neh. 7:65). Nehemiah's prohibition was a permanent one, since the Urim and Thummim, which hung on the High Priest's breastplate, disappeared with the destruction of the First Temple. His reference to the Urim and Thummim was the ancient equivalent of the modern Yiddish phrase "until the coming of the Messiah," meaning "no time soon."

The most holy things to which Nehemiah referred were the priestly gifts that could only be eaten in the Temple. Significantly, Nehemiah did not prohibit the priests from eating *teruma,* the special grain allotment to which priests were entitled, since it could be eaten outside the Temple precincts and the city of Jerusalem. Priests with physical blemishes or disabilities, who were disqualified from Temple service, were permitted to eat *teruma*; Nehemiah was, in effect, classifying the undocumented priestly families as blemished priests.

---

34. Some commentators believe that the title and subsequent ruling were Zerubbabel's and not Nehemiah's. See, for example, Zer-Kavod, *Ezra UNeḥemia,* 20–21; Sean E. McEvenue, "The Political Structure in Judah from Cyrus to Nehemiah," *Catholic Bible Quarterly* 43 (July 1981): 364; Rashi and Metzudat David (Ezra 2:63), s.v. *hat-irshata.* Metzudat David and Rashi on Ketubbot 42b argue that the term refers to Nehemiah; the Talmud asserts otherwise.

Nehemiah's solution was a politically astute move that won over a group of priests whom he otherwise would have alienated – despite the fact that he could claim that he was adhering to religious tradition. Yet it also demonstrated a generosity of spirit that was unusual not only in his time but in ours as well. He could have barred these individuals entirely from the priesthood. He could have excluded them from the Jewish community. He chose to do neither.

Nehemiah recorded the grand total of all he listed as 42,360. This figure was higher than the actual sum of the listed returnees, who numbered slightly more than 31,000. There is no obvious way to resolve the discrepancy. It is possible, however, that the difference of some 11,300 may reflect the returnees who preceded Zerubbabel, or perhaps members of the Ten Tribes who returned with him.[35] In any event, the tally of returnees, even though it does not appear to have included spouses or children, represented a not insignificant number, which itself points to the wider leadership challenge that Nehemiah faced as he tried to reconcile the conflicting economic and political interests of the various echelons of Judahite society.

In addition to the Jews who returned with Zerubbabel, there were also 7,337 servants who accompanied their masters to Judah, as well as livestock of various kinds. Listed separately as well were 245 male and female singers (Neh. 7:67). Classical and traditional commentators pass over this passage in silence. The sage Samuel argues in the Talmud that a woman's voice is a manifestation of lewdness (Berakhot 24a); as a consequence, to this day many strictly Orthodox Jews will not listen to a woman singing. Some halakhic decisors have argued that it is permissible to hear the singing of an unmarried woman, so long as it is not part of the prayer service.[36] In line with this view, the female singers would have been unmarried. Others have ruled that men may hear groups of women sing; in that case, it might be presumed that the

35. See Zer-Kavod, *Ezra UNeḥemia*, 21.

36. *Beit Shmuel, Shulḥan Arukh Even Ha'ezer* 21:1, s.v. *kol*. For a discussion, see Yechiel Yaakov Weinberg, *She'eilot UTeshuvot Sridei Aish*, vol. 1 (Jerusalem: Committee to Publish the Works of Rabbi Yechiel Yaakov Weinberg, 5759/1999), 216–17.

women vocalists sang as a choir.[37] In recording a list that specifies female singers, Nehemiah appears to have accepted the permissibility of such singing, at least in some circumstances.

DONATIONS FOR THE TEMPLE

Nehemiah also notes that some of the heads of the clans gave donations for the work, as did many of the community's ordinary citizens. In a departure from the nearly identical list in the Book of Ezra, Nehemiah states that he – i.e., the *tirshata* – donated to the treasury: "Gold – one thousand drachmas, basins – fifty, priestly robes – five hundred and thirty" (Neh. 7:70). It is noteworthy that Nehemiah's contribution and the others that are listed had nothing to do with the reconstruction of the walls. As will be noted below, his generosity may have extended to building homes for the people he planned to resettle in Jerusalem.

It is not clear why Ezra did not mention Nehemiah's donations. It is possible, as one traditional commentator speculates, that there may have been two sets of donations; alternatively, he posits that the original list was edited by Nehemiah to account for his and other later donations.[38]

There may be another explanation, however. Just as Nehemiah minimized Ezra's role in the community's development, Ezra may have done the same with respect to Nehemiah. The two were contemporaries, and, as Nehemiah's memoirs would later indicate, they jointly officiated over a major communal ceremony. In that case, Nehemiah had no alternative but to mention Ezra; however, where he did not have to do so, he did not. And Ezra seems to have done the same. Indeed, since his activities in Jerusalem preceded Nehemiah's, he was the first to gloss over the other's contributions to the stabilization of Judahite society.

One can only conclude that there was no love lost between the two men. They were so very different from each other. The one, a scribe, may well have been a bookish sort – like Jacob, a "man of tents" (Gen. 25:27), steeped in his religion; someone, for that matter, with whom later generations of rabbis could easily identify. The other was

37. Ibid., 217.
38. Malbim, Neh. 7:70, s.v. *umiktzat*.

a man of action. He was more than ordinarily religiously knowledgeable, but he was first and foremost a man of the world, wise to the ways of politics and economics in a manner that eluded Ezra. Ezra ignored Nehemiah's charitable gifts; Nehemiah reciprocated by virtually ignoring Ezra in his memoir.

Nehemiah had led the reconstruction of the wall, outwitted his opponents, arranged for Jerusalem's security, and completed the census. He now undertook a very different but nonetheless important task that also was geared to strengthening the community's sense of national and religious identity.

Nehemiah 8–9
Religious Revivalist

EZRA, NEHEMIAH, AND THEIR ROLES IN THE CEREMONY

Upon the completion of the genealogical research, and the accompanying lists, we might have expected that Nehemiah would have increased the population of Jerusalem beyond the small numbers that had returned to the city with Zerubbabel. After all, that had been his announced intention prior to commencing the census. He did not do so immediately, however, even though he may have prepared houses for the new residents of Jerusalem, as Josephus and Ben Sira later claimed.[1] The bulk of the population remained settled in their towns, and before any resettlement was undertaken Ezra led the community in a major ceremonial event.

What that event was, however, has posed problems for both traditional and modern biblical commentators. Different versions appear in the retellings by Ezra and Nehemiah, though both have the ceremonies taking place in the seventh month (Tishrei). As told by Ezra, the ceremony that took place after the genealogical review and its accompanying list related to Zerubbabel's construction of the altar (Ezra 3:3–11). Nehemiah's account has the review and list followed by

1. Josephus, *Antiquities*, XI:182 (see chap. 1, n. 30); *Ben Sira* 49:8–19. See also Galil, *Daniel, Ezra UNeḥemia*, 254.

the public reading of the Torah. It may be useful to digress in order to outline various solutions that have been offered to reconcile this seeming contradiction, and thereby to place Nehemiah's version in a credible context.

Some commentators resolve the contradiction by asserting that Ezra and Nehemiah both came to Judah twice, first with Zerubbabel under Cyrus, and then as leaders in their own right. In this view, what Nehemiah relates regarding the genealogy, lists, and the two ceremonies that followed are really part of the historical record of Ezra's activities at the time of his first return; Nehemiah recounted these events decades later. This view most closely conforms to the talmudic tradition, but is barely consistent with the fact that the return under Cyrus preceded the return under Artaxerxes by over six decades. One would have to assume that Ezra first came to Judah as a toddler and then returned as an aging leader and presided over the Torah-reading ceremony as a very old man.

A second traditional view sees Nehemiah's discussion of the ceremonies as distinct from Ezra's account, relating events that took place in Nehemiah's time. In this construct, Nehemiah employed the closing language of the list of the arrivals under Zerubbabel to introduce the story of the public reading because it coincidentally took place on the day that work had commenced on the altar decades earlier. This interpretation, though somewhat forced, is more consistent with the plain meaning of the text.

Both of these approaches still cannot resolve the question of why Nehemiah, who certainly did not lack an ego, was willing to give so much prominence to Ezra. He gave Ezra the stage to read the Torah, and gave him sole billing when he recorded the event afterwards. This is especially interesting because he and Ezra do not appear to have been close. Moreover, the twelve verses that deal with the Torah-reading ceremony also appear in the apocryphal book of 1 Esdras immediately following its repetition of the last verses of the canonical Book of Ezra. This leads some scholars to conclude that the entire event really had nothing to do with Nehemiah at all; rather, its retelling was grafted onto Nehemiah's book by a subsequent editor to render him and Ezra contemporaries. Moreover, Josephus includes the Bible-reading ceremony in his passages on Ezra and, like Nehemiah, omits Nehemiah's name entirely, as does Esdras.[2]

On the other hand, there is no reason to assume that Ezra and Nehemiah were not contemporaries, as is clearly indicated by the texts of both their books. Certainly, the dates that most scholars give for the arrival of each man are close enough to allow for them to have functioned simultaneously once Nehemiah arrived on the scene. As for Josephus, it is not entirely clear that his omission of Nehemiah necessarily implies that Nehemiah was not on the scene. To begin with, it is possible that this section of Josephus was tampered with to conform to the passages in Esdras, which preceded it by at least a century; other parts of Josephus are known to have been the subject of subsequent tinkering. On the other hand, Esdras itself might have been tampered with. Alternatively, Esdras may have omitted mention of Nehemiah because it reflected a tradition in Judaism that venerated Ezra and ignored Nehemiah.

It is noteworthy that Josephus does not mention the two leaders together, "since the net result of this would be to detract from the achievements of each of them."[3] This explanation is highly plausible. Nehemiah would, in any event, have played second fiddle to Ezra at the ceremony, since being neither a priest nor the community's leading sage he was not as qualified to lead the Torah reading. He may well have preferred to leave the limelight to Ezra. In so doing he was clearly demarcating the bounds between religious and secular leadership and affirming his own role as the national leader, rather than implying that he was in any way part of Ezra's supporting cast.

In addition, whatever their personal relationship might have been, the two men not only shared a common objective – to restore the identity, and the glory, of the Jewish people – but also confronted the same enemies and rivals. Despite being a priest himself, Ezra clearly stood apart from the priestly establishment. In this regard his interests

2. Josephus, *Antiquities*, XI:154; see also Marcus's comments in fn a. See also Cross, *From Epic to Canon*, 160–61 (see chap. 1, n. 16). It should be noted that, in general, Esdras devotes far more space to Nehemiah than does Josephus; see Feldman, "Josephus' Portrait," 188 (see chap. 3, n. 11).

3. Feldman, "Josephus' Portrait," 193.

were identical with those of Nehemiah, who was likewise opposed by the establishment. That alone was enough to bring them together in an alliance of necessity, just as shared interests have brought together other leaders over the centuries – Washington's and Lincoln's cabinets being but two of many examples of leaders who may have actively detested one another but of necessity worked together in a common cause.

Finally, precisely because it was Ezra who was the leading religious functionary, it was natural that the people would look to him, rather than Nehemiah, to lead a religious ceremony. As Nehemiah records, when "the entire people assembled as one man in the square before the Water Gate...they asked Ezra the scribe to bring the scroll of the Teaching of Moses which the Lord had charged to Israel" (Neh. 8:1).

Ezra's leading role in the ceremony underscored the fact that the religious leadership of Judah came from the Diaspora. There were no home-grown religious leaders, nor, for that matter, authoritative local religious practices and traditions. Both had to be imported from Babylonia.[4]

THE TORAH READING

Ezra's public reading of the Torah took place on the first day of Tishrei, that is, Rosh HaShana. He stood on a tower, flanked by six laymen on his right and seven on his left. The fact that they were laymen was a sign not of Ezra's political support, but rather of Nehemiah's. The audience was the entire congregation, not only men and women, but also children "who could listen with understanding" (Neh. 8:3).[5] Ezra spoke from dawn until midday, by which time the assembled throng had become hot and tired and were losing their concentration. Evidently the crowd was quite large and those in the rear had difficulty hearing Ezra; to enable everyone to hear, Nehemiah assigned the Levites to transmit what Ezra was saying. The fact that the Levites, like the laymen, were assigned a major

4. Bedford, "Diaspora: Homeland Relations," 157. The situation was repeated centuries later in late-nineteenth-century America, when virtually all Orthodox Jewish rabbis were immigrants from Eastern Europe.
5. See Ralbag, Neh. 8:2, s.v. *vekhol*. Malbim (Neh. 8:3, s.v. *lifnei*) asserts, however, that "men and women" referred to ordinary Jews for whom simple teachings sufficed, while "who could listen with understanding" referred to the rabbinic sages who were expert in the complexities of Torah.

role in the ceremony is similarly evidence of Nehemiah's political hand; their prominence was due to their support of Nehemiah's authority – as opposed to the priests, who were suspect.

The Pentateuch nowhere mentions Torah reading on Rosh HaShana, whereas it does in connection with Sukkot (Deut. 31:1–12). On the other hand, Ezra's ceremony involved neither ritual sacrifices nor the blowing of the shofar, both of which are explicitly mandated in Leviticus (23:23–25) and Numbers (29:1–6). In the traditional view, the Torah that Ezra read aloud is the very same Torah that Jews possess to this day. Indeed, Ezra's Torah reading took on tremendous significance in later generations, when he was credited with reviving the knowledge of Torah among the Jewish people (Sukka 20a). Moreover, the Talmud cites his Torah reading as the basis for its assertion that Ezra instituted the practice of public Torah readings on Mondays and Thursdays (Bava Kamma 82a).

Ezra's innovation, or *takana*, of having midweekly Torah readings was one of ten laws and practices that traditional Judaism ascribes to him. Only a few of these practices have endured among most Jews. The ten are outlined in Tractate Bava Kamma (ibid.):

> They should read [the Torah publicly] at the Sabbath afternoon service; that the Torah should also be read on Mondays and Thursdays; that the court should sit on Mondays and Thursdays; that clothes be washed on Thursdays; that garlic be eaten on the eve of the Sabbath; that a woman should rise early and bake; that a woman should wear an apron; that a woman should shampoo and then immerse herself [in the *mikve*, or ritual bath]; that peddlers should visit the villages; that men suffering from an issue should immerse themselves [in the *mikve*].

The two that are standard traditional Jewish practices relate to the Torah readings, which, as noted, are derived from verse 1, and the female practice of shampooing before ritual immersion. Other customs that have survived among the very pious include women wearing an apron when cooking and men's frequent use of the *mikve*.

It is noteworthy that Ezra is recorded as having "brought the Teaching before the congregation" (Neh. 8:2), as opposed to "the Scroll of the

Teaching." Nor does the verse refer to the people as requesting "the Scroll of the Teaching." This omission has led some traditional commentators to assert that Ezra taught the people both the Written and the Oral Law.[6]

Nehemiah relates that Ezra stood on a wooden platform specially made for the purpose of his Torah reading, and that he addressed the people in the square before the Water Gate (Neh. 8:1). The Water Gate was actually a Temple gate, but it appears to have doubled as a city gate. It was situated on the southern side of the Temple, near where the *netinim* resided; they had helped to repair it. The people, for their part, stood as Ezra opened the scroll.[7]

A midrash cites the reference to the purpose-built platform in conjunction with a passage in Deuteronomy (23:24) to underscore the biblical basis of the Temple maintenance fund (*bedek habayit*).[8] Special monies had to be collected to provide for the platform's construction, because, as Nehemiah soon discovered, the maintenance fund had not been properly sourced since the construction of the Second Temple. Fully sourcing the fund became one of Nehemiah's major priorities.

It is not clear where exactly the platform was placed, however. The Talmud records two views. The majority view, enunciated by the rabbis, and notably R. Ḥisda, is that the platform was placed inside the Temple grounds, in the Women's Chamber. R. Eliezer b. Yaakov, citing the same passage in Nehemiah, argues that the platform stood on

6. Malbim, Neh. 8:2, s.v. *et*.

7. Rashi (Neh. 8:5, s.v. *ukepitḥo*), Ibn Ezra (first interpretation of *ukepitḥo*), and Rabbi Saadia (Mathews, *Commentary*, 27) reject the usual translation of the Hebrew *amdu* as "stood" in favor of "became silent." In doing so they underscore two halakhic principles: that one is permitted to remain seated during the Torah reading and that one is forbidden to speak during the reading (*Shulḥan Arukh, Oraḥ Ḥayim* 146:4, 146:2). Ironically, while many Orthodox Jews stand during the reading, their synagogues have for centuries been notorious for their noisiness during services and during the reading of the Torah, despite the pleas, admonitions, and even imprecations of their rabbis and leaders.

8. Rabbi Zechariah ben Shlomo HaRofeh, *Midrash HaḤefetz: Vayikra-Devarim*, trans. and ed. Meir Havatzelet (Jerusalem: Mossad Harav Kook, 1992), 432. Havatzelet questions the relationship of *bedek habayit* to verse 4, since the passage discusses Ezra's Torah reading (n. 67). In fact, the midrash refers to the words "for that purpose," which clearly signify construction for a special need relating to the Temple ceremony.

the Temple Mount, but not in the Temple itself.[9] Both rabbis apply their respective positions to the public reading of the Torah in the *Hak'hel* ceremony, which took place at the beginning of Ḥol HaMoed (the intermediate days) of Sukkot immediately after the sabbatical year (*Shemitta*). Each argues that just as Ezra read the Torah aloud on a wooden platform to an assembly consisting, as noted, of "men and women and all who could listen with understanding" (Neh. 8:2), so too did the king read aloud on such a platform to an assembly that the Torah describes as "the people – men, women, children" (Deut. 31:12). Moreover, R. Ḥisda argues that the reading must have taken place in the Women's Chamber, because it was only in that section of the Temple grounds that the king was permitted to sit, which he did as he read the Torah aloud (Tosefta Sota 7:8).

On the other hand, most scholars do not place the Water Gate, and the square to which it opened, next to the Women's Chamber;[10] perhaps R. Ḥisda had a different tradition regarding its location. In any event, what is clear from both talmudic positions regarding Ezra's reading is that, unlike the *Hak'hel* reading, it was not a ritual event per se. It was, rather, an extraordinary occurrence, arising from the urgent need to win the people's allegiance back to the Torah. Indeed, this seems to have been the case. When Ezra blessed God, the people responded by uttering "Amen, Amen" with their hands upraised, and then bowed and prostrated themselves "with their faces to the ground" (Neh. 8:6).

Even if Nehemiah saw value in having Ezra lead the event, why did he organize it in the first place? And why did he do so before he had resettled a larger Jewish population in Jerusalem? At first glance, the segue to Ezra's reading of the Torah seems out of place; why read the Torah just after the wall was completed? Some non-Jewish biblical scholars have asserted that the entire episode was inserted into Nehemiah's memoir at a later date. Yet it is arguable that only after the wall was repaired would Ezra, with Nehemiah's support, have felt sufficiently confident to lecture

9. Yoma 69b; see also Sota 40b and *Ḥasdei David* on Tosefta Sota 7:8, s.v. *bima*.
10. See, for example, Rabbi Steinsaltz's sketch of the Temple, in Adin Steinsaltz, *Talmud Bavli: Masekhet Yoma* (Jerusalem: Israel Institute for Talmudic Publications, 1982), 164.

the people from the Torah itself. Until the city was finally fortified, there remained some doubt as to whether the adherents of Ezra and Nehemiah, who sought to maintain the ethnic and religious integrity of the Jewish community, would prevail in the face of the many who had married into the local population. After all, Sanballat's relatives by marriage included leading Jewish figures; his close collaborator, Tobiah, was Jewish himself. Nonetheless, Tobiah was a leading proponent of intermarriage, and both had done all they could to undermine Nehemiah's efforts. Under these circumstances, it was questionable whether a Torah reading would have had much effect on a populace whose loyalty might still have been up for grabs. Only when Nehemiah finally prevailed – with Sanballat, Tobiah, and the rest nursing the wounds of defeat – was it likely that the people would be receptive to a reiteration of the centrality of the Torah and reinforcement of their commitment to its teachings.[11]

It is also probable that during the dozen years between Ezra's failure to prevent intermarriage and Nehemiah's arrival, Ezra may have helped develop the Levites' expertise in the Torah, as well as in the Oral Law and in what centuries later came to be known as the "sea of halakha." Such a halakhic approach appears to have developed in the days of Haggai and Zechariah, both of whom dealt with halakhic-type queries. Indeed, in one such case, the latter prophet explicitly addressed questions regarding the observance of post-biblical fasts. In effect, Ezra may have spent the thirteen years between 458 and 445 BCE building a base of what might be termed Levitical halakhists.[12]

Ezra's inculcating the Levites in the law had the political effect of systematically creating a cohort that was both loyal to the Torah and opposed to the policies and practices espoused by Sanballat, Tobiah, Eliashiv the High Priest, and their supporters. When Nehemiah arrived, therefore, he had a ready bloc of allies who not only were economically disadvantaged, as the Levites surely were, but also were his natural political partners in seeking to reassert the community's national and religious identity. Of course, Nehemiah recognized that he needed to expand his influence beyond his committed political base. Since Ezra

11. See Galil, *Daniel, Ezra UNeḥemia*, 259.

12. Ibid.

was partly responsible for creating that base through his religious leadership, and had considerable religious authority in the eyes of the larger community, it made perfect sense for him to lead a religious event that would serve as a vehicle for mobilizing the community before it settled back into the routines of daily life.

A CEREMONY BOTH POLITICAL AND RELIGIOUS

Nehemiah, with Ezra's wholehearted participation, organized the ceremony as much for political reasons as religious ones. Able politicians throughout the ages have mustered popular support by evoking a nation's real or perceived days of past glory. Nehemiah did nothing less in orchestrating the Torah-reading ceremony. The reading itself echoed that of Josiah, who was looked upon as one of the great kings of the Davidic dynasty ("Like unto him was there no king before him, that turned to the Lord with all his heart… neither after him arose there any like him"; II Kings 23:25). Indeed, having Ezra read from an elevated wooden platform recalled Josiah's doing the same thing during the glory days of the First Temple.[13] It prompted the celebration of Sukkot "for the first time since the days of Joshua the son of Nun," when the Israelites first entered the land as victorious conquerors (Neh. 8:17). And it called for the giving of portions to the poor, a practice associated with the Jews' victory over Haman as recounted in Esther. Indeed, the ceremony was also a "triumph" in the Roman sense. It "marked Nehemiah's victory over those local enemies… who had tried again and again… to sabotage the creation of the walls."[14] In drawing around himself the cloak of Israel's past greatness, as well as its recent success, Nehemiah effectively offset the implicit claim of the priests to be the legatees of the nation's glorious history by virtue of their identification with the Temple.

For the ceremony to have its intended effect, however, Nehemiah needed Ezra's assistance to give it legitimacy in the eyes of the Torah sages and their supporters. There were two more reasons for Ezra to lead the ceremony. Nehemiah certainly appreciated the value of Ezra's

13. The use of such a platform, or *bima*, for the Torah reading has since become standard practice in the synagogue.
14. Wiesel, *Sages and Dreamers*, 129 (see chap 6, n. 52).

effort to transform the Levites into a new scholarly class, and would have made every effort to capitalize on it. Ezra, for his part, would have had no reason not to cooperate with Nehemiah if it meant that his twelve-year project of reaching out to the Levites would succeed.

Ezra cooperated at the ceremony by acting as the "star," the reader on whom all eyes focused. Yet Nehemiah demonstrated that he was the true master of ceremonies by announcing to the people – with the vocal support of the Levites – both the impending celebration of the Sukkot holiday and the details of its celebration, including the gifts for the poor. With Ezra's critical assistance, Nehemiah augmented his own temporal authority, derived from the Persian court, with spiritual authority as an associate of the nation's leading Torah scholar. At the same time, he rallied the various factions that he looked to for support – the poor, the Levites, and the growing class of scholars, at whose head Ezra stood – adding to them as many of the rest of the community as he could.

The ceremony prompted the reactions that Nehemiah – and Ezra – had hoped for. Nehemiah records that "Ezra blessed the Lord, the great God, and all the people answered, 'Amen, Amen,' with hands upraised. Then they bowed their heads and prostrated themselves before the Lord with their faces to the ground" (Neh. 8:6). The combination of solemnity and enthusiasm was palpable. The people heard Ezra utter the Tetragrammaton, the name of God normally only pronounced by the High Priest when inside the Temple, notably on Yom Kippur (Yoma 69b). He also recited what later rabbinic commentators assumed were the traditional blessings that precede and follow the Torah reading in synagogue.[15] Their emphatic "Amen" underscored their commitment to heed its teachings. The Levites and a few laymen, rather than the priests, then translated what Ezra had just read from Hebrew into Aramaic, and explained the teachings to the people, who remained standing the entire time. The translation into the lingua franca must have been very disturbing to Nehemiah. He viewed Hebrew as the national language of the Jewish people, the language that should have been as much a part of their everyday life as Aramaic. Later in his memoir he stresses the

15. Ralbag, Neh. 8:6, s.v. *vayevarekh*.

importance of the Hebrew language to the people; at this time, however, he must have judged it premature to do so.

As for the nature of the Levites' explanation, some later rabbinic commentators emphasize that it reflected the emendations of the text, as well as the interpretations of Oral Law, by means of which the rabbis traditionally explained the Torah's teachings.[16] Indeed, one medieval commentator asserts that the Levites were resuscitating details of the Oral Law that "were given to Moses and were forgotten because of the tribulations of the exile until Ezra and his associates [re]established them."[17]

The sages of the Talmud drew upon the nature of the Torah reading to formulate the way in which it should be conducted in the synagogue. They dissected the passage in Nehemiah that states that the Levites "read from the scroll of the Teaching of God, translating it and giving the sense; so they understood the reading" (Neh. 8:8). The sages asserted that "read from the scroll" indicates the text itself; "translating it" means the authorized Aramaic translation (which in later centuries included midrashic elements); "giving the sense" means the cantillations; and "so they understood the reading" means the traditional reading where it varies from the text.[18] In this regard it is worth noting that the rabbis also ascribed to Ezra the change from the ancient version of Hebrew script to the "Assyrian version" that remains in use today.[19] Likewise, the rabbis stated that it was Ezra who determined the proper use of vowels in the text, since the Torah scroll has no vowels.

A CALL TO CELEBRATE

It was subsequent to the Levites' translation and explanation that Nehemiah finally inserted himself into the narrative regarding the ceremony. The people had responded to the Torah reading by weeping. It is possible, as one commentator suggests, that they had just heard Ezra

16. Malbim, Neh. 8:8, s.v. *basefer*.
17. Mathews, *Commentary*, 27 (see chap. 4, n. 11).
18. Statement of R. Zeira in the name of R. Ḥananel in Y. Megilla 27b; see also Megilla 3a; Nedarim 37b.
19. Sanhedrin 21b and 23a and Sota 7b; Tosefta Sanhedrin 4:7; Y. Megilla 10a–b. For a discussion, see Galil, *Daniel, Ezra UNeḥemia*, 262; see also *Encyclopedia Talmudit*, s.v. *Ketav Ashuri*.

read from the curses outlined in Deuteronomy for those who sinned.[20] In any event, they recognized that as it was Rosh HaShana, it was the Day of Judgment, and in recalling their transgressions they wept out of fear of heavenly retribution.[21]

Nehemiah, referring to himself not in the first person, as previously in his memoir, but in the third-person coupled with the appellation *hatirshata*, says that he joined Ezra and the Levites in telling the people not to weep, because the "day is holy to your Lord God" (Neh. 8:9). Nehemiah may have quoted himself in this way to underscore his political role in the ceremony, in contrast to the ceremonial role of the others. In this regard, while he certainly shared with Ezra and the Levites the apprehension that the people not convert what was meant to be an uplifting event into a day of mourning, he likely was also deeply concerned that they not become demoralized. He still needed to repopulate the city, but he had to maintain the people's enthusiasm in order to do so successfully. With this goal in mind, he went further than Ezra and the others, encouraging the people to "go, eat choice foods and drink sweet drinks and send portions to whoever has nothing prepared, for the day is holy to our Lord. Do not be sad, for your rejoicing in the Lord is the source of your strength" (8:10). Moreover, by asking them to share their food with the less fortunate, he not only fostered a sense of community but demonstrated to the people, yet again, his commitment to social justice.

The sages interpret Nehemiah's remarks to indicate that he was doing more than exhorting the people to eat – he was legislating that it was forbidden to mourn or fast on a holiday, and particularly on the two days of Rosh HaShana.[22] At the same time, by doing so after Ezra

20. Ralbag, Neh. 8:9, s.v. *ki*.

21. Rashi, Neh. 8:9, s.vv. *hayom*, *bokhim*.

22. The general ban was enunciated by R. Akiva in Y. Taanit 13b. See also Mathews, *Commentary*, 27. Later decisors focused on Rosh HaShana itself. Rabbi Asher ben Yehiel (known as the Rosh), citing Rabbi Hai Gaon, took issue with Rabbi Natrunai Gaon, who held that while fasting was forbidden on the first day of Rosh HaShana, it was permitted on the second day. See Rosh, Rosh HaShana, chap. 4, no. 14, s.v. *ulehitanot bishnei yamim tovim shel Rosh HaShana*. See also Bar Sheshet Perfet, *She'eilot UTeshuvot Rivash*, nos. 513, 766. For an extended discussion and an outline

had read the Torah through midday, Nehemiah was outlining the principle that holy days should be equally divided between spiritual and physical nourishment.[23] In addition, his exhortation led the sages to conclude that people should not hesitate to borrow money in order to celebrate the festivals; God would reward their faith by covering their debts (Beitza 15b). Moreover, they should make a special effort to give charity to the poor.[24] Finally, Nehemiah's emphasis on "choice foods and sweet drinks" foreshadowed the Jewish tradition to eat particular foods on Rosh HaShana whose names hinted at good and sweet things to come in the New Year.[25] That Nehemiah might have set standards for the community would not have been out of character; he would subsequently do so on a range of important religious issues.

The community naturally responded positively to Nehemiah's encouragement. Most people prefer joy to weeping, and the Jews not only ate, drank, and shared their good fortune with others, but went one step further by doing so with great merriment (Neh. 8:12). Nehemiah had correctly anticipated the people's reaction.

On the next day, the second day of Rosh HaShana (which resulted from the addition of a day to the previous month of Elul due to the late arrival of witnesses to the new moon),[26] the people, including their leaders, gathered once again to hear Ezra read from the Torah. He focused on the passages relating to the upcoming Sukkot holiday. The early returnees with Zerubbabel had observed Sukkot, but, as noted, no one had done so with booths since the days of Joshua son of Nun.

The people responded enthusiastically. Heeding Ezra's call "to announce and proclaim throughout all their towns and Jerusalem as

of the views of later decisors, see Rabbi Shabtai Sheftel Weiss, *Ḥidushei Yom Rosh HaShana BeSefer Ezra UNeḥemia* (Novellae Regarding Rosh HaShana in the Book of Ezra and Nehemiah), *Yeshurun* 31 (Elul 5774/2014): 745–46.

23. Dictum of R. Joshua, Pesaḥim 68b.

24. Weiss, *Ḥidushei Yom Rosh HaShana*, 751–52.

25. Dicta of Abaye in Keritot 6a and Horayot 12a. See also Rabbi Shmuel Edels, *Ḥidushei Halachot V'Agadot Maharsha*, Horayot 12a, s.vv. *amar*, *yehei*; Meiri, *Beit HaBeḥira*, Horayot, 282 (see chap. 1, n. 6); and Mathews, *Commentary*, 27.

26. Rashi (Beitza 6a, s.v. *miyemot*) interprets the Talmud as concluding that this was the last instance of the addition of a day to Elul; after that year, Rosh HaShana automatically became a two-day holiday.

follows, 'Go out to the mountains and bring leafy branches of olive trees, pine trees, myrtles, palms and [other] leafy trees to make booths as it is written'" (Neh. 8:15), they did just that, and "then made themselves booths on their roofs, in their courtyards, in the courtyards of the House of God, in the square of the Water Gate, and in the square of the Ephraim Gate" (8:16).

One might wonder why Ezra did not read the portion of the Torah dealing with Yom Kippur, which follows Rosh HaShana and precedes Sukkot. It is also somewhat strange that Nehemiah could state unequivocally in his memoir that Sukkot had not been celebrated with booths "since the days of Joshua son of Nun" (Neh. 8:17). This would imply, somewhat implausibly, that throughout the era of the judges and the entire Davidic dynasty an explicit biblical command was completely ignored – by David himself, no less.

Some Bible scholars have argued that Ezra was not reading from the Scripture as we know it. With respect to Yom Kippur, they assert that "Yom Kippur had not yet attained a firm place in the liturgical calendar."[27] This purely speculative argument presupposes that the Pentateuch was a late composition by multiple authors and/or editors.

The omission of Yom Kippur can be explained as consistent with the traditional Jewish view that God dictated the Torah to Moses. The entire narrative highlights events that were unique. The ceremony on Rosh HaShana was itself unique. It was not the ceremony *of* Rosh HaShana, involving the shofar, but rather a ceremony that took place *on* Rosh HaShana. The festival of Sukkot was uniquely celebrated in Jerusalem, incorporating not only the previously long-standing practice of commemorating Sukkot with sacrifices in the Temple, as the Book of Ezra makes clear (Ezra 3:4), but also incorporating the previously neglected elements of the holiday, namely, the booths and the four species.

27. Blenkinsopp, *Ezra-Nehemiah*, 291. Other modern scholars, however, argue that "the Day of Atonement was fully known and celebrated despite the omission of reference to it in Nehemiah 8" (Cross, *From Epic to Canon*, 171). See also S. Mowinckel, *Studein zu dem Buche Ezra-Nechemia I: Die Nachronistiche Redaktion des Buches die Listen* (Oslo: Universitet Forlag, 1964).

On the other hand, there was nothing unique about the observance of Yom Kippur that year; and so there was no need to mention it. For the same reason, it is not accidental that Nehemiah says very little about Shemini Atzeret, the holiday that follows Sukkot, other than that it was observed "as prescribed" (Neh. 8:18). As with the shofar on Rosh HaShana and the fasting on Yom Kippur, there was nothing unique, and nothing much to be said, about Shemini Atzeret. It was probably mentioned only as an appendage to the verses on Sukkot, since the holiday is, in reality, an appendage of sorts.

REVIVING THE SUKKA

Biblical scholars, noting Nehemiah's assertion that the Jews sat in booths on Sukkot for the first time in nearly a millennium, likewise have asserted that the Sukkot festival appears to have been something new, and unfamiliar, to the assembled throngs. Again, however, it is arguable that the text simply focuses on commandments that the people were failing to carry out rather than those, like the Sukkot sacrifices, which they had been fulfilling for some time. Moreover, it is possible that Nehemiah was simply exaggerating for maximum effect to demonstrate the impact of his arrival on the community's religious behavior[28] – since Ezra, despite having been on the scene for over a dozen years, had not been able to motivate the people to carry out this particular commandment.

Not surprisingly, the sages of the Talmud were also troubled by Nehemiah's assertion regarding the last time the people had sat in booths on Sukkot. The rabbis could not possibly acknowledge that such heroic figures as Samuel, David, Solomon, Hezekiah, and Josiah – to name but five – did not admonish the people to keep all the commandments relating to Sukkot. Therefore, they too do not take Nehemiah's statement literally. Instead, they somewhat tenuously connected it to a dispute between R. Yishmael b. R. Yose and R. Eliezer b. R. Yose as to whether Ezra resanctified the land upon his arrival there. Moreover, R. Eliezer employs the verse homiletically to argue that Ezra was able

28. Zer-Kavod, *Ezra UNeḥemia*, 108.

to abolish the "evil inclination regarding idol worship."[29] At least one modern scholar adopts a roughly similar approach to the verse, not taking it literally but instead arguing that "the reference to Joshua may be motivated by the idea of the restoration as a second taking possession of the holy land, the first being in the time of Joshua."[30]

There are some additional puzzling aspects both to Nehemiah's instructions to the people and to their response. To begin with, Nehemiah said nothing about the need to gather palms, myrtles, willows, and the citron, which together constituted the four species that were integral to the festival ritual. Nehemiah had indeed mentioned myrtles and palms, but only in the context of building the sukka. In addition, Nehemiah records that people built booths not only on their roofs and courtyards but also in the public domain, notably the courtyards of the House of God, the square of the Water Gate, and the square of the Ephraim Gate (Neh. 8:16). Yet according to tradition, not only was Jerusalem considered to be a special entity and not part of any tribe – much like the federal cities of Washington and Brasília are not part of any state – but in addition, all of Jerusalem was considered to be communal property, and a sukka could only be built on private property. How, then, could Nehemiah have authorized sukka construction on people's roofs or in their courtyards, much less in what were manifestly public places?

The sages of the Talmud deal with the absence of any mention of the four species by identifying Nehemiah's reference to palms as connoting the lulav, and by citing his admonition to the people that they acquire leafy trees as referring to the myrtles of the four species. They posit that his reference to myrtles connoted a different type of myrtle that was used for sukka construction. Indeed, according to R. Ḥisda, who identifies the two different species of myrtle, Nehemiah's instructions provide the clearest textual source for determining what types of coverings are permitted for a sukka (Sukka 12a). In any event, having

29. Sanhedrin 64a. In this context, see also R. Hillel's dictum in the name of R. Shmuel b. Naḥmani (one of the Talmud's great storytellers), as to why the *heh* is dropped from Joshua's name. Y. Shevi'it 17a; see also the commentary of *Penei Moshe*, s.v. *pagam*.

30. Coggins, *Ezra and Nehemiah*, 110 (see chap. 1, n. 14).

mentioned two of the four species that had just figured in Ezra's reading from the Torah's commandments relating to Sukkot, Nehemiah, in the sages' later interpretation, may have concluded that the people would naturally seek out the remaining two species as well.

Nehemiah's authorization of booths in public places led the rabbis to conclude that this reflected another of Ezra's innovations. In other words, prior to Ezra's ruling, Jews did not build their sukkot on anything but private property. Ezra and Nehemiah recognized, however, that the festival offered them a powerful opportunity to promote a sense of community and religious commitment among the people. Private observances could not have achieved this objective. Indeed, in modern times, the communal sukka that is a fixture in synagogues continues to foster a feeling of shared *simḥat haḥag*, "joy of the festival"; this is especially appropriate for the days of Sukkot, which are termed *zman simḥateinu*, "the period of our joy," and about which the Torah exhorts, you shall be filled with joy (*vehayita akh sameaḥ*). Human nature has not changed all that much over the millennia, and the public sukkot of Nehemiah's day fostered the same emotions.

A FINAL PRAYER

Ezra continued the daily Torah readings throughout the seven days of Sukkot and on the eighth day, Shemini Atzeret, as well. Instead of dismissing the people once the latter festival was over, Ezra and Nehemiah kept them in Jerusalem for two more days. On the second of these days, Nehemiah led the people in fasting, dressed in sackcloth and with earth upon them (Neh. 9:1). This was exactly what the people had been inclined to do the week before. At the time, they were prevented from doing so by Ezra and Nehemiah because of the holiday. Indeed, they were not permitted to fast on the day after the festival either. Now, however, on the twenty-fourth of the month of Tishrei, the two leaders let the people vent their pent-up feelings of remorse and indeed encouraged them to do so.

There is no clear relationship between this special day of fasting and prayer and either Yom Kippur or the festivals that follow it. It was a once-only event, not meant for repetition in future years. Scripture recounts similar unique public gatherings that were convened by Elijah and Josiah.

Nehemiah's objective in organizing the ceremonies on this day was not merely to sustain the community's emotional support. Rather it was, as it had been throughout the festival that had just ended, to solidify the people's commitment to their religious and national heritage. Once again, it appears that he let Ezra lead the ceremony. Neither Nehemiah's name nor Ezra's is mentioned in connection with this special day of fasting. Scripture recounts only the names of the prominent Levites who led the people. Despite the fact that the Levites were his people, it was not Nehemiah's place as a layman to be in charge of the ceremonies.

There was no need to mention Ezra. He had just led all the rituals of the preceding week; naturally it was to be expected that he would continue to do so. Moreover, the ceremony centered around the bane of Ezra's original mission, namely, the epidemic of intermarriage that plagued the community. Ezra's eponymous book concludes with his spectacular failure to terminate the marriages of Jewish males to non-Jewish women. Twelve years later, with intermarriage still rife, Ezra, this time backed by Nehemiah's political power, naturally seized the opportunity to force the issue again.

This time the people seem to have responded to Ezra's entreaties. As Nehemiah recounts, "those of the stock of Israel separated themselves from the foreigners, and stood and confessed their sins and the iniquities of their fathers" (Neh. 9:2). Virtually all commentators agree that "stock of Israel" connotes the men, while the foreigners were their wives and children. It is striking, however, that Nehemiah does not explicitly mention women, as both his memoir and the Book of Ezra do elsewhere. It is possible that this separation was intended only for the purposes of the special assembly;[31] more likely it was meant to be final. In any event, Ezra's initial attempt to prevent intermarriages clearly had failed, and, as Nehemiah's memoir later makes clear, if this separation was intended to be permanent, it too failed. Nehemiah had to intervene more forcefully to settle the matter once and for all.

---

31. See Blenkinsopp, *Ezra-Nehemiah*, 296; such a temporary separation was not entirely implausible – witness God's commandment that the people separate themselves from their wives before the giving of the Torah.

One wonders why it was that the women generally remained loyal to their heritage while the men were so attracted to non-Jewish women. This appears to have been the case throughout post-exilic Jewish history, and the traditional commentaries reflect that reality. Indeed, it was the pattern of intermarriage until the late twentieth century, when, apparently for the first time, Jewish women were marrying out at an increasing rate – though that of men still remained higher.

Spurred on by Ezra, the men of Judah separated themselves from their wives and children, whom Nehemiah, and no doubt Ezra, labeled "foreign." The shattering of family units, no matter how much it was in conformity with Jewish norms, must nevertheless have been a traumatic event. Although Nehemiah does not elaborate, it is hard to believe that no tears were shed as husbands and fathers abandoned their families. Indeed, Nehemiah was to find sometime later that many of these families reunited, and he consequently decided upon a different method of combating the men's proclivity to marry out of the faith, focusing on the prevention of future intermarriage rather than dissolving those that had already taken place.

In the meantime, once the men had separated from their non-Jewish families, albeit it proved to be only temporarily, Ezra and the Levites continued with the ceremony. Once again they stood on a raised platform, in their places, and read "from the scroll of the teaching of the Lord their God for one-fourth of the day, and for another fourth they confessed and prostrated themselves before the Lord their God" (Neh. 9:3). Various rabbinic commentators view the program for the day as a model for all future fast days. According to one view, the first fourth of the day was to include the reading of the Torah (which indeed has been incorporated into the morning service of all fast days), the middle half was for contemplation of one's errors and sins, and the final fourth was dedicated to confession and prayer for forgiveness.[32] Others prescribed an even more rigorous schedule: one-fourth of the day for reading the Torah; one-fourth for confession; one-fourth for relating the past (*haggada*) and for the additional reading from the Prophets (*haftara*); and one-fourth dealing with the needs of the poor.[33]

32. Ralbag, Neh. 9:3, s.v. *vayikre'u*.
33. Mathews, *Commentary*, 28.

After the Torah reading, the Levites proceeded to exhort the assembled community to "Rise, bless the Lord your God who is from eternity to eternity: 'May Your glorious name be blessed, exalted though it is above every blessing and praise!'" (Neh. 9:5). The phrase "Rise, bless the Lord your God who is from eternity to eternity" may have been uttered responsively during the ceremony, first by the Levites and then by the assembled congregation.[34] It was incorporated into the standard congregational refrain after blessings uttered in the Temple service.[35] Indeed, the Talmud cites this refrain as support for its assertion that the congregation did not recite "Amen" during the Temple services (Taanit 16b). The phrase has since been incorporated into the High Holiday services.

Similarly, according to the Talmud, the phrase "May Your glorious name be blessed" is the origin of the Temple refrain "Blessed be His name and glorious sovereignty for ever and ever" (Berakhot 63a), which has since become the refrain uttered after the first verse of the *Shema* ("Hear, O Israel…") and is uttered three times at the conclusion of the Yom Kippur service.

Indeed, many of the passages in the long prayer that followed this initial exhortation were likewise incorporated into the siddur – for daily services, for Shabbat, for holidays, or for all three. Moreover, some elements of the prayer, such as the phrase "from eternity to eternity," were reformulations of passages from already extant Scripture, in this case Psalms (41:14 and 106:48), which added an element of familiarity for the assembled community and reinforced its sense of connection with past glories.

Ezra's recitation of the Jews' history, couched in the language of a prayer to God, incorporated a dual message. First, it offered a recapitulation of Jewish history as a function of the divine hand that guides it. In addition, it emphasized the Jews' persistent refusal to comply with God's statutes, their resulting punishment, and, with it, God's patient

34. Zer-Kavod, *Ezra UNeḥemia*, 110.

35. The response to blessings in the Temple service was "Blessed be the Lord God of Israel from eternity to eternity, blessed are You who redeems Israel"; see Taanit 16b. See also Ralbag, Neh. 9:5, s.v. *kumu*.

willingness to forgive. The opening passages of Ezra's prayer – "You alone are the Lord. You made the heavens, the highest heavens, and all their host, the earth and everything upon it, the seas and everything in them. You keep them all alive, and the host of heaven prostrate themselves before You" (Neh. 9:6) – have since become an integral part of the daily morning (Shaḥarit) service, including on festivals and fast days. In the Shaḥarit service, these passages serve as a prologue to the recitation of the biblical passages from Exodus that summarize the crossing of the Red Sea and cite the Song of the Sea that followed it. Similarly, Ezra's statement, beginning with God's covenant with Abraham to give him "the land of the Canaanite, the Hittite, the Amorite, the Perizzite, the Jebusite, and the Girgashite – to give it to his descendants" (9:8), with a recollection of the crossing of the Red Sea, also constitutes a major reading in the morning prayer. These verses also are read aloud on the occasion of a circumcision, whose Hebrew term *brit* (meaning "covenant") appears in this verse.

Ezra's prayers are also the source of many homiletical teachings. For example, the phrase "You keep them all alive" led the talmudic sage R. Ami b. R. Yitzḥak to assert that the angels are sustained by the splendor of God's essence (the *Shekhina*); R. Ḥanina b. Abba of Jaffa states that this phrase highlights the fact that God forces the soul to remain within the confines of the body.[36] In a similar vein, the rabbis interpret Ezra's use of the word "and" in his recounting of God's giving the people the laws, both on Mount Sinai and thereafter – "and You made known to them Your holy Sabbath" (Neh. 9:14) – to assert that the Israelites kept two Sabbaths prior to accepting the Torah.[37] Or again, the midrash draws upon Ezra's review of Israel's sins, notably their worship of the Golden Calf, which includes the passage, "They made themselves a molten calf and said, 'This is your God who brought you out of Egypt,' thus committing great impieties" (Neh. 9:18). One midrash seizes upon the plural noun "impieties" to assert that there were, in reality, thirteen calves, one for each tribe and one for the people as a whole.[38]

36. *Midrash Shoḥer Tov*, 138–39.

37. See commentary of Rabbi Isaac Katz, *Midrash Shoḥer Tov*, 181.

38. Dictum of R. Simon b. Yoḥai, *Midrash Shoḥer Tov*, 19.

Complementing and reinforcing the message of historical continuity – and therefore of national memory – are many other passages in the prayer that are reminiscent of phrases appearing in the Pentateuch, the Psalms, and elsewhere in the Scripture. Indeed, some are virtually identical to passages in earlier books of the Scripture. Interestingly, Josephus omits this entire prayer in his *Antiquities*, possibly in order to minimize the record of his people's sins in a book intended for a non-Jewish readership.

Although many of the above-mentioned passages appear in the section of the daily prayer that is meant solely to praise God, they were, in the context of Ezra's prayer, part of his admonition to the people regarding their sinfulness. Nevertheless, while scolding the people, Ezra also stressed God's compassion: "Refusing to obey, unmindful of Your wonders that You did for them, they stiffened their necks, and in their defiance resolved to return to their slavery. But You, being a forgiving God, gracious and compassionate, long-suffering and abounding in faithfulness, did not abandon them" (Neh. 9:17). Ezra emphasized that God's graciousness and compassion "are qualities which are never separable in the Bible from the thought of God."[39] Echoing the same idea later in his lengthy prayer, Ezra acknowledged that "surely You are in the right with respect to all that has come upon us, for You have acted faithfully, and we have been wicked" (9:33). His confession has resounded through the ages: it is recited in the confessional *Seliḥot* prayers of the days preceding Rosh HaShana (the Ten Days of Repentance) and in the Rosh HaShana and Yom Kippur services.

In the end, though, his prayer also had to recognize the reality in which the people found themselves. Accordingly, he concluded his prayer with a nationalist entreaty to God. "Today we are slaves," he said, "and the land that You gave our fathers to enjoy its fruit and bounty – here we are slaves on it! On account of our sins it yields its abundant crops to kings whom You have set over us. They rule over our bodies and our beasts as they please, and we are in great distress" (Neh. 9:36–37). Some biblical scholars are puzzled by Ezra's negative reference to a government known to have been a benevolent power. After all, Artaxerxes himself had granted both Ezra and Nehemiah permission to reorganize

39. Abraham J. Heschel, *The Prophets*, vol. II (New York: Harper Torchbooks, 1975), 65.

and strengthen the community in Judah. These scholars conclude that the outright claim to possession of the land, and the noxiousness of foreign dominance, are proof that the prayer could not have been part of the original material of the Book of Ezra (or Nehemiah), "for while Ezra-Nehemiah never loses sight of the unacceptability of foreign domination, allusions to it are carefully nuanced ... and are outweighed ... by the benevolent and providential aspects of Persian rule."[40]

In fact, however, the prayer was highly nuanced. It did not call for the overthrow of the Persian regime, and indeed mentioned no Jewish leader by name. There is thus no focus for an alternative authority, which is often central to a call for revolution and invariably the key to a revolt's success. Moreover, Ezra clearly posed no threat to Persian rule; he could not even get the people to follow him on matters of religion. The reference to foreign domination was meant primarily as a spur to penance rather than a call to arms.

Yet if the people did repent, Ezra seemingly implied, they would indeed merit God's help to restore their sovereignty over the land. There was no denying that the Jews were servants in their own land, paying taxes to foreign overlords, however benevolent the Persian overlords may have been. Foreign rule even reached down to their cattle and their own bellies. His phrase "they rule over our bodies and our beasts as they please" recalled the plea of the Egyptians to Joseph that he take their bodies as indentured servants in exchange for food, for that was all that was left to them.

Ezra's sentiment hardly was, or is, uncommon. Even the best-treated elites of a conquered people will not only resent their putatively inferior status, but often are the ones who take up the leadership of revolutionary causes. The Nehrus of India, the Bandarnaikes of Sri Lanka, Mandela in South Africa, and Jinnah of Pakistan all came from the upper echelons of their respective societies. Thus, while Ezra was not trying to raise the revolutionary standard, the import of his message was nevertheless clear: though free to practice their religion, the Jews were not free. Subjugation, however benevolent, is still subjugation. Ezra therefore concluded with a recognition of his people's downtrodden status, and their determination to serve God again, even in poverty.

---

40. Blenkinsopp, *Ezra-Nehemiah*, 301.

Nehemiah 10
The Jewish Constitution

A SOCIAL AND BIBLICAL COVENANT

Ezra ended his role in the spectacle after leading the people through emotional highs and lows, concluding with the undeniable reality that the people were not sovereign in their own land, but rather were "slaves" to their Persian overlords. Now it was Nehemiah's turn. He proceeded to preside over one of the least known yet most critical developments in Jewish political history since the fall of the Davidic dynasty, the destruction of the Temple, and the exile to Babylonia. He did nothing less than introduce a new constitution, the first of its kind in Jewish history, and perhaps the first of its kind anywhere.

A constitution is more than a code of law. It marks a commitment by a people to organize their governance according to agreed-upon principles. Nehemiah's covenant (*amana*), for that was what the constitution was called, involved a blend of practical social legislation and biblical jurisprudence. It reflected Nehemiah's determination to fashion a functioning, viable society that drew its lifeblood from its religious heritage but was not frozen in place by it.

Nehemiah's covenant more closely resembles a constitution than did the previous covenants to which the people of Israel had agreed – for example, the covenant on Mounts Gerizim and Eival prior to Moses's passing, or Jeremiah's covenant – not only because, unlike the others, acceptance was not accompanied by sacrifices, but because it went beyond imprecations to address a commitment to uphold very specific laws and practices. Moreover, while the covenant certainly committed the people to the keeping of Torah generally, its explicit list of obligations is noteworthy for its focus on the practicalities of supporting a functioning society. It specified commitments to provide financial support of various kinds to the Temple and its functionaries but did not focus on the nature of Temple ritual per se. It outlined several new restrictions to preserve the sanctity of the Sabbath, but limited them to what clearly upheld the integrity of a religious society. It demanded that there be no further dilution of the people's ethnic identity, but did not mandate radical solutions for doing so.

It is significant that the pledge extended the bounds of the Torah in some respects but not in others. It mandated extra-biblical practices with respect to the delivery and distribution of tithes, the scope of the law of giving first fruits, and the prohibition of conducting business on the Sabbath and festivals. But the pledge represented a significant step back from Ezra's ultimately unsuccessful demand that the Jewish men part from their non-Jewish wives. This demand was also extra-biblical, since the Jews had not intermarried with the indigenous Seven Nations of biblical days. Nehemiah accepted the principle that intermarriage with any non-Jewish nation was a threat to social cohesion. Nevertheless, while the pledge forbade new mixed marriages, it did not shatter those already in place.

The pledge has been called

> the archetype of the modern legal constitution... that is, it contains a lengthy preamble presenting the history of the nation... and its aspirations... followed by a detailed listing of basic laws, ordinances, and regulations required to give the covenant executive power. In addition to the Torah, which was defined as the accepted basic law, there was a sequence of social and economic legislation appropriate to the time and, only thereafter, a list of important persons setting their seals in the name of the people. By setting their seals, they pledged themselves to the first written

> constitution in history, the beginning of the modern concept of law as a mutual agreement among free men.[1]

This observation underscores the significance of the covenant in several respects. It implicitly accepts that social and economic values can be validated outside the narrow framework of the Torah. To some Jews today, such a notion is nothing less than anathema, if not blasphemy. Indeed, they can point to a midrash that seems to bolster their case. The midrash may possibly reflect the sensitivity of the rabbis to the implications for their own authority of the fact that people autonomously determined whether they were prepared to accept the binding nature of the covenant. The Midrash reinterprets the initial words of the covenant's opening sentence, "In view of all this, we make this pledge and put it in writing" (Neh. 10:1). Sidestepping the passage's literal meaning as a reference to the final, depressing words of Ezra's prayer, the rabbis saw the passage as an indication that because they accepted what they were commanded by the Torah, they were credited as if they had accepted the covenant's mandate of their own free will.[2] In this way, it was the leadership – Nehemiah – that was the source of authority; authority did not derive from the people.

In fact, however, the very nature of a constitution is that its acceptance is fundamentally an act of free will. If a constitution is indeed genuine – and not all are; that of the former Soviet Union is just one example of one that was not – it represents the very opposite of an authoritarian society governed from the top down. That was the case with respect to Nehemiah's covenant; not everyone signed the pledge, and there were many who refused to do so. Again, such a measure of free will has been unthinkable in certain Jewish circles since the late eighteenth century.

Even if the people were the source of the covenant's authority, it nevertheless reflected the fact that Nehemiah never veered from his primary objective. He sought to strengthen the fabric of society within the law. Where the law needed expansion and extension, he expanded and extended; where previous overextension threatened to undermine society, he contracted its scope. He certified his actions through vox

1. Steinsaltz, *Biblical Images*, 1–2 (see chap. 1, n. 3). See also Wiesel, *Sages and Dreamers*, 131.
2. Cited in Mathews, *Commentary*, 29.

populi, which truly was also vox Dei. But his document was a civil, not a religious, one – and that may be why Ezra was not one of its signatories.

A leading political scientist has this to say about the covenant and Nehemiah's intent in promulgating such a document:

> Covenant is less a theological concept than a theo-political one.... it seeks to both legitimize political life and direct it into the right paths; to use theo-political relationships to build a bridge between heaven and earth ... without letting either swallow up the other.... Humans abandon ... natural for federal liberty in order to live up to the terms of their covenants.... Leaders of the people are limited in their governmental powers to serving the people under the terms of the covenant. Thus the idea of constitutional or limited government is derived from the idea of government.[3]

He goes on to assert that Nehemiah reformed the *keter malkhut* (the role – literally "crown" – of the sovereign). Together with Ezra, Nehemiah "reconstituted the Israelite polity on a fully republican basis.... [In] their republic ... God is restored as undisputed king, with constitutionally more faithful human agents."[4]

It is unlikely that these interpretations of Nehemiah's approach, and perhaps even a modern version of the approach, would sit well with those who would advocate a theocracy in the modern State of Israel. In their view, all legislation must flow from the Torah; societal stability must never be a mitigating factor with respect to the breadth of religious authority; and man is not free to choose to submit to what Jean-Jacques Rousseau first termed the "social contract."

THE COVENANT'S SIGNATORIES

Like so many constitutions in future generations and in states around the world, the covenant was appended with a host of signatures. The

3. Daniel J. Elazar, *Covenant & Polity in Biblical Israel: Biblical Foundations & Jewish Expressions,* vol. 1: *Of the Covenant Tradition in Politics* (New Brunswick, NJ and London: Transaction, 1996), 1.
4. Ibid.

document was signed by the priests, the Levites, and the community's senior officials. Who all these people were is the subject of conflicting interpretations. The midrash claims that there were a total of 120 signatories, and identifies them as the Men of the Great Assembly.[5] The Jerusalem Talmud speaks of eighty-three signers (Y. Ḥagiga 20a). An actual count of the names listed yields eighty-four, however. The total comes to eighty-five if the name Shephatiah is added; it does not appear in the Hebrew text, but is in the *Peshiteta* translation. The latter figure corresponds to the number of "elders" who, the Jerusalem Talmud asserts, agonized over the propriety of adding Purim to the religious calendar (Y. Megilla 7a).[6]

There are difficulties with these interpretations, however. To begin with, as noted, Ezra was not one of the signatories – yet the Talmud names him as a member, indeed the founder, of the Great Assembly. In addition, according to the Talmud, Mordekhai of Purim fame was a member of the Great Assembly, yet he too is not listed. A more recent traditionalist interpretation, drawing on the Jerusalem Talmud, counts eighty-three signatories, seventy from the Sanhedrin and thirteen ex officio, whose positions are listed by Maimonides.[7] This explanation may avoid the awkwardness associated with the claim that the signatories were the Great Assembly, but it suffers from the difficulty that the number it addresses does not correspond to the Hebrew text, nor, for that matter, to any translation.[8]

5. See Wiesel, *Sages and Dreamers,* 130–31. Zeitlin (*Rise and Fall,* 24) also sees the signatories as Men of the Great Assembly, as does Yoel Bin-Nun, "*Anshei Knesset HaGedola Hem Ḥotmei HaAmana BeMaamad Ezra UNeḥemia*" (The Men of the Great Assembly Were the Signatories of the Covenant in the Presence of Ezra and Nehemiah), *Mishlav* 36 (2001): 5–20.
6. See Galil, *Daniel, Ezra UNeḥemia,* 276.
7. Malbim, Neh. 10:2, s.v. *ve'al.*
8. Galil, *Daniel, Ezra UNeḥemia,* 271–72, and others assert that the signatories could not have been the Men of the Great Assembly. It is argued that Nehemiah was a secular leader, and since he was the first to sign the document, it could not have been linked to the Great Assembly, which was a rabbinic group. Yet the Talmud considers Nehemiah part of the Assembly. It is also argued that the High Priest was always associated with the Assembly; proof is cited from Avot 1:4, which refers to Simon the Just (a High Priest) as a "remnant of the Great Assembly." This argument too falls flat, since the fact that Simon was a member in no way signifies that his predecessors likewise were members ex officio, as it were.

Whatever the actual number of signatories, the first signature was that of Nehemiah. He signed as the *tirshata*, the governor, perhaps to render the document official not only in Jewish but also in Persian terms. Two of the following three names – Zedekiah and Azariah – were, like that of Nehemiah, the names of individuals. Apart from the named Levites, however, the remainder of the names were clans, not individuals. Who signed for the clans is unknown.

Zedekiah may possibly have been another name for Zadok, whom Nehemiah subsequently appointed as treasurer (Neh. 13:13). As one of Nehemiah's top officials and a scribe, Zadok merited the number-two position on the list. Others see the name as that of a priestly family, though the evidence to support this assertion is uncertain.

While Zadok the scribe appears to have signed after Nehemiah, the fact that the far more famous scribe, Ezra, does not appear on the list has led some modern scholars to conclude that the chapter that describes the covenant, while part of the "Nehemiah memoir," is misplaced and belongs at the end of the book, since it bears several similarities with the final chapter of the memoir. Others consider the source of this chapter to be entirely independent of either Ezra or Nehemiah. The "Chronicler," the mythical editor of Chronicles who supposedly also wrote the books of Ezra and Nehemiah, inserted it into the narrative, "representing the Chronicler's view of the completion of Ezra's mission in which ... the law book figures prominently."[9]

The omission of Ezra's name may, however, have resulted from the fact that this covenant was a civil rather than religious document. Alternatively, it is possible that the Azariah, who signed the covenant after Zedekiah, was actually Ezra, though, as has already been pointed out, it is difficult to argue that the two names are interchangeable.[10] If Azariah was another name for Ezra, the question arises why he signed

9. For a discussion, see Shaver, *Torah*, 84–85 (see chap. 4, n. 7); see also Cross, *From Epic to Canon*, 160, who ascribes the insertion to the "final" editor, "Chronicler 3."

10. For example, Joshua is also called Jeshua; King Uzziah is also called Azariah. See Blenkinsopp, *Ezra-Nehemiah*, 311. On the other hand, Zer-Kavod does not conclusively assert that it is Ezra, possibly because the name Ezra in Aramaic does not include a letter to connote God, as does the Hebrew Azariah (and as does Rabbi Saadia, for example, which is also an Aramaic name).

only after Zedekiah and not before him. Surely, as noted, he was the more prominent of the two. That he did not sign first may be yet another indication of Ezra's waning influence in Judean society, particularly in light of the fact that the covenant was not a religious document. While Ezra certainly played a prominent role in the public ceremony that had just taken place, this was no indication of his real power now that Nehemiah was the undisputed leader of the community. By this time, Ezra may have become a figurehead, representing on paper, as it were, the spiritual side of the community, but having little practical influence over its administration.

As noted, in addition to the priests and the Levites, senior officials – more accurately, the clans they represented – also signed the covenant. They were listed as "the heads of the people" (Neh. 10:15) and their appearance on the list must have had political significance. The previous lists of those who returned with Zerubbabel counted seventeen clans. The covenant, on the other hand, listed only fourteen of those clans. In place of the three it omitted, three other – evidently new – clans appeared as signatories. Another difference from previous lists, likewise with possible political implications, is that some additional clans beyond the seventeen were listed as covenant signatories. Many of the clans were named for people who were involved in the construction of the wall.

Apparently the societal rifts were far from healed, and not all the clans were willing to sign the pledge.[11] Some clan leaders may even have been prevented by their followers from participating in the ceremony.[12] On the other hand, the clans that supported Nehemiah appear to have been staunch supporters of his new constitution. Nehemiah sought to reinforce the power of the pledge by collecting the signatures of the newly established clans that were obviously loyal to him; indeed, he most assuredly had a hand in the establishment of this new elite.

At least one of the clans that signed the covenant, Meshezabel, may have had divided loyalties. Meshullam son of Berechiah, a prominent member of the clan, took part in the construction of the wall, but

11. Zer-Kavod, *Ezra UNeḥemia*, 119.

12. Galil, *Daniel, Ezra UNeḥemia*, 279.

nevertheless was also linked by marriage to Nehemiah's enemy Tobiah. Though clan generally took precedence over all other loyalties, as remains evident in much of the contemporary Arab Middle East, this appears not to have been the case with the Meshezabel clan. That they signed the covenant indicates that Nehemiah was making inroads even among those closest to his adversaries.

In addition to the signatories, "the rest of the people, the priests, the Levites, the gatekeepers, the singers, the Temple servants, and all who separated themselves from the peoples of the lands to [follow] the Teaching of God, their wives, sons, and daughters, all who know enough to understand" (Neh. 10:29) took an oath to uphold the covenant. The oath that the mass of the people took in place of their signatures underscored the action of their leaders, who pressed their brethren to follow the Torah.[13] Some biblical scholars have asserted that the taking of an oath seems to have been "based on actual Temple practice."[14] In truth, Scripture frowns upon oath-taking. An oath was permitted in this case because "it is permitted to strengthen one's resolve to perform a mitzvah by swearing to fulfill it."[15] The Jews swore both to "follow the Teaching of God, given through Moses the servant of God, and to observe carefully all the commandments of the Lord" (Neh. 10:30). "Follow" (or "fulfill") refers to positive commandments; "observe," to negative ones. The traditional view is that the Jews swore to observe all the commandments, not merely those enumerated in the covenant.[16]

THE CONTENT OF THE COVENANT: NEHEMIAH'S CONCERNS

The actual text of the covenant was a list of selected issues that reflected Nehemiah's primary concerns. It was not exhaustive and certainly did not address the gamut of religious law. First on the list, and clearly uppermost in Nehemiah's mind, was the issue of intermarriage. The reference to "all who separated themselves" may have been to converts to Judaism

13. Ralbag, Neh. 10:30, s.v. *maḥzikim*.
14. Grabbe, *Ezra-Nehemiah*, 58.
15. Rabinowitz, *Nechemiah*, 172 (see chap. 1, n. 24).
16. Rabinowitz, loc. cit.

together with their families.[17] Alternatively, the reference may have been to Jews who indeed had married out of the faith but nevertheless committed themselves to the future purity of the nation. They had not abandoned their non-Jewish wives and children, and were not asked to.

From this perspective, Nehemiah and his pledge were less demanding than Ezra's policy, which required complete separation from non-Jewish spouses. Focusing solely on what he considered to be the negative impact that intermarriage had on the cohesion of the Jewish community, Ezra had sought to break up intermarried families, presumably without regard to the impact of such breakups on the people themselves or their children. He failed miserably. He simply was overreaching as he sought to bring an end to what had become a widespread practice throughout the Jewish community, at all economic and social levels.

Recognizing that the absolute dissolution of so many family units would be far more destructive to the community than the results of the scourge of intermarriage, Nehemiah took a different, more practical approach – but in modern halakhic terms it would be considered highly controversial. He focused on the future, not the present, and had the signers of the covenant pledge: "We will not give our daughters in marriage to the peoples of the land, or take their daughters for our sons" (Neh. 10:31). This pledge applied to all non-Jews, not only the biblically banned Seven Nations.[18] It targeted the male heads of households, who in ancient times – and indeed until the twentieth century – invariably determined whom their daughters could marry, and negotiated marriage terms, and dowries, with the parents of their sons' prospective wives.

No doubt many of the men who were prepared to give their daughters in marriage to non-Jews or to accept non-Jewish women for their sons had themselves married non-Jewish women. For them, intermarriage was as much a norm as inmarriage. Nehemiah shrewdly recognized that were he to attempt to force these men to divorce their

17. Zer-Kavod, *Ezra UNeḥemia,* 120; Rashi, Neh. 10:29, s.v. *vekhol.* Blenkinsopp, *Ezra-Nehemiah,* 314, points out that this is an allusion to proselytism in the early Second Temple period.

18. Malbim, Neh. 10:31, s.v. *vaasher.*

wives, not only would they resist (as they had resisted Ezra), but they would continue to marry off their children to non-Jewish spouses. So Nehemiah compromised and obtained a pledge that he hoped would bring an end to intermarriage in the next generation (a generation was roughly a decade, given the practice of betrothing children at an early age). He would later discover that he had been no more successful than Ezra.

The difference between Ezra and Nehemiah on the question of how to receive converts has continued to reverberate throughout the centuries. It is a challenge with echoes in contemporary Diaspora Jewish life and is at the heart of some of the most bitter disputes both within Israel and between Israel and the main Diaspora communities. Ezra's response to intermarriage foreshadowed that of contemporary Orthodox leaders. On the other hand, Nehemiah's approach would not be acceptable to many Orthodox rabbis today, though some, notably the great Sephardic decisor Chief Rabbi Ben-Zion Uziel, advocate a far more welcoming approach to the children of non-Jewish mothers who wish to convert than the more rigid stance taken by the majority of Ashkenazic rabbinic leaders.[19]

It is noteworthy that Maimonides credits Ezra, not Nehemiah, with instigating the pledge not to intermarry and applying it to all non-Jews[20] – not only to the biblically proscribed Seven Nations, who, in any event, no longer were identifiable, since they had been exiled by the Assyrian king Sennacherib.[21] It is possible that Maimonides identified Ezra as the author of the injunction because Nehemiah does not explicitly state that he formulated the covenant; perhaps, too, Maimonides could not conceive of a layman like Nehemiah formulating any religious legislation in the presence of Ezra, the acknowledged religious leader. It is equally possible, however, that Maimonides simply conflated the two men, since in the twelfth century the two books had not yet been treated separately.[22]

---

19. Rabbi Ben-Zion Uziel, *Mishpetei Uziel*, vol. 2: *Yoreh De'ah* (Tel Aviv, 1935), no. 14, 157.
20. *Mishneh Torah, Hilkhot Isurei Bia* 12:1; Avoda Zara 36b.
21. "Sennacherib jumbled all the nations"; Berakhot 28a.
22. Interestingly, the Talmud credits neither Ezra nor Nehemiah, attributing the more extensive ruling against intermarriage either to the "Hasmonean Bet Din" or to the first-century BCE Academy of Shammai, known as Beit Shammai. See Shabbat 17b; see also Avoda Zara 36b and Rashi ad loc., s.v. *d'oraita*.

Nehemiah's second major concern was the wholesale violation of the Sabbath. "The peoples of the land who bring their wares and all sorts of foodstuffs for sale on the Sabbath day – we will not buy from them on the Sabbath or a holy day" (Neh. 10:32). In actuality, the people were not violating a biblical law. When the sages of the Talmud banned trade or any form of business on the Sabbath, it was to prevent the associated writing – deeds, receipts, bills of sale, and so forth – that constituted the actual biblical injunction. Nehemiah was imposing on the people what later came to be termed a rabbinic injunction.[23]

Nehemiah's action was taken by later generations of rabbis as a basis for their assertion of the power to legislate "protective measures," or, as they often called it, "a fence," around biblical law to ensure that biblical commandments were not violated (Avot 1:1; Nidda 3b). At the same time, however, it was the traditional view that the rabbinic prohibition was already in effect well before Nehemiah's day. The people now accepted a further restraint beyond that on doing business in general, namely, to refrain from the purchase of any produce that non-Jews had brought to the Jerusalem market on the Sabbath as well as on those days of the festivals when most forms of work were proscribed.[24]

Nehemiah next turned to two major agricultural issues that had vexed the community since his arrival. His focus was on the sabbatical year (*Shemitta*), whose special status the rich systematically ignored, both by continuing to plow their fields in violation of the explicit biblical prohibition to do so and by refusing to cancel debts, as the Torah also mandated. Of course, by refusing to cancel debts, the rich were able to continue to exploit poor tenant farmers who otherwise would have been relieved of their financial burden every seven years.

That Nehemiah was able to get the leaders of the community to agree in writing to "forgo [the] produce of the seventh year and every outstanding debt" was a signal and revolutionary accomplishment. Violations of the sabbatical year had already become commonplace

23. Malbim, Neh. 10:32, s.v. *ve'amei*. See also Ralbag 10:31, s.v. *vaasher*. Ralbag (10:32, s.v. *vekhol*) also includes in the covenant the commitment to observe the sabbatical year with respect both to letting the land lie fallow and to forgiving debts.

24. Rabinowitz, *Nechemiah*, 173.

during the last days of the First Temple. Moreover, there may have been a tradition – certainly it is represented in the Talmud – that because the Jubilee year could not come into force until the land was fully settled by Jews, neither could the sabbatical year.[25] Thus the biblical strictures related to the sabbatical year could legitimately be ignored. Nehemiah essentially ruled that the link between the two types of years was insufficiently strong to obviate the laws of *Shemitta*; the laws of the Jubilee year might not be in force, but those of the sabbatical year surely were.[26]

The commitment made in the covenant came to the fore in the early twentieth century, when the question of *Shemitta* reemerged for the first time in fifteen hundred years as Jews began to resettle Palestine, establishing agricultural kibbutzim and moshavim. Rabbi Abraham Isaac Kook, the first Ashkenazic chief rabbi of Palestine, ruled that it was possible to circumvent many of the strictures relating to *Shemitta* by means of selling land to local Muslims (*heter mekhira*).[27] Even Rabbi Kook did not issue a blanket relaxation of the law, however. For example, he circumscribed this leniency by stipulating that it only applied to what was essential for the preservation of existing settlements, not to their expansion.[28]

Issues relating to *Shemitta* have become increasingly complex with the creation of the State of Israel and the increasing sophistication of the agricultural sector; at the same time, Rabbi Kook's ruling has not gone unchallenged, particularly in the past two decades. Some, drawing upon the ruling of Rabbi Abraham Isaiah Karelitz (1878–1953, better known by his works entitled *Ḥazon Ish*) around the time of the state's creation, have recommended alternative ways to avoid the impact of *Shemitta*. Others have argued against any form of circumvention.[29]

---

25. See Malbim, Neh. 10:32, s.v. *venitosh*.
26. Ibid.; Arakhin 32b; Rabinowitz, *Nechemiah*, 174.
27. Rabbi Abraham Isaac HaCohen Kook, *Mishpat Kohen* (Jerusalem: Mossad Harav Kook, 5753/1985), no. 58, 119–24.
28. Ibid., 124–25.
29. For a discussion, see Rabbi Yinon Veisman, "*'Heter Mekhira' o 'Otzar Beit Din'*" ("Permit to Sell" or "The Court's Storehouse"), *Teḥumin* 27 (5767/2007): 36–45. The literature relating to *Shemitta* in modern Israel has literally exploded, and continues to grow, especially prior to each new *Shemitta* year.

In any event, Nehemiah's ruling provided the foundation for all subsequent discussion of this issue.

The next set of commitments in the covenant dealt with contributions to the Temple, whose operations appear to have been underfunded. The signatories stated:

> We have laid upon ourselves obligations: To charge ourselves one-third of a shekel yearly for the service of the House of our God – for the rows of bread, for the regular meal offering, and for the regular burnt offering, [for those of the] Sabbaths, new moons, festivals, for consecrations, for sin offerings to atone for Israel, and for all the work in the House of our God. (Neh. 10:33–34)

The pledge represented an act of good will, because the people were voluntarily accepting a new set of obligations; for this reason, and from this verse, the rabbis deduced that "good deeds are equivalent to all the commandments."[30]

Another rabbinical deduction was based on the fact that while the covenant spoke of multiple obligations, the passage only involves one, namely, a single contribution from every Jew. Accordingly, the rabbis of the Talmud concluded that the use of the plural form was an indication that charity (the third of the shekel) is equivalent to compliance with all the commandments (Bava Batra 9a).

The actual sum mentioned, a third of a shekel, posed problems for traditional commentators, since the biblical commandment was for a half-shekel to support Temple operations and maintenance. Some argued that the third of a shekel was an additional levy, especially meant for the operation and maintenance of the Temple and the activities mentioned in the pledge.[31] Another view was that the weight of the shekel had changed, and Nehemiah's third of a shekel was equivalent to

30. Mathews, *Commentary*, 29.

31. Ibn Ezra, Neh. 10:33, s.v. *shlishit*. Ibn Yahia appears to be of the same opinion (ad loc., s.v. *vehe'emadnu*); see also Metzudat David ad loc., s.v. *vehe'emadnu*; Malbim ad loc., s.v. *shlishit*.

the old half-shekel.[32] Still another view was that it was the minimum acceptable charitable donation.[33] Finally, the Talmud seems to indicate that the one-third-shekel tax replaced the annual half-shekel commitment; moreover, in line with Nehemiah's preferences, the new allotment replaced the royal treasury as the source of Temple sacrifices.[34]

The "rows of bread" to which the covenant referred was the shewbread (*leḥem hapanim*), which was a Temple fixture, and had to be replaced every week.[35] Some translate the "regular meal offering" as also incorporating drink offerings; the offering actually consisted of both a meal offering and a libation of wine.[36] Yet another interpretation is that the words really indicate the incense that was also part of the Temple offering. Finally, the consecrations have been interpreted as indicating the special communal peace offerings and sin offerings.[37] Whatever their specific indication or meaning, the words in this portion of the covenant reflect Nehemiah's determination that the people become far more invested in the Temple and its ritual than they had been prior to his arrival and their assent to this goal. Since the centrality of the Temple was crucial to the sense of national identity, it was imperative that the people be attached to it in a material way.

The next passage in the covenant was a statement that incorporated a commitment. It said that the people "had cast lots [among] the priests, the Levites, and the people, to bring the wood offering to the House of our God by clans annually at set times in order to provide fuel for the altar of the Lord our God, as it is written in the Teaching" (Neh. 10:35). These lots were cast to establish a permanent rota so as to ensure that the Temple pyres could be maintained without interruption.[38] To that end, the wood was replenished nine times a year, but not on festival days.[39]

---

32. Ralbag, Neh. 10:33, s.v. *latet*. Malbim on Neh. 10:33 also offers this explanation.
33. Rabinowitz, *Nechemiah*, 174, citing *Shulḥan Arukh, Yoreh De'ah* 249:1–2.
34. Urbach, *The Halakhah*, 52 (see chap. 5, n. 24).
35. Ralbag, Neh. 10:34, s.v. *leleḥem*; Metzudat David ad loc., s.v. *leleḥem*.
36. Metzudat David, Neh. 10:34, s.v. *uminḥat*. See also Rabinowitz, *Nechemiah*, 17.
37. Ralbag, Neh. 10:34, s.v. *velakodoshim*.
38. Ibid. 10:33, s.v. *latet*.
39. The Talmud identifies the nine dates: 1 Nisan; 20 Tammuz; 5, 7, 10, 15, 20 Av; 20 Elul; and 1 Tevet (Taanit 26a).

Everyone was included in the rotation so that they could derive merit for supporting the Temple's operations.[40] Nehemiah, as was his wont, sought to distribute the financial burden of Temple upkeep as widely as possible, so as to minimize its impact on any one segment of society. For their part, the people committed to maintaining the rota. The wood offering that the people promised to provide is not mentioned in the Pentateuch, "perhaps," as one scholar has surmised, "because it would be illogical to do so in a context conventionally identified with the wilderness"[41] – although the Torah outlines numerous commandments that only are applicable in the Land of Israel.

The people next undertook to

> bring to the House of the Lord annually the first fruits of our soil, and of every fruit of every tree; also the firstborn of our sons and our beasts, as is written in the Teaching; and to bring the firstlings of our cattle and flocks to the House of our God for the priests who minister in the House of our God. (Neh. 10:36–37)

The core of these obligations was biblical; clearly they were not being properly fulfilled. Because the word "annually" appears to be a redundancy, the Talmud seizes upon it as really referring to the previous requirement to replenish the Temple woodpile. It asserts that the prophets extended a privilege to the families that had already been providing wood to the Temple since their return from the exile: the privilege of bringing the annual firewood donation, even if there was enough wood already available (Taanit 28a).

The commitment to bring first fruit, like the one regarding the wood, extended beyond the obligation outlined in the Torah. The Torah only demands the first fruits of the vine, the fig, olive, and pomegranate trees, and the date palm. The covenant called for the provision of first fruit from every tree. This wider obligation was another example of Nehemiah's commitment to what later became commonly identified as "rabbinic" – that is, extra-biblical – ordinances, which over time have

40. Ibn Yahia, Neh. 10:35, s.v. *vehagoralot.*

41. Coggins, *Ezra and Nehemiah,* 123.

become so thoroughly intertwined with those of the Bible that it is often difficult for non-scholars to distinguish which is which.

The next undertaking was of a biblical nature. The people would redeem the firstborn of their sons for five shekels – the custom of *pidyon haben*, still in practice. They would also redeem the firstborn of their animals, including non-kosher animals, "and ... bring the firstlings of our cattle and flocks to the House of our God for the priests who minister in the House of our God" (Neh. 10:37).

The covenant then continued with yet another commitment designed as a subvention for the operation and maintenance of the Temple:

> We will bring to the storerooms of the House of our God the first part of our dough, and our gifts [of grain], and of the fruit of every tree, wine, and oil for the priests, and the tithes of our land for the Levites ... who collect the tithe in all our towns subject to the royal service. (Neh. 10:38)

There is some uncertainty as to whether all or some of these gifts remained biblical obligations after the Babylonian exile, as were the redemption of the firstborn and the provision of first fruit to the priests. Maimonides rules that all gifts to the priests, as well as to the Levites, from the Second Temple era onward are post-biblical, that is, "rabbinic" obligations. His great critic, Rabbi Abraham ibn Daud (1125–1198), better known as Raavad, was of the view that gifts of grain, wine, and oil remained biblically obligatory, while other gifts to the priests and Levites, as well as the donation of dough, were rabbinic innovations imposed on the people.[42] Regardless of origin, the system that Nehemiah established for bringing gifts to the priests was innovative; it ensured that the priests would not have to leave their posts in order to search the fields for the gifts that were their livelihood.[43]

---

42. *Mishneh Torah, Hilkhot Terumot* 1:26 and *Hasagat HaRaavad*, loc. cit.; *Mishneh Torah, Hilkhot Maaser* 1:7. See also *Yalkut Shimoni* II:697 and Rabinowitz, *Nechemiah*, 176–77.
43. Num. 18:26–29; Metzudat David, Neh. 10:40, s.v. *velo*.

Nehemiah was not merely accommodating the priests. His primary concern was that the order of the Temple ritual not be interrupted. He did not want the priests scurrying to and fro in search of gifts while abandoning their responsibilities in the Temple.

The covenant continued with the revival of biblical practices designed to ensure the smooth functioning of the Temple ritual and of the functionaries who conducted and supported the ritual. It focused on the Levitical obligation to convey to the priests a tenth of the gifts they received, or, as the covenant termed it, "the tithe of a tithe" (Neh. 10:39). The covenant provided that "a priest must be with the Levites when they collect the tithe, and the Levites must bring up a tithe of the tithe to the House of our God, to the storerooms of the treasury" (ibid.). By mandating the presence of a priest when the Levites received the tithe, Nehemiah ensured that the Levites would not avoid their obligation to tithe their own tithe.[44] They were commanded to bring the tithe of their tithe to the Temple storeroom, where, as the covenant indicated, "the equipment of the sanctuary and of the ministering priests and the gatekeepers and the singers" (10:40) also was stored; the Persian imperial taxes, too, were kept there while awaiting shipment to Ecbatana or Susa or one of the other Persian capitals.[45]

This law is particularly noteworthy in that it demonstrates that while Nehemiah drew his political support from the Levites, he did not view their support as a vehicle or a reason for bending the laws in their favor. In this regard he differed from many politicians, not only in past centuries but also in contemporary times.

Some traditional commentators surmised that the priests also were entitled to the tithe that had in the past been the preserve of the Levites.[46] This opinion is based on the talmudic ruling that the Levites were penalized for not accompanying Ezra from Babylonia (Ezra 8:15)

44. Ralbag, Neh. 10:39, s.v. *vehaya*.
45. See Joachim Schaper, "The Temple Treasury Committee in the Times of Ezra and Nehemiah," *Vetus Testamentum* 47 (April 1997): 203–5. See also Urbach, *The Halakhah*, 45, and the discussion below, chapter 14.
46. Malbim, Neh. 10:39, s.v. *vehaya*.

and lost their exclusive right to the tithe.[47] It is unlikely that Nehemiah would have gone so far as to offend what he had himself helped to create as his core constituency. It was one thing to enforce the biblical standard and monitor the behavior of the Levites; he would not allot to the Levites what was not rightfully theirs. It was quite another thing, however, to deprive them of their income. It is possible that the penalty was imposed only for a brief period, and was rescinded by Nehemiah when he returned to Judah for his second tour of duty.[48]

Having outlined a series of commitments on the part of the society's various estates to maintain and support the Temple and its activities, the covenant concluded with a summary statement: "We will not neglect the House of our God" (Neh. 10:40). The series of events that Nehemiah described, beginning with Ezra's peroration and concluding with the covenant, may have served as a model for later, similar ceremonies in ancient Judea. Most notably, the Qumran scroll known as the "Community Rule" established "requirements for entry into the community, with special liturgical functions for Priests and Levites.... The ceremony ends...with solemn undertakings entered into by all those present."[49]

The brief final sentence of the covenant encapsulates the essence of Nehemiah's approach to what in our time is often termed "nation-building." Strengthening the city walls, even populating the city, did not, in and of itself, provide the cohesion necessary to restore a true sense of nationhood to the Jews who had left Babylonia. Their uniqueness as a people lay in the combination of their national and religious heritage.

---

47. This was the opinion of R. Elazar b. Azariah, himself a priest. R. Akiva disagreed (Yevamot 86a–b). *Tosafot,* s.v. *mai,* suggest that even according to the view that it was the poor who benefited from the tithe that the Levites forfeited, poor priests were eligible to be among those who received it. A discussion in Ḥullin 131b indicates that R. Elazar reflected the prevailing view and practice during the later Temple period. For a modern critical exposition of the statement in the Talmud, see Blenkinsopp, *Ezra-Nehemiah,* 318.
48. See comments of Rabbi Yosef Karo, *Kesef Mishneh,* s.v. *veEzra,* in *Mishneh Torah, Hilkhot Maaser* 1:4.
49. Coggins, *Ezra and Nehemiah,* 122.

It was not enough simply to fulfill commandments that forged closer religious bonds among the people but did not pull them toward a central magnet that would foster their collective religious and national identity. To achieve this objective, institutions needed to be established that embodied the history that had forged a religious nation in the first place, "a nation of priests and a holy people" as the Torah aptly put it (Ex. 19:6). The Temple – with its ritual and its functionaries – embodied that heritage, and was the heartbeat of the people.

Subsequent history has shown that the Jewish people could survive without a Temple. It was the genius of the rabbis, notably R. Yoḥanan b. Zakkai, whose accommodation with Vespasian allowed for the flourishing of Torah at Yavne, that enabled the survival of Jews and Judaism. But while the Temple existed, it was meant to be the true focus of the people. The fact that Nehemiah had to include a commitment couched in what was essentially a double negative – "We will not neglect" – indicates the degree to which the Temple had in fact been neglected. By preserving the Temple and all that it stood for, Nehemiah safeguarded Jewish identity for another five hundred years.

Nehemiah 11
Repopulating Jerusalem

BRINGING THE LEADERSHIP TO JERUSALEM

Nehemiah had held off on taking any action to repopulate the near-empty city of Jerusalem, which naturally would have involved the uprooting of families from their ancestral homes, until he obtained the commitments outlined in the covenant. With the future of the Temple's operations and its maintenance now ensured, in addition to the walls having been restored and fortified, Jerusalem held the promise of being a secure magnet for religious as well as commercial activity. Repopulating the city represented another essential stage in restoring its ancient glory[1] so that it once again would be Isaiah's "holy city" (Neh. 11:1; Is. 48:2).[2] Jerusalem's new and potentially even more attractive status perhaps rendered it a far easier sell to those who might otherwise drag their heels about taking up residence there.

Nehemiah began with the clerical and lay leaders, whom he describes as "the officers" (Neh. 11:1). It made sense for the Temple functionaries – the priests and Levites – to live near their place of work. Some already were living there, and Nehemiah supplemented their number. Nehemiah also needed men who could muster for service if

1. See Oded Lipschits, "Literary and Ideological Aspects of Nehemiah 11," *Journal of Biblical Literature* 121 (Autumn 2002): 424, 431, 440.
2. The term appears in only one other place in Scripture, Dan. 9:24.

the defense of the city became necessary; it made no sense to fortify the city if no one manned its ramparts.[3]

Among the priests who had previously moved to the city was Ezra's father, Seraiah, "son of Hilkiah son of Meshullam son of Zadok son of Meraioth son of Ahitub, chief officer of the House of God" (Neh. 11:11). Seraiah was one of the three officers for the priestly houses of Jedaiah, Pashhur, and Immer. His title, "chief officer" (in Hebrew, *nagid*), could also designate a secular ruler – for example, in later generations, the talmudic commentator who served as grand vizier of Granada was Rabbi Shmuel "HaNagid."

Some contemporary scholars argue that this title implies that the priests had powers beyond the religious sphere – similar to bishops in the Middle Ages, or today, to imams in Iran, for example. Such a concept would parallel the notion of *daat Torah*, which requires rabbinical blessing for activities ranging from the most mundane to matters of national security strategy, and which has become prevalent in the contemporary yeshiva world. This is unlikely to have been the case, however, because Nehemiah's governmental and quasi-religious role was the antithesis of clerical rule, whether the Iranian version or that which comes under the rubric of *daat Torah*. While he was a religious man – indeed, he legislated and enforced religious ordinances – he was first and foremost a secular leader, and that certainly was how the people perceived him.

It likewise was natural for other leading officials to live in Jerusalem – there was no commuting to work in those days. The challenge for Nehemiah was to get artisans and others who would support the local economy to settle in the city for practical reasons.[4] There was, of course, the obvious need to populate empty parts of the city; the new walls extended the city's area, parts of which were bereft of inhabitants, and these areas had to be settled for security reasons.[5] In addition, Nehemiah wanted to ensure that Jerusalem did not become an isolated bastion for the elite, who would have to call in outsiders to perform routine day-to-day

3. See Williamson, *Ezra, Nehemiah*, 354.
4. Blenkinsopp, *Ezra-Nehemiah*, 323.
5. Rashi, Neh. 11:1, s.v. *eḥad min haasara*. See also Myers, *Ezra/Nehemiah*, 186 (see chap. 1, n. 35).

tasks, as was the case with the helots of ancient Sparta, or, more recently, apartheid-era South Africa, where blacks lived in impoverished townships outside the main cities and commuted to serve the urban white class.

Among the officials who moved to the city were three new deputies whom Nehemiah appointed to manage civil affairs in Jerusalem: Joel son of Zichri, of the tribe of Judah, for the tribesmen; Zabdiel son of Haggedolim for the priests; and Uzzi son of Bani son of Hashabiah son of Mattaniah son of Micha, of the Asaphite singers, to oversee the Levites, and particularly to distribute Artaxerxes's funds for Temple expenses.[6] Uzzi was a scion of an especially prominent family. Asaph, David's contemporary, had authored numerous psalms. He is reputed to have been an old man who had "fasted and prayed" that the Holy City be rebuilt in his days.[7] Mattaniah was the lead Levite of the first round of *mishmarot*, the yearlong rotation of priestly and Levitical service in the Temple.[8] He was head singer and the first to sing, as well as head Levite, in charge of the gatekeepers and singers.[9]

The singers, whom Nehemiah identified apart from the general community of Levites, had a special subvention supporting their role in the Temple services that may have been the direct result of Nehemiah's arrival on the scene and his alliance with them. Apparently Artaxerxes, no doubt at Nehemiah's instigation, "issued a royal order… concerning the daily duties of the singers."[10] The order consisted of a stipulation that the general public provide daily support for the needs of the singers. The separate reference to the singers appears to have been a political statement, specifically indicating Nehemiah's support and concern for their welfare. Evidently, the singers were second-class members of the

6. Ralbag, Neh 11:22, s.v. *ufekid*.
7. Mathews, *Commentary*, 30.
8. Ibn Yahia, Neh. 11:17, s.v. *rosh*.
9. Zer-Kavod, *Ezra UNeḥemia*, 127. See also Rashi, Neh. 11:17, s.v. *rosh*.
10. Neh. 11:23. Ralbag (s.v. *vaamana*) asserts that Artaxerxes issued the order. Rashi, s.v. *al*, says it was Darius, though he may simply have been following talmudic lore in conflating Darius with Artaxerxes and, for that matter, Cyrus. Others assert that the reference is to King David's order, such as those referenced in 12:24 and 12:45. (See Blenkinsopp, *Ezra-Nehemiah*, 327; Zer-Kavod, *Ezra UNeḥemia*, 128; and Galil, *Daniel, Ezra UNeḥemia*, 294.)

Levitical clan; they may not have had the same privileges or benefits as the others. Since Nehemiah relied heavily on the Levites, particularly as a countervailing force to the priests, he may have sought to bring about unity and comity within the Levitical camp.

Finally, Shabbethai and Jozabad were two other prominent Levites who moved to the city. Nehemiah describes them as in charge of the "external work of the House of God" (Neh. 11:16). These responsibilities were in contrast to work in the Temple itself.[11] They involved managing the treasury accounts, Temple security, supply and inventory control, and administrative and ritual law. They were also responsible for the provision of supplies – for example, wood for the altar. Both men had already achieved prominent positions under Ezra. Shabbethai had assisted Ezra in his unsuccessful attempt to nullify intermarriages (Ezra 10:5). Jozabad had taken control of the Temple valuables that Ezra had brought with him from Babylonia (8:33).

In addition to these appointments, Nehemiah named Judah son of Hassenuah, a Benjamite, to be the second-in-command of the city. Judah's appointment as deputy was yet another reflection of Nehemiah's political acumen; the Benjamite tribe needed some official representation. In fact, the practice of appointing deputies from a clan other than that of the leader is still common in the Arab world, particularly in the Gulf sheikhdoms.

There was one other leader whom Nehemiah listed among those moving to the city, though it appears he had done so prior to the governor's arrival. Nehemiah described Petahiah son of Meshezabel, of the sons of Zerah son of Judah, as an "adviser to the king concerning all the affairs of the people" (Neh. 11:24). Some commentators speculate that Petahiah held this office in the generation prior to that of Nehemiah.[12] According to this view, he was the official who addressed the concerns of Jews in the entire province, possibly as an official seconded by the governor to the court of Persia.

Several medieval commentators saw Petahiah as a counterpart of the *shtadlan* of their day; his role was to represent the concerns of the

11. Williamson, *Ezra, Nehemiah*, 352.
12. Galil, *Daniel, Ezra UNeḥemia*, 294–95.

Jews to the Persian king.[13] Another view is that his role was to forward to the king all of the province's payments, a far less significant office.[14] Still another view held he was "appointed by the king for all matters that the people required, matters that were outside the purview of the Temple."[15]

Finally, Petahiah may have moved to Jerusalem because he had also been designated as the leader to muster his tribesmen from Judah to defend the city in case of attack. In this regard, Judah son of Hassenuah, the Benjamite whom Nehemiah appointed as second-in-command of Jerusalem in peacetime, would have been the proper choice to be reassigned as Petahiah's deputy in wartime, so that he could conscript his fellow Benjamites for military duty. Moreover, Judah may previously have reported to Petahiah as his deputy prior to Nehemiah's arrival on the scene; in that case, Nehemiah may simply have retained the chain of command while assigning it a new mission. Such practice remains common in modern times among government civilian and military personnel; a commander or official who is reassigned often takes his or her deputy along to the new assignment.

It is, however, unlikely that Petahiah had a major role at the Persian court prior to Nehemiah's arrival. Nehemiah never mentions by name any of his predecessors who served as governor of Judah, presumably to highlight his own significance. He would surely have been disinclined to mention a predecessor at the Persian court. Moreover, Nehemiah is unlikely to have given such a predecessor any kind of serious new responsibility, whether as a representative or as a reserve military commander.

On the other hand, Nehemiah would have had less difficulty appointing Petahiah as *his* representative or even as an official adviser to the king on Jewish affairs. The court knew that Nehemiah was the most important person in the Jewish community, particularly because his power, which was very real, derived from his secular position at the court rather than from his Jewish affiliation. The same has also been the case in recent American administrations: the official representative

13. Rashi, Neh. 11:24, s.v. *lekhol*; Metzudat David, Neh. 11:24, s.v. *leyad*.

14. Ralbag, ad loc., s.v. *vehenai*.

15. Malbim. Neh. 11:24, s.v. *UPetaḥia*.

to the Jewish community has little influence, whereas Jews holding other offices in government are often extremely powerful. In like manner, Nehemiah would not have seen Petahiah as any sort of competitor, though he would not have considered him of significant assistance at the Persian court either.

RELOCATING MEMBERS OF THE GENERAL POPULATION

Having identified the leaders who would be moved to the city, the issue before Nehemiah was how to find a basis for determining, as well, who of the ordinary people would be transferred to settle Jerusalem. Many of these people had been involved in the construction of the wall. Nevertheless, the community was a rural one, and movement to the city was likely to be disorienting for people accustomed to living on the land, as it still is today for the millions in the Developing World who have migrated to cities from the countryside. Accordingly, Nehemiah hit upon a lottery scheme, thereby ensuring that he could not be accused of singling out individuals to be drafted away from their farms and rural roots to live in Jerusalem. As he recounted, the "rest of the people cast lots for one out of ten to come and settle in the holy city of Jerusalem, and the other nine-tenths to stay in the towns" (Neh. 11:1).

The final section of the covenant had ended with a tithe; Nehemiah was now implementing a tithe of a very different sort. In addition, he was building upon the people's commitment not to leave or neglect the Temple; Nehemiah's ordinance ensured that the city itself, likewise, would not be forsaken.[16] It is not clear, however, whether the lottery meant that one-tenth of the population outside Jerusalem was to be transferred there, or whether the lottery was designed to ensure that the population of Jerusalem comprised one-tenth that of the entire province.[17] Since the population of the province was approximately forty-five thousand, including the few hundred already residing in Jerusalem, the transfer involved some four thousand souls.[18]

---

16. Blenkinsopp, *Ezra-Nehemiah*, 322; Zer-Kavod, *Ezra UNeḥemia*, 124.
17. Myers, *Ezra/Nehemiah*, 186.
18. Reditt, "Nehemiah's First Mission," 671 (see chap. 2, n. 27); Myers, *Ezra/Nehemiah*, xxxiv and 13–16.

It is equally unclear whether the people willingly acceded to this plan, though they had no choice, of course. Nehemiah records that "the people gave their blessing to all the men who willingly settled in Jerusalem" (Neh. 11:2). This does not necessarily mean that everyone who was transferred was happy about it; perhaps the reason the other nine-tenths blessed those who were relocating was that they were relieved that they themselves were not forced to do so.

Indeed, the Talmud indicates that those who moved recognized that the transition would not be an easy one, and for that reason they were blessed by the rest of the community.[19] Several medieval commentators on the Talmud, reflecting conditions in their own time that had probably not changed for centuries, explained the hesitation on the part of those who relocated to Jerusalem. A walled city like Jerusalem was not a pleasant place. The air was fetid, the overcrowded buildings cramped together. There was no greenery to speak of, neither gardens nor orchards.[20] Prices were higher because food had to be brought in from the outside. Indeed, the overall cost of living was significantly greater,[21] driven in part by peer pressure that led to conspicuous consumption and, in turn, increased the demand for goods. As one medieval commentator put it, "in cities people must conform to the standards of the rich, both in outlays and in dress."[22]

On the other hand, it is possible, though less likely, that since the leaders of the community were already in Jerusalem, others sought to move there as well, and Nehemiah had to draw lots to prevent an excessive inflow into the capital.[23] Nehemiah's reference to the people who willingly settled in the city does seem to indicate that many people volunteered to move there. Perhaps they did so in order to be part of the new armed guard that Nehemiah was organizing, to supplement his own militia in line with Persian policy to fortify cities such as Jerusalem.[24]

19. Statement of R. Yose b. Ḥanina, Ketubbot 110b.
20. Rashi, Ketubbot 110b, s.v. *yeshivat*; and *Tosafot Rid* ad loc.
21. Meiri, *Beit HaBeḥira*, vol. 8: Ketubbot, 502.
22. Attributed to a student of Rabbeinu Yonah, cited in Rabbi Bezalel Ashkenazi, *Shita Mekubetzet: Ketubot*, vol. 2 (New York: Pollak Brothers, 5721/1960), 332.
23. Galil, *Daniel, Ezra UNeḥemia*, 286.
24. Urbach, *The Halakhah*, 27.

As Nehemiah noted, among those moving to the city were both "the clan of Perez who were living in Jerusalem – 468 valorous men" (Neh. 11:6) and that of "Amashsai son of Azarel son of Ahzai son of Meshillemoth son of Immer, and their brothers, valorous warriors" (11:13–14). Their role clearly was to provide Nehemiah with a strategic reserve, available when needed to supplement the men on full-time active duty. It is possible, indeed, that lots were cast to augment the number of those who volunteered to move to Jerusalem in order to fill the remainder of the 10 percent quota.[25]

In any event, the notion of having one-tenth of the population in the national capital is certainly in line with modern population flows. So too is the phenomenon, especially in the Developing World, of poorer people migrating in droves from the countryside to urban areas. The capitals of many major states today represent between 8 and 12 percent of the total national population.

The people who moved to Jerusalem received a major benefit, the equivalent of a modern tax incentive. It appears that as a reward for their willingness to settle in the city, the biblical law of houses in walled cities was not applied to Jerusalem. This law provided that a house in a walled city passes into the perpetual ownership of the purchaser if the vendor does not buy it back within a year of the date of purchase. Jerusalemites were permitted to reacquire their homes at any time.[26]

The majority of the population remained on the land. The Benjamite settlements were in the north, while the tribe of Judah occupied seventeen settlements, including Hebron (*Kiryat Arba*). All of the tribe's settlements, apart from Hebron, were to the west and south of Jerusalem. In fact, Jews appear to have settled quite far southward, beyond the actual bounds of the province. The southern settlements were under Edomite-Arab control. Evidently, the Jews in these places were happy to live in the outlying districts of the province. One reason this may have been the case is that they appear to have met with little opposition, even though they were returning to their ancestral holdings. Moreover, they benefited from the freedom of movement accorded to all subjects of

25. Williamson, *Ezra, Nehemiah*, 351.
26. See Lev. 25:29; Bava Kamma 82b.

the Persian Empire.[27] That they maintained contact with the Jews under Nehemiah's rule is not surprising, given his charismatic leadership, his emphasis on nationhood and national and religious identity, his position as a senior Persian official, and, of course, the central religious role of the Temple in Jerusalem.

---

27. Myers, *Ezra/Nehemiah*, 189, 191.

Nehemiah 12

The Ceremony to Dedicate the City Wall

BRINGING OUT THE POPULATION

With his plan to repopulate Jerusalem being implemented, Nehemiah orchestrated yet another ceremony: the dedication of the city walls. The walls signified much more than security for the city, or indeed, for the Jewish population of the province. Much like the improvements made to the walls of the Old City subsequent to the Six-Day War, the walls represented a symbol of resurgent nationalism as well as religious revival. Nehemiah, ever eager to instill a sense of both into the Jewish community – as well as to cloak himself in pageantry and tradition harking back to Solomon's dedication of the First Temple – seized upon the opportunity to stage yet another spectacle According to the midrash *Megillat Taanit*, the ceremony took place on the seventh of Elul.[1]

1. *Megillat Taanit* 6:1. Another version of *Megillat Taanit* states that the ceremony took place on the fourth of Elul, while *Megillat Taanit* 2:1 gives the seventh of Iyar as the date of the dedication. The scholion, an ancient commentary appended to the Megilla, initially does not determine in which month the dedication took place, but from the citation of verses in its commentary on chapter 6 of the Megilla, it appears that that scholion favors the Elul date. For a discussion, see Solomon Zeitlin, "Megillat Taanit as a Source for Jewish Chronology and History in the Hellenistic and Roman Periods," *Jewish Quarterly Review*, new series 10 (October 1919–January 1920): 239,

The stars of the dedication were Nehemiah's political allies, the Levites, who strengthened his hand vis-à-vis the priests. Nehemiah realized all along that there were limits to the constraints he could place on the priests because of the ritual tasks that the Torah mandated for them. Accordingly, rather than attempting directly to reduce the power of the priesthood, Nehemiah focused on building up that of the Levites. For the purposes of the dedication, Nehemiah reached out to the Levites "wherever they lived…and brought [them] to Jerusalem to celebrate a joyful dedication with thanksgiving and with song, accompanied by cymbals, harps, and lyres" (Neh. 12:27). Transporting the Levites to the celebration was as much an act of underscoring his power relative to rival factions as it was of further empowering the Levites.

Nehemiah's practice of mobilizing support remains common to this day. In Western countries it takes the form of "bringing out the vote" at election time. It was important even in the Soviet Union: in 1957, Nikita Khrushchev, seeking to cement his position as the country's most powerful leader, was able to defeat his "anti-party" foes with the help of Central Committee members who were "sought out and brought" to Moscow by Marshal Georgy Zhukov's military airlift forces.

Nehemiah relates that the Levites came from as far as the Jordan plain, the countryside around Jericho, the villages surrounding Bethlehem, and from the environs of Jerusalem itself.

"The priests and Levites purified themselves; then they purified the people, and the gates, and the wall" (Neh. 12:30).[2] The purification of individuals involved their descending into a *mikve*, or ritual bath, as

248. Vered Noam, who prefers the version that lists the fourth rather than the seventh of Elul as one of the dates of the dedication, is uncertain whether either day refers to Nehemiah's era. It is possible, she says, that a third date, the sixteenth of Adar, listed by the Megilla as the date on which the wall began to be built, is actually the only one that refers to Nehemiah's era or is in addition to one of the other two. See Vered Noam, "Megillat Taanit – The Scroll of Fasting," in Shmuel Safrai et al., *The Literature of the Sages: Second Part: Midrash and Targum, Liturgy, Poetry, Mysticism, Contracts, Inscriptions, Ancient Science and the Languages of Rabbinic Literature* (Assen, Netherlands: Fortress Press, 2007), 343–46.

2. Metzudat David reads the passage to say that the priests and Levites urged the people to purify themselves.

specified in Leviticus and elsewhere.[3] Purification of the gates probably involved the sprinkling of water, or of blood from a sacrifice. Purification was traditionally the province of the priests in the Temple, and it is probable that to the extent the Temple gates and other Temple areas were reconstructed and had to be purified, the task fell to the priests. But purification of the city's walls and gates was an entirely different matter. It was a fundamentally secular activity, involving precincts outside the Temple. Accordingly, Nehemiah probably assigned the task of purifying the city gates to the Levites; the religious overtones attached to the ceremony, and the centrality of the Levites to its conduct, would not have been missed by the population at large. Similarly, the Levites may have been charged with purifying the walls, likewise an unprecedented form of purification, to ensure that the city was ritually pure.[4] Assigning this role to the Levites provided a further indication of their newfound stature.

THE WALK ALONG THE WALLS

The dedication ceremony involved the circumambulation of the wall, a ritual that was common in the dedication of ancient cities and buildings.[5] It is remotely possible that the ceremony took place in Tishrei, soon after the completion of the wall. On the other hand, the logistics involved in beginning the resettlement of Jerusalem, as well as importing Levites from outlying districts and purifying them, would suggest that the ceremony was held later, perhaps even as late as the following Elul.[6] Most commentators believe, however, that the ceremony was held during Nehemiah's first year in office.[7]

---

3. Meztudat David is one of the few traditional commentators explicitly to refer to ritual bathing; Neh. 12:30, s.v. *vayetaharu.*
4. Rashi, Neh. 12:30, s.v. *ve'et.*
5. Blenkinsopp, *Ezra-Nehemiah*, 346.
6. Rabbi Saadia claims the dedication took place on the fourth of Elul; since the wall was completed on the twenty-fifth, he must be referring to the following Elul. See Mathews, *Commentary*, 30.
7. For a discussion, see Zer-Kavod, *Ezra UNeḥemia*, 137; Myers, *Ezra/Nehemiah*, 202; Blenkinsopp, *Ezra-Nehemiah*, 343–44.

The ceremony was preceded by the stationing of the officials from Judah and Benjamin on the walls, which served as a kind of assembly point for them to follow the marchers. Then two processions of thanksgiving, both of which included Levitical choristers, and each bearing a bread offering larger than the one normally offered in the Temple ritual,[8] began their march at the same point on the southwestern corner of the wall near the Valley Gate. The wall was wide enough to accommodate the marchers.[9] Each procession appears to have included an armed escort that marched alongside the singers, providing them with protection in the event of a surprise attack from beneath the walls' exterior face.

Though beginning at the same place, the two processions headed in opposite directions around the wall. The double procession created a precedent that the Talmud later remarked upon: it was a necessary requirement to legitimize the expansion of the city.[10] Additionally, the Talmud notes that expansion of the city or of the Temple precincts requires the presence of the king or prince, the High Priest bearing the Urim and Thummim, the Sanhedrin (of seventy-one judges), two thanks offerings, and songs of thanksgiving (Shavuot 14a). One of the thanks offerings would be eaten; the other would be burnt (Shavuot 15b).

Nehemiah's ceremony met some, but not all, of these requirements. As the provincial governor, he personally may have qualified as the "prince." Rabbinic lore has the Sanhedrin in attendance as well, while the marchers had the thanks offerings and the Levites provided the singers. There were, however, no Urim and Thummim, which the High Priest had worn during the First Temple era; they had disappeared during Nebuchadnezzar's conquest of Judea and his destruction of Jerusalem and the Temple.[11]

---

8. Metzudat David, Neh. 12:31, s.v. *vaamida*.
9. Ralbag, Neh. 12:31, s.v. *vetahalukhot*. Ralbag's interpretation, at least insofar as he asserts that people walked on the wall, has since been verified by Kathleen Kenyon's archaeological findings, which found the wall to be sufficiently wide for two or three people to march abreast upon it. See Blenkinsopp, *Ezra-Nehemiah*, 345.
10. Shavuot 14a–15b passim. See also Mathews, *Commentary*, 30.
11. Although Josephus argues that the Urim and Thummim were in use through Maccabean times (Josephus, *Antiquities*, III:8:9), the Talmud unequivocally asserts that they were lost during the Babylonian conquest. See Y. Sota 44a and *Korban HaEida*

Behind the marchers with one of the two bread offerings was Hoshaiah, the senior officer,[12] "and half the officers of Judah" (Neh. 12:32). They were accompanied by some of the young priests (or their families), with trumpets. Priests were biblically commanded to sound the trumpets on festivals and the New Moon (Num. 10:10); here again, Nehemiah was seeking to give a religious patina to what was, in effect, a political ceremony. Likewise, it was no coincidence that a leading Levite, "Zechariah son of Jonathan son of Shemaiah son of Mattaniah" (Neh. 12:36), who was descended from Asaph the singer in King David's era, was, like his great-grandfather Mattaniah, the lead singer;[13] his family accompanied him in song.[14] To further underscore the connection with Judah's glorious religious and national past, the Levites "played the musical instruments of David, the man of God" (12:36). Half the people followed in the train of the Levites and the official participants.

Despite his emphasis on the importance of the Levites, Nehemiah once again accorded special recognition to Ezra. As he recorded in his memoir, "Ezra the scribe went ahead of" the singers (Neh. 12:36). Since the official party was joined by the trumpeters and singers, and Ezra marched in front of the singers, this naturally placed him immediately behind those carrying the bread offering, a fitting place for the religious leader. Of course, Nehemiah's assigning a prominent role to Ezra was yet another way of adding religious significance to the secular ceremony. In fact, Ezra may not have realized that he was being given a

---

ad loc., s.v. *zeh*; Yoma 21b. A number of medieval commentators take the position that the Urim and Thummim did exist during the Second Temple era; however, they did not function as an oracle but rather were part of the priestly vestments. For a discussion and review of the sources, see *Encyclopedia Talmudit*, s.v. *Urim V'Tumim*.

12. Zer-Kavod, *Ezra UNeḥemia*, 138n12, speculates that Hoshaiah was Zerubbabel's grandson, making him a scion of the House of David.

13. Zer-Kavod, *Ezra UNeḥemia*, 139, notes that Mattaniah was the lead singer in Jeshua's time. Blenkinsopp, *Ezra-Nehemiah*, 345, argues that the chronology "makes no sense" because Zechariah would have been active seventy-five years after his great-grandfather Mattaniah. A generation in those days was something under twenty years, however, and if the position was indeed inherited, there is no chronological problem.

14. Metzudat David, Neh. 12:36, s.v. *ve'eḥav*.

part to play, as his previous behavior had shown some degree of political naiveté. No matter; he was accorded a great deal of respect, and that was certainly how the public must have seen it.

The procession led by Ezra marched from the southwestern corner of the wall to the Dung Gate, which was located at the southeastern corner. From there they marched to the Fountain Gate, on the eastern side of the wall, where they ascended the steps of the City of David; those steps evidently had been transported from the south for the purpose of the ceremony.[15] They then passed on to the Water Gate on the east and then west into the Temple area.

The second procession marched on the wall in the opposite direction from the first. With no counterpart to Ezra in the second procession, Nehemiah, as the senior official, marched directly behind those carrying the second bread offering.[16] He was joined by half the officials, while the remaining half of the community followed them. The procession marched to the northwestern part of the wall above the Tower of Ovens to the Broad Wall, headed eastward along the north wall, and then turned south above the Gate of Ephraim, which had figured in the Sukkot ceremony (Neh. 8:16). It then passed the Jeshanah Gate, the Fish Gate, the Tower of Hananel, the Tower of the Hundred, and the Sheep Gate, halting at the Gate of the Prison Compound.

"Both thanksgiving choirs halted at the House of God" (Neh. 12:40), as did Nehemiah and the prefects, the priests who blew the trumpets, and the Levite choristers. Nehemiah, the officials, the priests, and the singers then entered the Temple to offer the sacrifices, with each group proceeding to the section of the edifice that was reserved for it. The celebration was a truly festive one, with the entire community, not just its male population, divinely inspired to celebrate: "For God made them rejoice greatly; the women and children also rejoiced, and the rejoicing in Jerusalem could be heard from afar" (12:43).

15. Zer-Kavod, Ezra UNeḥemia, 139.

16. A contemporary Bible scholar notes that the dual procession underscores the case for Ezra and Nehemiah having been contemporaries, since the absence of one of them "would leave one of the processions without a leader"; Yamauchi, *Persia and the Bible,* 253 (see chap. 1, n. 26).

THE TREASURIES

On the day of the celebration, or shortly thereafter,[17] Nehemiah oversaw the appointment of Levites to serve as officials who would look "after the chambers that served as treasuries for the gifts, the first fruits, and the tithes" (Neh. 12:44) that the people brought from the fields to Jerusalem. While the priests bore the responsibility for managing the sacrifices and rituals properly, as well as for ensuring the purity of the Temple and preventing the entry or insertion of any ritually impure people or items, the Levites furnished the "singers and gatekeepers [serving] in accord with the ordinance of David and Solomon his son" (12:45). The Levites who served in the Temple as a result of David and Solomon's innovations received priority over other Levites when the offerings were distributed.[18]

The people's willingness not only to contribute gifts to the Temple, but to bring the gifts to Jerusalem, stood in stark contrast to the state of neglect that Nehemiah had found upon his return to Judah from Persia. Indeed, Nehemiah, in his memoir, may well have wished to highlight the changes that his leadership had brought about. He attributed the popular willingness to contribute the biblically mandated gifts as arising from the fact that "the people of Judah were grateful to the priests and Levites who were in attendance" at the celebration (Neh. 12:44). No doubt, too, the people recognized the increased status that Nehemiah had accorded to the Levites in particular and responded accordingly.

Nehemiah's appointment of the Levites to positions involving the receipt of gifts from the people and their distribution to Levites serving in the Temple was consistent with his long-standing policy of showing preference to his supporters. The timing of the appointments was opportune as well. As he noted, the people appreciated the prominent role of Levites in the dedication of the walls, in addition to that of the priests, as was only to be expected.[19] Finally, granting oversight

17. Neh. 12:44 can be translated literally as "on that day."
18. See Malbim's discussion, Neh. 12:45, s.v. *David*. The Talmud and halakha cite laws enacted by the "Court of David" – for example, the laws restricting fraternization between the sexes (*yiḥud*). See Avoda Zara 36b, *Shulḥan Arukh, Even Ha'ezer* 22:1.
19. See Galil, *Daniel, Ezra UNeḥemia*, 309.

and control over the gifts addressed yet another challenge that Nehemiah had to overcome: the paucity of Levites performing rituals at the Temple. This was due to economic conditions. Malachi had bemoaned the fact that the populace were not paying their tithes (Mal. 3:8); the Levites simply were unable to earn their keep from the gifts brought by the public and had been forced to seek income elsewhere. Even if the gifts were being offered, they were not being brought to Jerusalem; this too forced the Levites to wander further afield in search of an income. Nehemiah, therefore, established a system to ensure not only that the priests would receive their due in the form of first fruits,[20] but so too would the Levites, who no longer would have to scour the countryside for tithes, but would oversee the storage of gifts in Jerusalem and draw their allotments from the storehouses.[21]

Nehemiah not only highlighted the role of the Levites but took great pains to emphasize his own role in ensuring the restoration of ancient practices. He compared himself to Zerubbabel, the scion of the royal family who had led the initial return from exile. Referring to himself in the third-person, he stressed in his memoirs that "in the time of Zerubbabel, and in the time of Nehemiah" – that is, when each was governor[22] – "all Israel contributed the daily portions of the singers and the gatekeepers, and made sacred contributions for the Levites, and the Levites made sacred contributions for the Aaronites," namely, the biblically mandated tithe from the Levite tithe (Neh. 12:47).[23] The gatekeepers and singers were not alone in receiving their due allotments

20. Ralbag translates the Hebrew as first fruits. Metzudat David translates "first bread" or challah.

21. Thus Ralbag, Neh. 12:44, s.v. *vayipakdu*. Zer-Kavod, *Ezra UNeḥemia*, 141, asserts that the storehouses were in each town.

22. Zer-Kavod, loc. cit.

23. The Levitical tithe to the priests is outlined in Num. 18:26. Several contemporary Bible scholars speculate that Neh. 12:47 provides the basis for the assertion in II Maccabees 1:18 that Nehemiah restored the city upon the first return from exile. This assertion may also be linked to the roughly similar talmudic tradition that treats Nehemiah as a contemporary of Zerubbabel. II Maccabees actually credits Nehemiah with rebuilding the Temple, restoring the sacrifices, and locating the miraculous fire that burned on the altar, which had been hidden away when the Temple was destroyed. See II Maccabees 1:18–29.

from Nehemiah's officials; other Levites who served in the Temple on an occasional basis were likewise remunerated from the storehouses in Jerusalem.[24]

It is noteworthy that in his entire discussion of the dedication and of the bringing of gifts that followed it, Nehemiah omitted any mention of the High Priests. Unlike the Levites, and perhaps many if not most of the ordinary priests, Eliashiv the High Priest was not part of Nehemiah's power base.[25] Far from it, his loyalty to Nehemiah's entire enterprise remained highly uncertain. As a consequence, it is not surprising that he led neither of the two processions along the wall that were the heart of the dedication ceremony.

24. Galil, *Daniel, Ezra UNeḥemia*, 309; Malbim, Neh. 12:45, s.v. *David*.

25. Galil, *Daniel, Ezra UNeḥemia*, 309.

Nehemiah 13

Departure and Return

DEPARTURE FOR SUSA

Nehemiah's mission was accomplished. He had completed and dedicated the wall, repopulated the city, restructured the economy, provided for the defense of Jerusalem, reorganized and regularized the operation and maintenance of the Temple, and appointed religious, civil, and military officials to ensure the smooth functioning of all that he had set in motion. It was time for Nehemiah to return to the royal court in Susa. It is not clear whether he did so of his own volition or whether he was recalled; most commentators, both classical and modern, assume that he was called to Susa. Regardless, he took his leave of Judah and headed back to Persia.

It appears that Nehemiah left without much fanfare. His memoir records no great departure ceremonies, nor is there any record of his receiving any farewell gifts. This is somewhat unusual; for example, Genesis recounts Laban's grievance with Jacob for stealing away in the night and preventing him from parting with his family "with festive music, with timbrel and lyre" (Gen. 31:27). Similarly, Pharaoh insisted on presenting an array of gifts to Joseph's brothers when they departed Egypt for Canaan, even though they would soon return with Jacob. Nehemiah had served as governor of the province for twelve years when he returned to Susa; one would expect something more from the community he served. Yet Nehemiah's silence on the subject clearly must reflect the community's silence.

One can only speculate why more of a fuss was not made when Nehemiah departed. Perhaps he thought more of himself than others thought of him. Perhaps he had pushed through too many reforms too quickly. While the people responded positively and emotionally when Ezra urged them to repent, their ardor may have cooled as quickly as it arose once the ceremonies were over. Similarly, many of those who drew lots to move to Jerusalem may have been less than excited about relocating to the city – or they may have become unhappy once they were settled there. And there can be little doubt that there was not much enthusiasm on the part of the men who were asked to separate from their non-Jewish wives and children. Nehemiah's departure meant that only Ezra remained behind. Though Ezra was fully committed to the reforms that had just been implemented, the people knew from his failures twelve years earlier that he had neither the political acumen nor the political support to force the reforms into solid institutional patterns.

As for Nehemiah, we do not know whether he returned to his former post as cupbearer or simply served as one of Artaxerxes's courtiers. We do not even know why it was, at this stage of his service as governor, that the king appears to have recalled him to the court. Perhaps his term had simply expired. He had initially given the king an estimate of how long he expected to be away from the court, in response to the king's question regarding how long he wished to be in Judah, but he did not include the estimate in his memoir. Clearly, he did not ask for a twelve-year term; he could not possibly have imagined he would have been away that long, and it is doubtful that the king would have granted him such an extended leave from his duties as cupbearer. His appointment certainly was not a permanent one, though there is no indication regarding its length and whether his term was renewed, or, alternatively, whether Nehemiah simply took it upon himself to remain in Judah until he was recalled. Once summoned by the king, Nehemiah had no alternative but to return to Susa.

It is remotely possible that Nehemiah's term had not expired, or – perhaps more likely – that he had obtained permission after some interval to renew his initial term and was now in his second term, which had not yet expired. Rather, responding to the king's orders, he returned to Persia on an extended leave of absence from Judah, or more accurately, what would today be termed "temporary duty," although such assignments are measured in months, not years. For example, Arsames, satrap of Egypt, and more senior than Nehemiah as proconsul of a far more important unit within the empire, took a three-year leave from his post to return to Persia. Nehemiah's leave could have been as long and, if the king so desired it, could have been longer still. But we simply do not know.

In any event, whether he was recalled or had taken temporary leave from his duties, Nehemiah gives no indication in his memoirs of how long he remained in Susa. It took anywhere from one to six months to travel to Susa, depending on the route; Nehemiah would have had to spend some time in court as well. It appears that, at a minimum, he was away for the better part of a year, and that is the estimate of the classical commentators.

However long his stay at the court may have been, at some point Nehemiah decided to ask the king for leave to return to Judah. It is not clear what prompted him to make this request. It is likely that he had maintained contact with his appointees in Jerusalem and was disturbed by the news that his entire set of reforms was being systematically unraveled by his old adversaries Tobiah and Eliashiv the High Priest.

Unlike his description of his initial interview with the king regarding the state of affairs in Jerusalem, Nehemiah's memoir offers no details of any further communication with Artaxerxes. Nor, for that matter, does it indicate whether he prayed to God prior to what must have been a mandatory audience with the king to obtain permission to return to Judah. Perhaps at this stage of his career Nehemiah was confident that the king would grant him the authorization he sought and thus concluded that no additional prayers were called for.

It also is not clear whether Nehemiah returned as governor. The classical commentators are silent on the issue, while modern biblical scholars are divided as to whether he retained his original appointment, was reappointed, or simply was given leave to return as a private citizen. The last of these possibilities seems implausible. More than anyone, Nehemiah understood the importance of a royal office; after all, though

Ezra had obtained permission to lead an *aliya* to Judah, he had no official standing and accomplished little that lasted until the time Nehemiah arrived on the scene.

A TROUBLING STATE OF AFFAIRS

Whether Nehemiah took up the remainder of his original term after having completed his temporary assignment, or had his governorship renewed, it was clear upon his arrival in Judah that his return had not been anticipated by the locals. It must have come to them as something of a shock. For what he found when he arrived left him deeply dismayed.

To begin with, despite all their protestations to the contrary, the people had once again returned to their non-Jewish wives. Nehemiah had not sought to force the issue the way Ezra had done. He obviously thought he had succeeded where Ezra had failed; clearly that was not the case.

In addition, Nehemiah found that during his absence, and obviously anticipating that he would not return, the priest Eliashiv, a relative of Tobiah by marriage,[1] "had been appointed over the rooms in the House of our God" (Neh. 13:4). He had assigned Tobiah a large room, one that had been used to store the meal offering, the frankincense, the equipment, the tithes of grain, wine, and oil, the dues of the Levites, singers, and gatekeepers, and the gifts for the priests. The people had stopped offering these gifts to the Levites, however, and the room had stood empty until assigned to Tobiah.

The room Eliashiv gave to Tobiah was probably next to his own. In addition, Eliashiv may also have given another room to his ally Sanballat. As a coconspirator with the other two men, Sanballat no doubt wanted, and was granted, a share of the revenues that they were skimming from the people's gifts, which may well have been the reason why gifts were no longer forthcoming.

Traditional commentators assert that the man Nehemiah calls Eliashiv was none other than Eliashiv the High Priest, Tobiah's ally and Nehemiah's old adversary. Some modern critics believe he was an ordinary priest, since the High Priest would not have bothered himself with

1. Zer-Kavod, *Ezra UNeḥemia*, 142, and Coggins, *Ezra and Nehemiah*, 138.

running the storage chambers.[2] But this underestimates the pettiness of even senior officials. Besides, it is doubtful that anyone but the High Priest would have had the authority, or the temerity, to install someone in the Temple precincts without approval from a religious authority. Moreover, given the wealth that resided in the storerooms, it could very well have attracted the personal interest of the High Priest.

As noted earlier, Tobiah, the so-called "Ammonite," was probably scion of a prominent family with a base in both Ammon and Jerusalem. It is possible that he was indeed descended from Ammonite stock; living in Ammon, he naturally would have heralded his lineage. Even if that were the case, he was also closely tied to the priests of Jerusalem, whether as an associate or as a kinsman. The argument that the Eliashiv mentioned in the text is none other than the High Priest is reinforced by the relationship with Tobiah; the latter, no doubt, consorted with the elite of Judah's community.

Of course, it was the very elite to which Tobiah belonged that had most strongly resisted Nehemiah's initial arrival, his effort to rebuild the walls, his social program, and his cooperation with Ezra to revive long-standing religious practice. In obtaining a room at the heart of the Jewish polity, Tobiah was in a position to rally the opposition to Nehemiah and to press for a resumption of the integration of the Jews into the wider Levantine community that Nehemiah's arrival had interrupted. In addition, the priests and their allies would logically have been the strongest opponents of Nehemiah's efforts to provide a stable income to the Levites, since the latter were among his staunchest supporters. Thus, in giving Tobiah control over the storerooms, Eliashiv and his circle at once both strengthened the opposition to Nehemiah and weakened the financial base of his supporters.

NEHEMIAH SPRINGS INTO ACTION

Nehemiah's first course of action upon his arrival in Jerusalem was to deal with Tobiah. He immediately "had all the household gear of Tobiah

---

2. For example, Myers, *Ezra/Nehemiah*, 214; Galil, *Daniel, Ezra UNeḥemia*, 311; Williamson, *Ezra, Nehemiah*, 386. Not all modern critics are of this view, however; see Coggins, *Ezra and Nehemiah*, 138.

thrown out of the room" that Eliashiv had allocated to him (Neh 13:8). Nehemiah was furious that a man whose uncertain origins banned him from membership in the community could be ensconced in the holiest precincts. Because Nehemiah was not the religious leader, several modern scholars have argued either that he arrogated to himself control of issues that were not really his prerogative – namely, determining who was entitled to the use of Temple spaces – or that he received permission from whoever was in charge, presumably Ezra, but did not credit him. The latter is certainly plausible, but Nehemiah may have been acting impetuously. In any event, in order to justify his actions, Nehemiah read from the Torah so as to quell any protests on the part of Tobiah's relatives and his allies among the senior bureaucrats. It was probably Tobiah's good fortune that he was not around when Nehemiah unceremoniously dumped his goods on the street. Given Nehemiah's rage, Tobiah might have found himself under physical attack.

Nehemiah then gave orders that Tobiah's room be purified, and restored the equipment of the House of God that had been moved to make room for Tobiah's occupancy. Nehemiah also restored the giving of the meal offering and the frankincense that apparently had been suspended when Tobiah moved into the Temple precincts. Nehemiah purified at least two other rooms as well, those of Eliashiv and of Sanballat, his long-time adversary. He also cleansed additional rooms that were adjacent to those of the three men.[3]

Nehemiah's next move was to restore the privileges that he had established for the Levites prior to his return to Persia. He found that the Levites had not received the gifts mandated for them, and as a result, "the Levites and the singers who performed the [Temple] service had made off, each to his fields" (Neh. 13:10). On the other hand, the priests continued to receive their gifts, no doubt as a result of Eliashiv's influence.

Nehemiah blamed the prefects in charge of Temple maintenance for not distributing their portions to the Levites, who had left their posts and duties at the Temple in search of food. Nehemiah recalled the Levites to their former posts and restored the arrangement whereby

3. Williamson, *Ezra, Nehemiah*, 387.

offerings for the Levites were brought to the Temple precincts. Faced with the wrath of their newly returned governor, the people complied with his demands, as they had previously, "and all Judah brought the tithes of grain, wine, and oil into the treasuries" (Neh. 13:12).

Nehemiah was generally a good judge of character. But no one is perfect in that regard, and political leaders throughout history have often regretted some of their personnel decisions. Nehemiah was no exception. Not all the men that he had chosen to oversee Temple operations had remained steadfast in ensuring the performance of the obligations set out either in religious law or the covenant. Had they carried out their mandates to the fullest extent, even if they had not been able to prevent the seizure of Temple rooms by Tobiah and his friends, they could still have ensured that the Temple would not face a financial shortfall and the Levites would not go wanting. Recognizing that some of his appointees were not as reliable as he had assumed, Nehemiah put the treasuries in the charge of the priests Shelemiah and Zadok – the latter, using the name Zedekiah, had signed the covenant immediately after Nehemiah and Pedaiah of the Levites. Hanan son of Zaccur son of Mattaniah was appointed as their assistant. In contrast to the men who had betrayed him, these three retained Nehemiah's trust, and he made it "their duty to distribute the portions to their brothers" (Neh. 13:13).

It is noteworthy that Nehemiah, while appointing a priestly scribe to serve as one of the troika responsible for allocating the gifts to the Temple, did not choose Ezra. Trust was not the reason that Nehemiah did not conscript Ezra to one of these positions. The great man may have died during Nehemiah's governorship or at some point while Nehemiah was away from the province. Even if he were still alive, such tasks were beneath him as the undisputed religious leader of the people.

Nehemiah also found that the people were violating the Sabbath; he "saw men in Judah treading winepresses on the Sabbath, and others bringing heaps of grain and loading them onto asses, also wine, grapes, figs, and all sorts of goods, and bringing them into Jerusalem on the Sabbath" (Neh. 13:15). He also found that people were selling goods that they had brought to Jerusalem. Such behavior, like so much else, had commenced after Nehemiah's departure for Susa and reflected the shallowness of the people's commitment to the religious duties that he had imposed on them. Indeed, their lax attitude toward the Sabbath was a throwback to the twilight years of the First Temple, when Jeremiah inveighed against the people's commercial dealings on that day (Jer. 17:20–27).[4] Nehemiah must have been frustrated and angry.

Treading winepresses was not a biblical violation, but rather a subcategory of the biblical prohibition against threshing, a violation of rabbinic law.[5] The populace, either innocently or willfully, simply had not absorbed this prohibited derivation of what the Torah defines as labor. Loading grain onto pack animals likewise was a violation of rabbinic, not biblical, law. It is not clear whether the actual loading took place on the Sabbath or whether the donkeys had already been loaded on the Friday and the violation, which was biblical, was that of causing beasts to work on the Sabbath.[6] For a time, the very act of loading, which involved moving utensils, was prohibited as a result of Nehemiah's ruling. This was later modified to prohibit only the movement of large saws and plowshares.[7]

As for selling goods on Shabbat, that too was, at a minimum, a violation of rabbinic law (Beitza 37a). One major medieval halakhic decisor ruled, however, that conducting business on Sabbath in the usual weekday manner is a biblical prohibition.[8] In that case, the sin that the people were committing was even graver, for it appears that Shabbat had become the regular market day. The fact that a biblical prohibition was being violated in so widespread a manner would have been a further indication of how far the community had regressed during Nehemiah's absence.

---

4. For a discussion see Lau, *Jeremiah*, 40–42 (see chap. 1, n. 33).
5. *Mishneh Torah, Hilkhot Shabbat* 21:12, and Shabbat 7b.
6. Ralbag, Neh. 13:15, s.v. *umevi'im*, states that the animals were loaded on the Sabbath; Malbim, on the other hand, asserts (s.v. *umevi'im*) that the animals were loaded on Friday and then carried the goods on the Sabbath, in violation of the prohibition against working an animal on the Sabbath. The prohibition is included in the fourth of the Ten Commandments; see Ex. 20:10 and Deut. 5:14.
7. Mishna Shabbat 17:4. For a discussion, see Urbach, *The Halakhah*, 24–25.
8. Cf. Rabinowitz, *Nechemiah*, 215.

Nehemiah, as was his wont, took no time before responding. He admonished them there and then for "selling provisions" (Neh. 13:15). Henceforth, he ordered, no such transactions could take place. In addition, he ruled that no goods should be brought to market, and if items were brought for sale he would declare them public goods (*hefker*), available to all at no cost.[9] Needless to say, his ruling caused much discomfort to the Jewish merchants.

The Jews were not alone in bringing their goods to the Jerusalem market on Shabbat. "Tyrians who lived there brought fish and all sorts of wares and sold them on Shabbat to the Judahites in Jerusalem" (Neh. 13:16). These may have been Phoenician traders who frequented the Levant.[10] They might have been Tyrian traders who had either settled among the Jews[11] or – again a reflection on the state of religious practice in the community – resided in Jerusalem especially on Shabbat so as to do business there.[12]

Having issued his orders regarding current merchandise and future sales, as well as having admonished both those who produced the goods and the merchants who sold them, Nehemiah then turned on his officials, whom he held ultimately responsible for the profanation of Shabbat. It is not clear whether they also bought goods on the Sabbath or merely permitted the common people to do so.[13] In all likelihood they were complicit in the transgression, since at a minimum they could have prevented the markets from opening. Given their previous lax ways, the nobles probably participated in, and perhaps even profited from, the Sabbath trade.

In holding his officials publicly responsible for the communal violation of Shabbat, Nehemiah demonstrated how different he was from so many top officials in our time, both in the West and in the Developing World. Oftentimes leaders are reluctant in the extreme to punish their subordinates, but instead throw the book at those at the bottom of the

9. Ibn Yahia, Neh. 13:15, s.v. *vaa'id*.
10. Rashi, Neh.13:16, s.v. *vehatzorim*.
11. Metzudat David, Neh. 13:16, s.v. *vehatzorim;* Malbim ad loc., s.v. *vehatzorim*.
12. Ralbag, Neh. 13:17, s.v. *vehenei*.
13. The latter is Malbim's view; Neh. 13:7–18, *ve'ariva*.

political ladder. True to his character, Nehemiah did not mince words: "What evil thing is this that you are doing, profaning the Sabbath day! This is just what your ancestors did, and for it God brought all this misfortune on this city; and now you give cause for further wrath against Israel by profaning the Sabbath!" (Neh. 13:17–18). From his perspective, the fact that most of the laws that had been violated were of post-biblical origin was no excuse. Indeed, his reproof provided the basis for the Talmud's derivation of another set of laws that have become central to the proper keeping of Shabbat, namely the laws of *muktze* (Shabbat 123b). These laws prevent the moving or even handling of objects normally employed for the various types of weekday labor on Shabbat.

The following Friday evening, as the sun was setting and "shadows filled the gateways of Jerusalem at the approach of the Sabbath" (Neh. 13:19), Nehemiah took steps to ensure the implementation of the orders given earlier that week. Accomplished leader that he was, he recognized that verbal admonitions and perorations were insufficient to achieve his objectives. His credibility rested on his ability to ensure that his orders were implemented to the fullest extent. Accordingly, he ordered that the doors inside the gates (similar to those inside contemporary Jerusalem's gates) be closed, and that they not be reopened until after the conclusion of Shabbat. Furthermore, to ensure that his orders were carried out effectively, he stationed at the gates a squad of trusted personal servants who were tasked with preventing goods from being smuggled in through the doors.

The Jerusalem market was important business both for the Jewish farmers of the surrounding countryside and for the Tyrian merchants. Nehemiah was risking the investments of those who had brought property in Jerusalem expressly for the purpose of conducting sales there. The merchants recognized that it was pointless to resist Nehemiah frontally; if Sanballat, Tobiah, and Geshem had failed to do so, they had no hope of succeeding against him. Instead the merchants resorted to a stratagem. On a couple of occasions the merchants – notably the sellers of perfume and the vendors of all sorts of wares – spent the night outside Jerusalem. Expecting the Jews to leave the city on the Sabbath, they acquired smaller, and presumably less noticeable, goods and smuggled them inside.[14]

14. Malbim, Neh. 13:20, s.v. *vayalinu*.

Nehemiah had no patience for such evasive stratagems. He "warned them, saying, 'What do you mean by spending the night alongside the wall? If you do so again, I will lay hands upon you!'" (Neh. 13:21). Nehemiah recognized that he was taking a major risk in alienating the Tyrians, who had their own connections to the Persian court.[15] He nevertheless felt sufficiently confident to issue the warning and, if necessary, carry out his threat. The merchants got the message, as no doubt did the Jews who collaborated with them. There were no protests registered in Persia; instead, "From then on," records Nehemiah, "they did not come on the Sabbath" (13:21). True to his character, however, and in light of the recidivism he had encountered upon his return, Nehemiah took no chances: he gave orders to the Levites to purify themselves – by immersion in a *mikve* – and come and guard the gates, to preserve the sanctity of the Sabbath (13:22).

TACKLING INTERMARRIAGE ONCE AGAIN

Nehemiah then addressed the most vexing challenge of them all, that of intermarriage. Nothing he had tried had succeeded any better than Ezra's efforts in bringing a halt to the scourge of the community. He found upon his return that Jewish males – always, it seemed, it was the males who were the perpetrators – had married what he termed "Ashdodite, Ammonite, and Moabite women" (Neh. 13:23). These were not, however, their actual origins, for all three nations had disappeared by the time of the Second Temple. Moreover, even during the First Temple era, there was no prohibition against marrying women from any of the three nations, so long as they converted to Judaism.[16] The implication is that these women had not done so.

To add insult to injury, as many as half the children of these marriages "spoke the language of Ashdod and the language of those various peoples, and did not know how to speak Judean" (Neh. 13:24) – that is, Hebrew. Their families had so thoroughly assimilated that they no

15. Cf. Rabinowitz, *Nechemiah*, 218.
16. Conversion may not have been accompanied by the rituals that now govern the process, which were only fully developed subsequent to the destruction of the Second Temple.

longer spoke the national language of their fathers, but instead spoke their non-Jewish parent's tongue. Since Aramaic was the lingua franca of the time, and was spoken by Jews in Babylonia, the reference here appears to be to the Jews' second language. Not only did they not use Hebrew regularly, they did not use it at all. It was not all that many years earlier that Xerxes's order that the Jews defend themselves in the aftermath of Haman's foiled plot had been promulgated "to the Jews in their own script and language" (Est. 8:9). It was doubly tragic that the Jews who had moved back to their native land had so quickly forgotten their native language.

Some neo-classical commentators argue that the children spoke a hybrid tongue that mixed Hebrew with the local language.[17] The modern counterpart of such a dialect would be Yiddish, a form of German with some French, Russian, and even English words, or Ladino, a form of Spanish and Portuguese; both languages are laced with Hebrew words and phrases. Yet even if what was being spoken in Judah was a combination of Hebrew and indigenous tongues, as opposed to a completely foreign language with no Hebrew content, that was not enough for Nehemiah. His insistence on the use of pure Hebrew as an everyday tongue, or at least as the language the Jews spoke in their homes, is an indicator of the importance he attached to language as an element in Jewish national identity. His view was the model for Eliezer Ben-Yehuda, the father of modern Hebrew. To this day, among non-Jews as well as for most Jews, nationalism and national identity are a function not only of religion, ethnicity, and shared history, but of language as well.[18]

Frustrated by his previous failures, Nehemiah went far beyond merely chastising those who had intermarried. He "cursed them, flogged them, tore out their hair, and adjured them by God, saying, 'You shall not give your daughters in marriage to their sons, or take any of their daughters for your sons or yourselves'" (Neh. 13:25). The curse was

---

17. Malbim, Neh. 13:24, s.v. *medaber*; see also Rabinowitz, *Nechemiah*, 219. Ironically, Yiddish, not Hebrew, was the language that Malbim himself spoke.
18. See for example, Macmillan, *War That Ended Peace*, 267ff (see preface, n. 1), and Strobe Talbott, *The Great Experiment: The Story of Ancient Empires, Modern States, and the Quest for a Global Nation* (New York and London: Simon & Schuster, 2008), 20ff. For a more extensive discussion of this subject, see appendix B.

tailor-made for the circumstances at hand, and was designed to instill fear into the populace. It may even have involved some form of excommunication; those who did not comply with Nehemiah's demands would be separated from the community and left to fend for themselves.[19]

There is some ambiguity regarding the precise nature of the floggings. The Talmud explains that the lashes were of rabbinic derivation, to enforce rabbinic authority (*makat mardut*).[20] There was no limit to the number of lashes administered in floggings of this type. Alternatively, some medieval commentators regarded the floggings as punishment for violation of the biblical prohibition on intermarriage, in which case no more than thirty-nine lashes could be administered.[21] Nehemiah's order that the offenders' hair be torn out was intended to cause additional pain and public humiliation.[22]

More than any other statement in Nehemiah's memoir, this one has been cited to indicate that he was an unrelenting extremist, what is now termed a "religious fundamentalist." Given the stakes, and the times he lived in, Nehemiah was nothing of the sort. His objective was essentially to humiliate the men who had married foreign wives so as to root out intermarriage once and for all. Intermarriage was not only a religious threat to the community; it was a political threat that could undermine the congregation's cohesion.

Another ruler, even one who was not a despot, might for these reasons have executed some of the offenders as an example to the rest. Nehemiah did nothing of the sort. Although he began with censure and progressively moved to more violent and humiliating forms of punishment, Nehemiah stopped short of capital punishment. His objective was not the death of the offenders, but rather their adherence to their vow to forswear intermarriage in the future.

---

19. Moed Katan 16a; Ibn Ezra on Neh. 13:25, s.v. *vaakallelem*; Ralbag, s.v. *vaakallelem*, asserts that Nehemiah excommunicated some of the perpetrators and flogged the others.
20. Moed Katan 16a. See also *Shulḥan Arukh, Ḥoshen Mishpat* 2:1 and Rabinowitz, *Nechemiah*, 220.
21. Ralbag, Neh. 13:25, s.v. *vaakallelem*.
22. See Ralbag, Neh. 13:25, s.v. *va'emretem*.

Nehemiah did not restrict himself to dealing with the men who had married foreign wives. He adjured the entire population of Jerusalem, which presumably had been called together to witness the floggings.[23] His message was straightforward: even those who had never intended to renounce their faith by virtue of marrying non-Jewish women were no less sinners for their act. Nehemiah gave the example of King Solomon: "Among the many nations there was not a king like him, and so well loved was he by God that God made him king of all Israel, yet foreign wives caused even him to sin" (Neh. 13:26). Nehemiah employed the example of King Solomon to demonstrate that even a man of strong character and religious commitment could not withstand the pressure upon his religious practice that marrying out of the faith would impose. If this could happen to King Solomon, it could happen to anyone.[24]

Moreover, as the entire Judahite community knew, as punishment for his sin, Solomon's family had lost its right to rule over all Israel. During the reign of his son Rehoboam, the kingdom was split in two, with Jeroboam ruling over the northern territories that came to be known as the Kingdom of Samaria. The northern kingdom fell to the Assyrians and its people were exiled; the kingdom of Judah met the same fate about 150 years later. The implication was clear: intermarriage would rend the community asunder with the worst possible consequences – dissension, schism, and ultimately another exile.

It should be noted that Nehemiah's reference to Solomon's sin was the cause of some awkward moments for the sages of the Talmud. The notion that members of the Jewish pantheon could sin was evidently seen by some as undermining rabbinic authority. According to a tradition exemplified by R. Samuel b. Naḥmani in the name of R. Yonatan, several Jewish leaders whom Scripture identified as sinners were nothing of the sort. Among them were David and Solomon, whose courts, by rabbinic tradition, had imposed the first set of rabbinic laws. R. Samuel argues that anyone who thinks that these men sinned is "mistaken," and he then ingeniously explains away their faults (Shabbat 56b). In the case of King Solomon, the Talmud asserts that his wives had converted to Judaism, but

23. Ibn Ezra, Neh. 13:25, s.v. *vaashbi'em*.

24. Rashi, Neh. 13:26, s.v. *gam*. Metzudat David, Neh. 13:27, s.v. *velakhem*.

because their intentions were suspect, their conversions were considered invalid and Solomon was, in consequence, "guilty" of intermarriage. While Scripture also explicitly states that Solomon built unauthorized altars for his wives' idols (I Kings 11:7–9), the Talmud asserts that he did not actually build them, but because he had not prevented their construction, he was held liable anyway. Not every talmudic figure appears to have adopted this revisionist view of Solomon (and of his father, for that matter), but it fits neatly into the argument made by some contemporary Orthodox figures who argue that history can be rewritten to serve higher religious purposes.[25]

Despite his high dudgeon at those who had broken their word and married non-Jewish women, Nehemiah did not alter the policy that he had followed during his first term as governor. He did not order the men to leave their families. His admonition focused on the future: he was against people allowing their children to marry non-Jews or marrying non-Jewish women themselves if they had not yet done so. Presumably he hoped that the women who married into the community would follow its religious standards; if they did, and if their children married Jews, the plague of intermarriage would finally come to an end.

In one case it was clear, however, that an elder had not prevented his offspring from marrying a gentile woman. And because of the prominence of the family in question, Nehemiah singled out the perpetrator for special treatment. The individual in question was a grandson of Eliashiv the High Priest; he was married to a daughter of Sanballat. The marriage, which must have taken place during Nehemiah's absence, was an act of defiance. The High Priest was signaling that his alliance with Nehemiah's enemy not only remained intact but was further sealed by this dynastic arrangement.

Nehemiah reacted by excommunicating the young man (whom he does not name in his memoir), driving him out of Jerusalem. As long as this scion of Eliashiv remained in the city, the germs of social and religious rebellion would fester. There were several other reasons for this

25. See Rabinowitz, *Nechemiah*, 220. For a discussion of contemporary efforts to rewrite Jewish history, see Jacob J. Schacter, "Facing the Truths of History," *Torah U-Madda Journal* 8 (1998–1999): 200–76. See also Marc B. Shapiro, *Changing the Immutable: How Orthodox Judaism Rewrites Its History* (Oxford and Portland, OR: Littman Library of Jewish Civilization, 2015).

man's expulsion. First, because the family in question was so prominent, and the marriage so symbolic, Nehemiah could not turn a blind eye to it as he did in all other cases; he had to insist that the young man leave his wife. When the man refused, Nehemiah was compelled to demonstrate to the community that such defiance could not be tolerated. In addition, by driving the young man away, Nehemiah prevented Sanballat from visiting his son-in-law in Jerusalem. Sanballat, Nehemiah's arch-nemesis, would have exploited any such visit to cause trouble in the community.[26]

Having banned any future marriages with non-Jews, Nehemiah purified the priests and Levites and put them to work in the shifts that he had arranged prior to his departure for Persia. He also restored the provision of wood offerings and first fruits to the Temple. It had been specified in the covenant but was honored only in the breach as soon as he left Judah. He set an exact timetable for the delivery of both these offerings and, to facilitate meeting the timetable, destroyed the barriers that the indigenous people had erected along the routes to Jerusalem in order to prevent the offerings from being brought in a timely fashion.[27]

THE MEMOIR'S CONCLUSION

Nehemiah's memoir ends abruptly. He closes with yet more pleas to God to remember him favorably for his good deeds, specifically recounting his restoration of the practices and regulations that he introduced in the covenant. Indeed, he pleads for remembrance no less than three times in the concluding chapter of his memoir.

Language very similar to that of Nehemiah's plea to God appears in the concluding phrases of the statue of the Egyptian notable and naval commander Udjahorresnet, as we saw earlier. The latter, like Nehemiah, had been sent by the Persian court on a delicate mission to his homeland to restore tranquility in the aftermath of serious anti-Persian disturbances. It is possible that Nehemiah wished these last verses to be preserved on a statue similar to that of Udjahorresnet.

As noted, the rabbis did not take kindly to Nehemiah's request, and for that reason did not recognize his memoir as a stand-alone book

26. Ralbag, Neh. 13:28, s.v. *vaavriḥehu*.

27. Rashi, Neh. 13:31, s.v. *ulevikurim*; Ibn Yahia ad loc., s.v. *korban*.

of Scripture. On its face it seems puzzling, however, for him to have been punished for a request that was far from unreasonable, particularly as it was put to God, not to other men. Yet Udjahorresnet's plea was also addressed to the gods ("O great gods who are in Sais! Remember all the useful things accomplished by the chief physician Udjahorresnet").[28] No doubt the rabbis, particularly the Men of the Great Assembly, were familiar with statues such as the one containing Udjahorresnet's inscription. They may well have concluded that Nehemiah indeed intended for a similar statue to be erected in his memory.

In any event, even if this were not the case, the rabbis who chose to delete Nehemiah's name from his work may have done so because he represented a lay threat to rabbinic religious authority. It was he – not Ezra the scholar, scribe, and rabbinic archetype and paragon – who imposed a constitution upon the people. It was he who implemented both biblical laws and later ordinances that had long been honored in the breach. It was he who innovated new practices beyond those Ezra had introduced. In this sense Nehemiah, for all his good deeds, represented a lay challenge as an alternative source of authority that the rabbis of a later era, struggling to preserve Judaism in the face of exile and persecution, simply could not countenance.

Nehemiah offers no record of his later years, no indication as to whether he once again returned to Persia or instead remained in Judah. A tradition dating back to the seventh-century compendium of laws entitled *Halakhot Gedolot*,[29] and subsequently recounted by the anonymous author of *Kol Bo* as having been first noted in the midrash

28. Blenkinsopp, "Mission," 415 (see chap. 4, n. 22).

29. *Halakhot Gedolot: Hilkhot Tisha B'Av V'Taaniyot* (Jerusalem: Machon Yerushalayim, 5752/1982), 233. There is some disagreement as to the author of *Halakhot Gedolot*. According to Rabbi Moses of Coucy, it was Rav Yehudai Gaon, who flourished in the eighth century CE, as Rabbi Moses of Coucy asserts in his *Sefer Mitzvot Gadol*. See *Rabbenu Moshe ben Rav Yaakov z"l MiCoucy, Sefer Mitzvot Gadol: Lo Ta'ase*, ed. Alter Pinhas Farber (n.p., 5751/1981), introduction, 4. Others assert that the ninth-century halakhist R. Shimon Kayyara was the author of *Halakhot Gedolot*; see, for example, Avi Sagi and Zvi Zohar, *Transforming Identity: The Ritual Transition from Gentile to Jew – Structure and Meaning* (New York: Bloomsbury, 2008), 158, and *Jewish Encyclopedia*, s.v. "Kayyara, Simeon" (http://www/jewishencyclopedia.com/articles/9254-kayyara-simeon).

Megillat Taanit,[30] gives the date of Nehemiah's passing as the ninth of Tevet. According to this tradition, which appears to have been widely accepted in Orthodox circles and is mentioned in the context of the *Seliḥot* prayers for the tenth of Tevet, Ezra died on the same day.[31] Interestingly, the *Seliḥot* only refer to Ezra, while *Megillat Taanit* mentions neither Ezra nor Nehemiah in conjunction with the ninth of Tevet. Indeed, one commentator on *Halakhot Gedolot* asserts that its reference to Nehemiah's passing is a later insertion.[32]

Whatever the origin of the tradition concerning the day that Nehemiah died, there can be little doubt why it arose. It was on the tenth of Tevet that Nebuchadnezzar first broke through the walls of Jerusalem in an operation that culminated in the destruction of the First Temple. It was Nehemiah who healed that breach nearly a century and a half later. In so doing, he not only ensured the security of the Jewish commonwealth for several hundred years, but also inspired those who again secured its walls, and the city they enclosed, after another hiatus of two thousand years.

30. *Kol Bo* (New York: Shulsinger/Feldheim, 5747/1987), 27.

31. See, for example, Rabbi Nosson Scherman et al., *The Artscroll Siddur*, 2nd ed. (Brooklyn, NY: 1990), 851n, s.v. "9 Teves." See also the Orthodox Union website, https://www.ou.org/judaism-101/bh-yom-yom/tevet/. The Chabad Torah Tots website states that both Ezra and Nehemiah died on the ninth of Tevet, 320 BCE; see http:www.torahtots.com/timecapsule/thismonth/tevet.htm#9.

32. Rabbi Ze'ev Wolf Lipkin, *Hagahot ben Aryeh* in *Halakot Gedolot*, 233n6. Lipkin, the father of Rabbi Israel Salanter, was *dayan* of Telz and Goldingen early in the nineteenth century.

Conclusion

Nehemiah's Legacy

Senior official, governor, statesman, legislator, religious enforcer, national leader, social reformer – Nehemiah was a man of many roles, and he excelled at them all. He was a visionary without being a prophet, a man who revived in his demoralized people the sense of religious and national commitment that had dissipated both during their years in exile and upon their return to their homeland. He struggled to establish a viable, pulsating, dynamic Jewish polity, one that embodied religious values and that practiced social and economic justice, and did so in the face of opposition from both the indigenous peoples and some of his leading coreligionists. And, as we have seen, his efforts foreshadowed the challenges that faced those who brought the State of Israel into existence – and continue to face its leaders today.

Nehemiah did not seek merely to restore the values of the Torah or the identity of the nation. He was an innovator in both the religious and the national and social realm. Indeed, with respect to some of his reforms, it might be said that he was literally millennia ahead of his time. His legacy can best be understood when one regards both dimensions, the religious and the national.

NEHEMIAH AS RELIGIOUS INNOVATOR

Although the Talmud was critical of Nehemiah, as has been noted, tradition has assigned him a place among the Men of the Great Assembly, to whom it attributes a host of religious innovations. Nehemiah was responsible for a significant number of these innovations, all of which were incorporated as adjuncts to the Oral Law, and took the form of rabbinic edicts. Nehemiah himself outlined some of these innovations; others were derived by the talmudic sages from the text of his memoir.

Most, though not all, of Nehemiah's religious edicts were incorporated into the covenant. These included the ban on commerce on Shabbat, the requirement that each individual contribute one-third of a shekel for the Temple upkeep, the provision of the wood offering, and the obligation to bring first fruits of every tree, not just those mentioned in the Torah, to the Temple in Jerusalem. In addition, Nehemiah imposed a ban on treading winepresses on Shabbat; again, doing so was not a violation of Torah law. He also prohibited loading grain onto pack animals on Shabbat. Finally, the ceremony that he organized to dedicate Jerusalem's reconstructed walls, which involved a dual procession, became the model for all future expansions of the city.

In addition to Nehemiah's explicit rulings, the rabbis derived a number of others either from those rulings or from his actions, as we have seen throughout the course of this volume. Among the most significant rabbinic derivations of Nehemiah's edicts was the principle of *shvut*, which, like Nehemiah's rulings, were additional restrictive laws for Shabbat and holidays meant to prevent the violation of biblical laws.[1] These laws drew upon Nehemiah's ban on conducting commercial relations on Shabbat, which, the sages reasoned, would inevitably lead to the violation of the biblical prohibition against writing on the holy day.

Another important rabbinic innovation, also derived from Nehemiah's rulings, was the series of laws relating to the concept of *muktze*. These laws, which applied to Shabbat, and generally to festivals as well, banned the handling, or even the moving of items that were either not appropriate for use on Shabbat or reserved for weekday use, with some

1. See for example, Shabbat 8a, 94b, 97a, 114b; Ḥagiga 16b. For a discussion of aspects of *shvut*, see *Encyclopedia Talmudit*, s.v. *Ain Shevut Bamikdash: Gedero Vedino*.

exceptions made for items that were identified for Shabbat use prior to its onset. Still another set of rabbinic bans relating to Shabbat pertained to the loading of pack animals. Nehemiah had banned the loading of articles of any kind. His ruling was later amended to prohibit only the movement of large saws and plowshares.

The Talmud draws upon Nehemiah's description of the military watches assigned to the defenders of the city, which began when the morning star rose, *amud hashaḥar,* and terminated at night, when three stars could be seen, *tzet hakokhavim.* These serve as the Talmud's basis for establishing certain laws relating to early morning, as well as when one day ended and the next would begin. The latter ruling, in turn, determined, for example, when Shabbat and festivals terminated, when the evening *Shema* prayer could be recited, and at what point in the evening the festival of Shavuot could commence upon the conclusion of the forty-ninth day of the Omer, which begins on the second day of Passover. Another rabbinic ruling derived from Nehemiah's narrative specified that Rosh HaShana was always a two-day holiday.

Nehemiah's request to the king that he be provided timber for the reconstruction of the gates and walls, as well as for his governor's mansion, led to an exemption in the Talmud. After considerable debate, the sages resolved that one could accept a gift from a non-Jew for a Temple repair project only near completion of the project and only if the donation was such that it could not be easily identified with the donor. The exemption was for a government donation, the subject of Nehemiah's request.

Nehemiah's dedication of the renovated walls led to yet another rabbinic ruling. The dedication ceremony had involved two processions headed in opposite directions around the wall. The double procession created a precedent that the Talmud later remarked upon: it was a necessary precondition for legitimizing the expansion of the city.

The rabbinic exemption of government officials from the ban on drinking non-sacramental wine produced – or even touched – by non-Jews (which itself was rabbinic) derived from the obvious fact that Nehemiah was a cupbearer, and therefore, as was widely understood in ancient times, had to taste the wine before handing it to the king. The actual rabbinic derivation of the exemption was from the Persian word *tirshata,* which described Nehemiah as the governor, but which the rabbis divided into the Hebrew words *heter shato,* meaning permission to drink.

Nehemiah's behavior and the extent to which it provides a basis for exemptions to rabbinic and even biblical prohibitions and strictures has taken on tremendous significance since the birth of the State of Israel, with the concomitant responsibilities of its diplomatic corps. It is also significant due to the increase in recent years of both the number and seniority of Jewish officials serving in the governments of Diaspora lands. Some commentators support blanket exemption from all rabbinic ordnances,[2] others circumscribe the exemption, while yet others apply it to some biblical prohibitions.[3]

Another rabbinic derivation from Nehemiah's memoir was the ruling that a sukka could be built in a public place. The sages argue that prior to Nehemiah's era, a sukka could only be built on private property. It was when, as Nehemiah recounted, the people built booths not only on their roofs and in their courtyards but also in Jerusalem's public domains – despite the fact that all of Jerusalem was considered to be communal property – that the restriction on building on communal property was lifted. Interestingly, but perhaps not surprisingly, the sages attribute this innovation to Ezra rather than to Nehemiah.

Finally, Nehemiah, like Ezra before him, banned intermarriage with all non-Jews, not only those who were members of the Seven Nations, which had disappeared by the time he arrived in Judah. The sages of the Talmud, under pressure from the Romans in particular, erected high barriers to intermarriage, but it was Ezra and Nehemiah who identified the importance of maintaining the cohesion of the Jewish people. The two men differed in that Ezra attempted – unsuccessfully – to force the breakup of marriages that had already taken place. Nehemiah was more politic; he focused on the need to prevent future intermarriages.

2. Mathews, *Commentary*, 27, commenting on Neh. 8:8.
3. For a discussion, see Dov S. Zakheim, "Practicing Jews Serving in the National Security Community: Modalities and Challenges," *Conversations* 14 (Autumn 2012/5773): 9–23.

Contemporary debates in Israel over intermarriage in many ways reflect the divergence of views between Ezra and Nehemiah. Those who would retroactively annul conversions are, in effect, breaking up families that in most, if not all, cases view themselves as Jewish. Their position is very much in the spirit of Ezra. Those who would ease the path to conversion for couples that are already married, whether in civil or non-Orthodox marriages, reflect what is arguably Nehemiah's more judicious approach to what is, at a minimum, a delicate situation, and at most – as it was for Nehemiah – an explosive one.[4]

Nehemiah's contribution to religious law and practice did not end with talmudic rulings. The prayers that he recorded, whether uttered by him, Ezra, or the Levites, have made their way into the daily, Shabbat, and holiday ritual of the Jewish people. While not cited in full, some of these prayers are among the most familiar in the prayer book. These include Ezra's *Vekarot Imo Habrit,* and the even more widely recited *Barukh Shem Kevod Malkhuto Leolam Va'ed* ("Blessed be His name and glorious sovereignty for ever and ever"), which the rabbis derived from the Levites' exhortation to the people after Ezra's reading of the Torah.

Nehemiah's influence continued after the talmudic age. His response to intermarriage became the basis for a major ruling by Rabbi Asher ben Yeḥiel (ca. 1250–1327), popularly known as the Rosh, who was the leading Spanish halakhic decisor in the thirteenth century, and whose decisions have continued to influence halakha ever since. Drawing upon the talmudic dictum that it was permissible for a court to flog, curse, excommunicate, and pull out the hair of a transgressor,[5] the Rosh ruled that in the case of a transgressor who could not afford to pay a fine, the community could

> punish him and fine him with floggings and with all means of persecution until he submitted to the law… as it is written "and I quarreled with them and I cursed them and I beat some of the men and I pulled out their hair" (Neh. 13:25).… Therefore the

4. For a discussion of both points of view, see Dov S. Zakheim, "Transforming Israel's Chief Rabbinate," *Conversations* 17 (Autumn 2013/5774): 81–114.
5. Moed Katan 16a.

> court in each city can persecute and trouble with all means of such persecution and exclusion anyone who defies their rulings.[6]

The sages of the Talmud noted that Nehemiah had forced the people to vow not to permit their children to marry non-Jews. On the basis of this action, they concluded that a court had the right to "bind a recalcitrant against his will."[7] In turn, medieval Jewish authorities drew upon the talmudic ruling to apply the sanction of *ḥerem,* the equivalent of an involuntary personal oath, to enforce communal ordinances.[8]

Nehemiah's influence is cited in two more contemporary rulings by Rabbi Yosef Eliyahu Henkin, a leading decisor in mid-twentieth-century America. Rabbi Henkin refers to Nehemiah in the course of arguing that Shabbat need not terminate more than seventy-two minutes after sunset, even on long summer days when the division of the day into twelve hourly units results in a longer period per unit. He notes that were it not for the passage in Nehemiah that half the men worked "and half of them held spears ... until the emergence of the stars" (Neh. 4:15), the rabbis would have treated sunset as the end of the day, and accordingly would have terminated Shabbat at that time, rather than at least an hour later, as is the common custom.[9]

In the course of another responsum, Rabbi Henkin cites Nehemiah's call to the people on Rosh HaShana to "go, eat choice foods and drink sweet drinks and send portions to whoever has nothing prepared, for the day is holy to our Lord" (Neh. 8:10). Rabbi Henkin bemoans the fact that the day's Musaf prayers were being so dragged out by songs and melodies that people had taken to eating after the first set of shofar blasts. Accordingly, Rabbi Henkin sought to ban eating prior

---

6. Yitzchak Shlomo Yodlov, ed., *She'eilot UTeshuvot LeRabbeinu Asher ben Yeḥiel, zt"l* (Jerusalem: Machon Ohr Hamizrach, 5754/1994), 39.
7. Samuel Morell, "The Constitutional Limits of Communal Government in Rabbinic Law," *Jewish Social Studies* 33 (April–July 1971): 92. Morell's source is Moed Katan 16a.
8. Morell, loc. cit.
9. Rabbi Yosef Eliyahu Henkin, *She'eilot UTeshuvot Gevurot Eliyahu al Arba Ḥelkei Shulḥan Arukh*, vol. 1 (Lakewood, NJ: Machon Harav Henkin, 5773/2013), no. 73, pp. 130–31.

to Musaf, however long the service lasted.[10] As noted earlier, the Rosh, citing Rabbi Hai Gaon, as well as later decisors such as Rabbi Isaac bar Sheshet (1326–1408; better known by his acronym Rivash) cited the same passage both to forbid fasting on Rosh HaShana and to promote the tradition of particularly eating foods whose homonyms portended good things in the new year. As he put it, "eat choice foods and drink sweet drinks so that your year will be prosperous and sweet."[11] As with the Rosh's ruling regarding the treatment of transgressors, and the talmudic citation upon which the ruling was based, it was not so much an explicit ruling by Nehemiah but rather his recounting of events that furnished the basis for halakha to be codified.

In sum, Nehemiah, though a layman, nevertheless bequeathed a significant religious legacy to his people. As he writes at the conclusion of his memoir, "I purged them [the priests] of every foreign element... and for the wood offering [to be brought] at fixed times and for the first fruits. O my God, remember it to my credit!" (Neh. 13:30–31). Indeed, his memoir has proved to be a valuable, if not critical, resource for halakhic legislation as well as communal prayer. That is no small accomplishment for a man who nevertheless saw his legacy primarily in national terms.

NEHEMIAH AS NATIONAL LEADER

However significant his accomplishments in the development of what later came to be termed "rabbinic Judaism," it is as a national leader that Nehemiah is rightly best remembered. Of course, Nehemiah's most famous achievement was his restoration of Jerusalem – its walls, its defenses, its population. In the face of powerful entrenched opposition, he converted what had become a desolate provincial backwater into the heartbeat of a nation that expanded and thrived for half a millennium, and provided the inspiration for generations afterward.

What he did for the city he also did for the Temple. When he arrived on the scene, it must have been in desperate need of upgrade

10. Ibid., 281, 284.

11. On the prohibition against fasting, see Rosh, Rosh HaShana 4:14, s.v. *ulehitanot bishnei yamim tovim shel Rosh HaShana*, and above, chap. 10, n. 40. On eating sweet things, see Rosh, Rosh HaShana 4:14, s.v. *vegam besefer Ezra*.

and maintenance; the sources of income to fund its maintenance had dried up. By reinstating long-standing practices, and initiating new ones, such as the provision of first fruits from all trees, Nehemiah created the regular funding streams necessary to ensure that Temple operations were fully funded and its maintenance assured.

Nehemiah was also a social reformer. As a man of action, he did not merely restate the words of the prophets but implemented them. He forced the upper classes to relieve the economic burden of the less fortunate. In so doing he not only enabled the poor to retain whatever meager land holdings they might have possessed, but also strengthened critical family ties by preventing the sale of loved ones into slavery and enabling those who already had suffered that fate to be redeemed. In effect, he created a social and economic safety net for less privileged members of the community.

One of Nehemiah's social reforms was also highly political: the increased status he gave to the Levites. By tradition a landless class, the Levites supported themselves from the gifts they received from their coreligionists; invariably, the vast majority of them were poor. Nehemiah incorporated them into the Temple apparatus and mandated that they receive the gifts to which Jewish law entitled them, thereby ensuring them a steady income. In addition, he included them in his armed security forces, gave them a major role in the ceremonies he orchestrated, and joined Ezra in transforming them into a scholarly class, thereby vastly increasing their prestige. In implementing these reforms, Nehemiah won the Levites' solid allegiance, which helped him offset the opposition of a significant element of the priestly class.

Nehemiah's nation-building efforts also afforded a place to the role of women in the community. He drafted the daughters of Shallum son of Hallohesh into the workforce that repaired the city's walls. Shallum was a prominent man; that his daughters were involved in the city's reconstruction afforded other, perhaps lesser-born women in the community a model of national service that they all could seek to emulate. He may even have included the womenfolk among the city's defenders, since they were drafted in family units. Moreover, he paid heed to the protests of the women whose husbands had been drafted into the work gangs repairing the walls; in addition to feeding their families, they were forced to cultivate the land on their own, and to do so in the face of greedy creditors and indigenous enemies. Nehemiah records that women singers were among the returnees with Zerubbabel. It is possible that the menfolk heard them as they sang.[12] In addition, Nehemiah (and Ezra) listed a woman, Soferet, as giving her name to one of the clans descended from Solomon's slaves that were among Zerubbabel's returnees. Her listing in this way indicates the important status granted to some women in post-exilic Judah; by the time of the return to Zion, these clans had to all intents and purposes been fully absorbed into the Jewish community.[13]

Finally, Nehemiah focused on the importance of Hebrew as the language of the Jewish household. Language is central to nationhood. As a leading rabbinic educator has written:

> It is impossible to ignore the historical connection throughout the duration of all three exiles [i.e., the Egyptian, Babylonian, and Roman exiles] between the abandonment of the Holy Tongue and the erosion of the national character of our people, and [as a consequence] the priority given to intermingling and identifying with the citizens of foreign lands.[14]

Indeed, some of the greatest rabbinic decisors also recognized the deleterious impact on Jewish identity when its historic language became, in effect, a dead letter.[15] By contrast, the revival of the language is seen as a part of the miracle of Israel's rebirth: as one rabbinic scholar puts it "the revival of the study of Scripture (Tanakh) in our time is part of the amazing biblical miracle of the ingathering of exiles and the return

12. Metzudat David on Neh. 7:67, s.v. *meshorerim*, asserts that the women had sung along the way as the people returned to their homeland. That they would do so as separate groups strains the imagination, since they were most likely to have been part of family units.
13. Galil, *Daniel, Ezra UNeḥemia*, 139–40.
14. Rabbi Ari Yitzchak Shvat, "*Targum VeḤibur Sifrei Kodesh BeLa'az*" (Translation and Authorship of Holy Books in a Foreign Language), *Teḥumin* 17 (5757/1997): 379.
15. Among them were Rabbi Akiva Eger and Rabbi Jacob Emden; see ibid.

to Zion, together with the revival of the language of Scripture in the land of Scripture."[16]

Nevertheless, many modern rabbinic leaders focused more on avoiding any knowledge of local languages than on the need to communicate in Hebrew. For them the solution was to speak Yiddish. In our day as well, there are those who insist that Hebrew serve only as the language of prayer and study, and who especially oppose the use of modern Hebrew as the national Jewish language (see appendix B).

The Jews of Nehemiah's day also had an alternative to the languages spoken by their non-Jewish wives, namely Western Aramaic. It was a language with which they were familiar, being the lingua franca of the Persian Empire. Indeed, large portions of Daniel and Ezra are written in Aramaic, while the Torah itself attributes an Aramaic expression to Laban. Nehemiah, on the other hand, insisted on Hebrew, focusing in particular on the children of mixed marriages, who tended to speak the language of their non-Jewish mothers. In so doing, he created the basis for a Jewish identity that has lasted two millennia, and in the process set a precedent for modern Jewish life: the return to Hebrew as the "natural language" of the Jewish people.

Nehemiah's efforts to modernize Jerusalem's infrastructure, his creation of a safety net for the needy, his emphasis on social justice, and his recognition of the role of women in society offer a model that modern leaders – Jewish and non-Jewish alike – would do well to follow. His commitment to maintaining his nation's cultural heritage, his emphasis on maintaining a viable military deterrent, and his efforts to recruit as much of society as possible into national service remain viable – indeed, commendable – policies for all modern states and those who lead them. As with so much else in Scripture, times and circumstances may have changed, but some lessons are eternal.

Nehemiah was not without flaws. He was self-centered. He saw himself as superior to his predecessors. He was stingy when it came to giving credit to others. No wonder the sages were reluctant to credit him with a book of his own.

---

16. Yoel Bin-Nun, "*Al Odot Mikraot*" (Regarding Biblical Texts), http://ybn.co.il/wp-content/uploads/2014/09/m2.pdf.

Nevertheless, just as Ezra restored the Torah to the Jewish people, so did Nehemiah restore their sense of identity and nationhood. For the Jewish people, Torah and nationality are intertwined and inseparable. Nehemiah, even more than Ezra, recognized this reality. For that reason, more than any other, his book remains required reading, and his role as a leading light of Jewish history will forever be secure.

Appendix A

Chronological Table

ACCORDING TO AGGADIC LORE, JEWISH TRADITION, HISTORICAL ACCOUNTS, AND CRITICAL SPECULATION

(All dates BCE)
Midrashic*
Traditional**
Critical#
Tosefot¶

586	Fall of Jerusalem
559	Cyrus becomes king of Anshan
550	Cyrus becomes king of Persia
539	Cyrus conquers Babylon

* Consensus view of aggadic literature and medieval and neo-medieval twentieth-century Jewish commentators based on *Seder Olam Rabba*. See also Moshe Yair Veinshtok, *Yemot Olam*, in *Seder Olam Rabba HaShalem LeHatana Rabbi Yose ben Rabbi Ḥalafta* (Bnai Berak: Mishor, 1990), 458–63; and Rabinowitz, *Nechemiah*, 32.

** View of Modern Orthodox commentaries and scholars, mainstream historians, some biblical critics.

\# View of many biblical critics.

¶ *Tosafot*, the medieval commentators, place Nehemiah's mission four years before Ezra's, foreshadowing the argument of recent biblical critics. See *Tosafot*, Rosh HaShana 3b, s.vv. *shnat* and *be'oto*.

539–38	Edict of Cyrus
	Initial return of Jews under Sheshbazzar
538–37	Zerubbabel and Joshua
535	Altar rebuilt
530	Cyrus dies; Cambyses rules
525	Persia conquers Egypt
522	Reign of Darius I Hystaspes
520	Zerubbabel
520–516/15	Temple rebuilt
486	Darius I dies; Xerxes I rules
465	Xerxes I dies; Artaxerxes I rules
458	Ezra's mission**
445–433	Nehemiah's mission**
402	Nehemiah's mission¶
398	Ezra's mission¶
371	Babylon falls; Darius the Mede rules*
370	Cyrus on Persian throne; edict of Cyrus*
368	Cyrus killed; "Ahasuerus" rules*
354	Darius I ("Artahsasta") rules*
348	Temple rebuilt*
347	Ezra's mission begins*
334–322	Nehemiah's mission*
333–323	Reign of Alexander the Great
318	Alexander the Great defeats Persians, rules Judah

Appendix B

Hebrew: The Jewish National Language

Nehemiah's emphasis on Hebrew as the spoken language of the community in Judah set a precedent that for centuries was honored in the breach and in contemporary times has been the subject of much halakhic and political dispute. Until its revival in the late nineteenth century, Hebrew was exclusively the language of prayer and religious scholarship. During the Persian and Hellenistic periods, most Jews spoke Aramaic or Greek or both. The Books of Daniel and Ezra have a heavy Aramaic component.

When Rome came to dominate the eastern Mediterranean, most Jews spoke one of the Aramaic dialects. The great translations of Scripture, of which Yonatan ben Uziel and Onkelos are the best known, were written in Aramaic. So too were the Talmud and the various midrashim. Whereas the Mishna, completed around 250 CE, was written in Hebrew, the Jerusalem Talmud, completed a century later, was written in a Western Aramaic dialect. The Babylonian Talmud, completed around 500 CE, was likewise written in an Aramaic dialect that was spoken in the Parthian Empire. Most halakhic decisions and other correspondence during the subsequent geonic period, which lasted into the eleventh century, were written in Aramaic or Arabic; fewer were written in Hebrew. Aramaic prayers also figured in the liturgy, most famously the various forms of the Kaddish, but also prayers like *Yekum Purkan*, recited on most Sabbaths.

Even as local vernaculars became the language of European Jewry – for example, Old French as recorded in Rashi's eleventh-century commentary – for several centuries Aramaic remained alongside Hebrew as the language of Jewish scholarship. The Zohar was probably the best-known Aramaic work to appear in medieval Europe, but Aramaic literature also included many religious poems, known as *piyutim*, of which the *Akdamot* and *Yetziv Pitgam*, both recited on Shavuot, may be the best known to synagogue goers. In addition, sacred songs (*zemirot*) such as *Yah Ribbon*, which is sung at Shabbat tables on Friday nights, continued to be written in Aramaic well into near-modern times.

Aramaic formulas also entered into holiday ritual. The nullification of leaven is recited in Aramaic upon searching for leaven on the night before Passover eve. A similar Aramaic formula nullifying the leaven is recited the next day following its burning. A familiar passage in the Passover Seder, "This Is the Bread of Affliction," is also recited in Aramaic. Finally, certain documents central to the rhythm of Jewish life, such as the *ketubba* in a marriage, and the *get* in a divorce, are still worded in Aramaic.

The Arab conquests of the eighth century led to the displacement of Aramaic in much of the Middle East, and Arabic became the second language of the Jews of that region. Leading Jewish scholars such as Rabbi Saadia Gaon in the tenth century and Maimonides two centuries later – as well as a host of lesser luminaries – wrote many of their volumes and responsa in Arabic. As for Hebrew, it continued to be restricted to prayer and scholarship, while Judaized forms of local languages, notably Yiddish, Ladino, and Judeo-Arabic, became the everyday language of the Jewish people.

These developments did not go unnoticed by rabbinic scholars. Maimonides, in particular, explained the need for an order of prayer in terms of the challenge that had confronted the Jews of Nehemiah's day. As he put it, the children of those exiled by Nebuchadnezzar had blended in with the Persians, Greeks, and other peoples among whom they had been dispersed, and as a result, they

> spoke an adulterated language that was a mixture of many tongues … unable fully to express [themselves] in a single language but rather

> in a garbled manner, as it is written, "and half of their sons spoke Ashdodite, and they did not know how to speak Hebrew, and [thus it was] regarding the language of each nation" (Neh. 13:24). And for this reason, when one of them prayed, he became tongue-tied when it came to outlining his needs or to praising the Holy One, Blessed Be He, in the holy tongue until the Hebrew became mixed with other languages. And when Ezra and his *beit din* witnessed this development, they arranged the eighteen benedictions in a set order... so that they should be organized for all and easily learned, so that the prayer of those who stuttered would be as complete as the prayer of the fluent. And for this reason [the rabbis] established that all the blessings and prayers should be organized for all Israel so that the subject matter of each blessing would be set out [even] in the mouth of the tongue-tied.[1]

At the same time, Maimonides cautioned against the use of Hebrew for anything other than holy pursuits. He chided as foolish those scholars who were reluctant to sing songs that praised God or good deeds if they were in Arabic but had no qualms about singing songs about forbidden or "disgusting" subjects as long as they were in Hebrew. As he put it, "speech is neither forbidden nor permitted, nor to be loved nor rejected nor the subject of a commandment on the basis of its language, but rather [on the basis of] its subject matter." He went on to argue that adding a passage from Scripture to an inappropriate poem in no way rendered it any less forbidden to be recited.[2]

The advent of modern Hebrew, almost single-handedly inspired by the Lithuanian-born journalist Eliezer Ben-Yehuda in the late nineteenth and early twentieth centuries (and also advocated by the proto Zionist rabbi, halakhic decisor, and teacher of Hebrew Rabbi Yehuda Alkalai),[3] posed a special challenge for those who viewed Hebrew as a holy language. Ben-Yehuda, and the Zionist movement, which adopted

1. *Mishneh Torah, Hilkhot Tefilla* 1:4.
2. Maimonides, *Commentary on Masekhet Avot* 1:17.
3. I am indebted to Rabbi Yoel Bin-Nun for pointing out Rabbi Alkalai's critical role in the revival of Hebrew as an everyday language. Interestingly, one of his descendants,

Hebrew as its language, were avowedly secular. How, then, was Hebrew to be treated by those who considered themselves committed to halakha?

The standard that Nehemiah set seemed to imply that Hebrew was meant to be a daily language, not merely a holy one. After all, although he did not break up marriages that already had taken place between Jews and non-Jews, he nevertheless insisted that the children of the intermarried couples speak Hebrew in their homes. Surely not everything that was spoken in such homes was holy.

On the other hand, Maimonides had made it clear that it is the subject matter, rather than the language used to express it, that matters most. For some in the Orthodox community, following this view, the conversational Hebrew of the Zionists was inherently profane. Since no one but the Zionists spoke Hebrew in anything other than a religious context, spoken Hebrew for non-religious purposes simply was not to be permitted.[4]

The creation of the State of Israel, with Hebrew as its official language, and as a major unifying factor for Jews who streamed to the state from the four corners of the earth, intensified the challenge to those who were only prepared to employ Hebrew for religious purposes. In fact, the challenge was not only within Israel itself, but throughout the Diaspora, where there had already been a growing movement within religious Zionist circles to translate religious texts into modern Hebrew and use it in study even before the creation of the state.[5] The reaction of many traditionalists both within Israel and outside it, and most notably in the Ashkenazic community,[6] was to dig in and emphasize both the teaching of Jewish subjects and daily speech in either the local vernacular or, preferably in the

---

Sven Alkalaj, became the new Bosnian Republic's ambassador to the United States and later that country's foreign minister. Minister Alkalaj related this fact to the author and is proud of his ancestry.

4. See Shternbuch, *She'eilot UTeshuvot*, vol. 1, no. 538, 366–67 (see chap. 9, n. 33). Rabbi Shternbuch served in South Africa and then headed the anti-Zionist *Edah Ḥaredit Bet Din* in Jerusalem. Rabbi Shternbuch has maintained close ties with the famously anti-Zionist Satmar Rebbe.
5. For example, the Yeshiva of Flatbush, founded in Brooklyn in 1927.
6. The Sephardic communities have long spoken Hebrew in an accent and manner similar to that of modern Hebrew; even *ḥaredi* Ashkenazim accepted their Hebrew as legitimate. See Shternbuch, *She'eilot UTeshuvot*, vol. 1, no. 538, 366–67.

case of religious studies, the Yiddish of their European fathers.[7] Indeed, there was even opposition to the written translation of Daniel and the Aramaic portions of Ezra into Hebrew.[8]

Opponents of the use of modern Hebrew, even for religious studies, have asserted, in the words of a contemporary decisor, not only that modern Hebrew is like any ordinary language, but that it "is worse than other languages because it is the language of the secular who have no part in God's Torah."[9] Another late-twentieth-century decisor writes, "Certainly it is not the holy tongue that the patriarchs, the prophets, or our fathers spoke."[10] In other words, there is a fundamental difference between the "Holy Tongue" and modern Hebrew. Indeed, this decisor cites the very passages of Nehemiah regarding the need to speak Hebrew to prove his point: "The people spoke part Chaldean [*sic*] and Ashdodite because they did not keep themselves holy... and it is impossible to maintain the holy tongue without holiness."[11] Some opponents of the use of modern Hebrew have gone so far as to question the use of any modern Hebrew word, unless it appears in some form in Scripture or in the halakhic literature of earlier generations.[12]

It is indeed ironic that Nehemiah is cited as the basis for opposing the use of Hebrew in everyday life. Of course, the opposition would have existed even if Nehemiah had made no mention of his concern to

7. See Rabbi Moshe Stern, *She'eilot UTeshuvot Be'er Moshe*, 2nd ed. (Jerusalem: Moznaim, 5764/2004), no. 140, 208–9, who relates a dispute that he had with the "heads of an institution in Boro Park because of their teaching Chumash in Hebrew translation in their school." The school was probably the Etz Chaim Yeshiva, a Modern Orthodox, pro-Israel institution. Rabbi Stern recounts that he took the leaders of the school to task in the presence of Rabbi Aharon Kotler, the leading *ḥaredi rosh yeshiva* in America, who sided with him, stating in Yiddish, "*Der Debretziner Rav iz gerecht*" ("The Debreziner Rabbi [Rabbi Stern] is right").
8. See Rabbi Eliezer Waldenberg, *She'eilot UTeshuvot Tzitz Eliezer*, 2nd ed., vol. 14, no. 1 (Jerusalem: n.p. 5745/1985), especially 4–7, and vol. 15, no. 3 (Jerusalem: n.p. 5745/1985), 8.
9. Shternbuch, *She'eilot UTeshuvot*, vol. 1, no. 538, 366.
10. Rabbi Menashe Klein, *Mishneh Halakhot*, vol. 9, no. 204 (Baltimore: Mishne Halachoth Gedoloth Institute, 5758/1998), 45. Rabbi Klein, the rabbi of Ungvar, was closely linked to the Satmar community.
11. Klein, loc. cit.
12. Ibid., vol. 6, no. 95, 52.

make Hebrew the language of the Jews of his time. To assert that the people were all righteous and holy flies in the face of Nehemiah's own testimony and rationale for mandating that Hebrew be spoken, namely, the rash of intermarriages within the community.

Nehemiah's memoir, and more generally, the sacred books of the Prophets and Writings (Nakh), deal with real life in the real world. Rabbi Yuval Cherlow – one of an ever-expanding cadre of religious Bible experts who not only have brought Scripture to life, but have done so by translating and expounding its classical Hebrew in the spoken language of the Jewish state – writes that Scripture speaks of

> national-social life, of the link between Torah and life, of the high status of societal morality, which serves as the basis for national existence, of governance and rule, of conquest and retreats, of prophecies that were of a temporary nature, of a living vibrant reality. All of the foregoing stands in contradistinction to the image of Judaism as it developed from the day we were exiled from our land, as a society that willingly abstained from universal politics, and established the study of Torah as the height of its glory. In such a society, there was virtually no place for the normal life of an individual or a state.[13]

The reality described in Nehemiah is far closer to that which obtains both in the State of Israel and in those parts of the Diaspora that are functioning democratic societies, and it is through the prism of modern democratic Jewish life that Nehemiah's stress on Hebrew as the living language of a vibrant, free people can best be understood and appreciated.

13. Yuval Cherlow, "*Mavo*" (Introduction), in Yoel Bin-Nun, *Pirkei HaAvot: Iyunim BeParshiyot HaAvot BeSefer Bereshit* (Chapters of the Fathers: Studies in the Accounts of the Patriarchs in the Book of Genesis) (Alon Shvut: Tevunot, 5763/2003), 8–9.

The fonts used in this book are from the Arno family

Other books in the
Maggid Studies in Tanakh series:

Joshua: The Challenge of the Promised Land
Michael Hattin

I Kings: Torn in Two
Alex Israel

Jeremiah: The Fate of a Prophet
Binyamin Lau

Ruth: From Alienation to Monarchy
Yael Ziegler

Maggid Books
The best of contemporary Jewish thought from
Koren Publishers Jerusalem Ltd.